D1691697

Hilal Alkan
**Welfare as Gift**

# ZMO-Studien

―

Studien des Leibniz-Zentrum Moderner Orient

Herausgegeben von
Ulrike Freitag

**Band 46**

This publication was supported by the Leibniz Open Access Monograph Publishing Fund.

Leibniz Gemeinschaft

ISBN 978-3-11-113816-9
e-ISBN (PDF) 978-3-11-115655-2
e-ISBN (EPUB) 978-3-11-115834-1
DOI https://doi.org/10.1515/9783111156552

[CC BY-NC-ND]

This work is licensed under the Creative Commons Attribution-NonCommercial-NoDerivatives 4.0 International License. For details go to https://creativecommons.org/licenses/by-nc-nd/4.0/.

Creative Commons license terms for re-use do not apply to any content (such as graphs, figures, photos, excerpts, etc.) that is not part of the Open Access publication. These may require obtaining further permission from the rights holder. The obligation to research and clear permission lies solely with the party re-using the material.

**Library of Congress Control Number: 2023947865**

**Bibliographic information published by the Deutsche Nationalbibliothek**
The Deutsche Nationalbibliothek lists this publication in the Deutsche Nationalbibliografie; detailed bibliographic data are available on the internet at http://dnb.dnb.de.

© 2023 the author(s), published by Walter de Gruyter GmbH, Berlin/Boston
This book is published with open access at www.degruyter.com

Cover image: Zaksheuskaya / Pexels.com
Printing and binding: CPI books GmbH, Leck

www.degruyter.com

Hilal Alkan

# Welfare as Gift

---

Local Charity, Politics of Redistribution, and Religion in Turkey

**DE GRUYTER**

To my grandparents, for being the best teachers about the gift

# Content

**Acknowledgements —— IX**

**Preface —— XI**

**Introduction —— 1**

**1  Fields and Methods —— 25**

**2  *Waqf* as Institution and Imaginary —— 45**

**3  *Hizmet*: A Contested Ethos of Service —— 65**

**4  "Our Poor": Criteria, Entitlement, and Justice —— 93**

**5  Embodied Ethics of Being a *Vakıfçı* —— 119**

**Epilogue —— 143**

**Bibliography —— 147**

**Index —— 161**

# Acknowledgements

This work is the materialisation of my incurred debts to so many people that any acknowledgement would be insufficient. I can only rely on the assumption that they know that their gifts were heartily accepted and very much appreciated. My greatest debt is to my research interlocutors, who patiently bore with my constant presence and answered my endless questions. My dear friends and hosts in Kayseri, Perihan Altun, Leyla Ekiz, Ahmet Gümüş, Nuh Hasyüncü, Fatma Kayar, and Pınar Akyurt graciously taught me about gifts more than they could have possibly intended. I also thank all of the staff, volunteers, and beneficiaries of the *vakıf*s who let me work with them.

Without the support of my doctoral supervisors at the Open University, Engin F. Işın and Umut Erel, this research project would not even have been possible. Their professional congeniality has taught me the value of true mentorship. This book owes a debt to their generosity. The Open University Research School has supported my doctoral studies with a full scholarship and provided a range of opportunities for academic development. Leibniz Zentrum Moderner Orient supported me with all the means necessary to turn my dissertation into a book, and with a stimulating intellectual atmosphere. I am particularly indebted to Ulrike Freitag, Katharina Lange, Samuli Schielke, Steven Serels, Canay Şahin, Nikolaos Olma, Aksana Ismailbekova, Nico Putz, Nora Lafi, Kadara Swaleh, Anandita Bajpai, and all my ZMO colleagues for their comments, questions, and critique. Svenja Becherer's endless support and patience made me see this process through.

I am extremely lucky to have Tatjana Thelen as my mentor and grateful for her valuable feedback on the book and for all the advice on academic life. Seçil Dağtaş became a close reader in the final stages of writing, and her careful comments helped me greatly in revising the introduction. Over the years we have lived in Berlin, Nazan Maksudyan proved to be not only a wonderful friend, but also the best co-author possible and a generous commentator. Feyza Akınerdem and Esra Demir have always been there to read, to discuss, to comment, but most importantly to hold me tight. They make feminist sisterhood real.

I had the right kind of people around me to sail through graduate school, most of whom have stayed in my life since then: Uli Beisel and Elena Vacchelli made trips to the British Library something to look forward to. Dear friends Banu Aydınoğlugil, Veysel Apaydın, Selma Altun, Billur Dokur, Simon Hutta, İrem İnceoğlu, Algın Saydar, Özlem Ünsal, Johanna Wadsley, Alex Wafer, Amy Watson, Besim Can Zırh, Çağda Zırh, Alev Kuruoğlu, Özge Özeke, and Burcu Arıkan were always there in days of joy and sorrow. My special thanks go to Vildan Erşen, who is my rock and chosen sister, and my lifelong friend Pınar Özgüner, who always bears with me. While I was turning the dissertation into a book, Esra Ertan, Edibe Benekçi, and Sezin Topçu shared my burdens in life so that I could have the mental space for writing.

I thank Thomas Pierret, Paulo Pinto, Kathryn Spellman Poots, and Baudouin Dupret, the organisers of the Ethnographies of Islam Workshop and the editors of the collection that followed, for their valuable comments and well-posed critiques. Lale Yalçın-Heckmann and Chris Hann hosted me in the Exploring Moral Economy and Civil Society in Eurasia Workshop at the Max Planck Institute for Social Anthropology in Halle, and provided precious feedback. I also thank Fabian Steininger, Jeremy Walton and Chris Gregory for their comments. Janine Su and Andy Tarrant were valuable in making the final manuscripts of both dissertation and book a more pleasant read through their language editing. Rafet Koca and Kübra Sarıyar helped me with the final stages of putting things in order and good shape.

Necati Zeybek and Nimet Zeybek have supported us at every turn and move in our lives. My sister Elif and brother-in-law Daniel made moving to Berlin feel like moving house in the same city. Our dear neighbour Saliha Erkmen looked after our daughter while I was completing the dissertation. I finished this book during my stay with two dozen family members, young and old, at my grandmother's summer house in Ayvalık. Such gifts of care are hard to fathom.

There are no words to fully appreciate and acknowledge what my mum Nurten, dad Mehmet, siblings Elif, Amine Seyhun, Abdullah Giray, and Alperen have given me. Their love is life sustaining.

Ozan, I am forever in your debt, for all the years, love, care, and intellectual stimuli. Azade and Aziz, you are the joy, you are the light. You have taught me how bottomless love can be.

# Preface

I am writing this preface in the aftermath of the earthquakes of 6 and 20 February 2023, which turned whole towns in southern Turkey and northern Syria to rubble, claiming more than 50,000 lives and displacing millions. Thousands of individuals and groups did everything they could to reach the disaster zone, completely unprompted, as soon as they heard the news. They pulled people from under the concrete, cooked meals, washed clothes, erected tents, and distributed whatever they brought along and whatever other people sent. Loose, ad-hoc networks mobilised volunteers, as much as established NGOs did. Pleas for help echoed and were magnified on social media, as did the responses to organise, deliver, and sustain. The state fell short of fulfilling its role to provide for those affected with catastrophic incapacity, ineptness, corruption, and inability to deal with the magnitude of the disaster. The question, "where is the state?" echoed everywhere. Once they were finally and belatedly in the field, state actors of all ranks proved quick to employ a paternalist, benevolent language. What I had observed in a medium-sized town more than a decade ago unfolded on a grand scale once again: gift-giving with its capacity to heal, console, and mend, as well as to humiliate, select, and exclude; with its reliance on informal networks and bridging/demolishing the distinctions between public and private property; through entitlements that go beyond citizenship rights, and interpellations that go beyond civic duties.

This book focuses on the provision of welfare by religiously informed local non-state agents to alleviate the effects of poverty. It identifies the mechanism that makes circulation of goods, services, and affects possible within that field as gift-giving and traces the vocabulary that smoothens tensions and enables shortcuts within those gift circles. It employs a close-up view of the intimate, embodied encounters between the workers/volunteers and beneficiaries of several aid institutions, as well as of the processes of resource creation. It is based on ethnographic research conducted within charitable organisations in the central Anatolian town of Kayseri between 2008–2009, which led to my doctoral dissertation "An Enchanted Welfare: Islamic Imaginary and Giving to Strangers in Turkey", appearing in 2013.

Although it was only just over a decade ago, my time in Kayseri feels like a whole different age. It was before the Syrian exodus and the settlement of 3.5 million Syrian migrants in Turkey. After 2013–2014, when the Syrians were left to their own fate in cities all around the country, a large proportion of non-state welfare provision was redirected to Syrian migrants. In my postdoctoral studies, I also shifted my focus and started working with informal neighbourhood initiatives aiding Syrian migrants in two Istanbul neighbourhoods. Although the context and the recipients were different, the circulation of gifts and care was the defining characteristic of that field, too.

It also feels like a different time because of the drastic changes in the Turkish (and global) political climate. Unlike today's overwhelming view of the country as authoritarian, in 2009 Turkey was considered a successful example of bringing moderate Islam and capitalist modernization together, and its European Union membership was still on the table. Not much later came some key political turning points: the Gezi uprisings of 2013, military operations in majority-Kurdish cities, an attempted coup against the government, and the great purge of the opposition, which also changed the course of my life and pushed me into exile in Germany.

While I was conducting my research and writing my dissertation, I was intrigued by the complexity of gift-giving, with its multiple facets and moral undertones that refer to several registers at once, although with oscillations and ambiguities. But, most importantly, I was attracted by the immediacy of the aid that was offered; its plain direction towards easing the suffering of a stranger here and now. What I observed was different from the neoliberal micro-credit schemes, job-trainings, and development programmes that pushed the poor to be productive and market-savvy under impossible conditions. The people I worked with were realistic enough to dismiss such visions. Poverty was real and immediate. Food had to be put on the table then and there, not in some uncertain future. I developed respect for what my interlocutors did and how they did it. I appreciated their moral determination, ethical dilemmas, and keen understanding of their own acts' insufficiency. What I observed in Kayseri was complex, potent, and plurivocal.

However, scale is always important. What happens between some volunteers and philanthropists in a small city becomes a different monster at the national level. On the dark side of "welfare as gift", one finds massive corruption, clientelism, and authoritarianism, all of which go against what my interlocutors believed and practised. Yet, similar mechanisms and networks were easily identifiable in both levels. As these darker aspects have become more visible at the national level every day, it has become increasingly hard to come back to the book (and of course, life, children, and migration came in-between, too). While it was buried in a folder for many years, the book was becoming too hot for me to touch.

For these reasons, I felt the urge to rewrite almost everything while preparing this book for publication. Not to change it substantively, but to shift the axis and adjust the tone. Also, of course to incorporate recent debates and literature. While I was at that task, the earthquakes happened. And I became paralysed, for several months. The grief was huge; being far away and unable to do anything except send money was excruciating. Not being able to give was a torment in itself. I once again saw that giving and caring are hardly volitional, that they are as much primal needs as learned duties. Reflecting on my own decade-old writing, which somehow addresses these questions, in the end, I decided to keep the ethnographic parts intact with light editorial touches, in order to keep this as an authentic picture of the time and place as possible. Yet, I wrote the introduction and the epilogue from scratch to engage with the academic and public discussions that have developed during the decade since, with a retrospective and critical eye on the conclusions I had once drawn. The outcome is an attempt to do justice to the people I worked with, and to their beliefs, dilemmas, and uneasy solutions, without overlooking the processes that have brought Turkey and its diverse peoples to where we are: a country with a state that masterfully employs the language of the gift while hollowing out generosity, trust, social bonds, and societal cohesion – the promises of the gift as critique – through violence, corruption, and polarisation.

# Introduction

A warm spring day in 2008. I am given a tour of Kayseri's charity scene. My guides, Neriman and Beyaz are excited, even enthusiastic.[1] They have promised to introduce me to countless people. Yet both of them are extremely busy, often with work that has nothing to do with the organisations they are employed by. So, we lag behind at every step, and every step teaches me something new. This is my second day in the city and my first in the field.

Earlier in the afternoon, I found Neriman at an informal branch of a private school where she had placed two orphan girls as interns. The girls lived in the state care home, but according to Neriman and her social worker contacts, the girls' serious psychological problems required special help. Neriman found a psychiatrist and a donor to pay for the sessions. She also found somebody to pay for the girls' internship, though the girls believe that the school pays them for the work they do. Neriman coordinates between state employed social workers, health care professionals, the head of the informal school, several donors, and the girls. I am slightly at a loss about the web of relations and wonder if any of this has anything to do with her job as the director of a charitable foundation. This foundation provides healthcare to the poor at its own private hospital and does not employ a psychiatrist; however, we do not have time for questions. Once Neriman has received an oral account of the girls' improvement, we take our leave to shortly stop by her office.

In her office, although we are only there to pick something up, Neriman ends up listening to a brother and a sister, both in their late thirties, who have showed up at her door unannounced. They work together at a soup kitchen. The man is officially employed there. However, his sister works "voluntarily", despite being a widow with several young children and barely having any income. Neriman is perplexed; the patron of the soup kitchen must be unaware of the situation, she says. Otherwise, he would never let this happen. The woman should be properly employed. She knows the patron, a wealthy industrialist, quite well and he always responds to her requests. She promises to call him. The man and the woman thank Neriman and leave.

After a short car ride, we meet Beyaz at a clothing shop. The owner had left a short while ago but apparently Beyaz received the donations he was expecting. He is cheerful as his van is full of new clothes. Neriman and Beyaz make small talk seasoned with several religious phrases and we leave. When I ask who the

---

[1] All the names of people and organisations are pseudonyms.

owner was, Beyaz says he was a friend of God (*Allah dostu*) who would never say no to their appeals for donations.

Our next stop is a historical Turkish bath that provides free laundry and bath services to impoverished women and children. The bath is run by the association Beyaz works for and maintained by one volunteer and two salaried women. The bath receives electricity and water for free thanks to an arrangement that was worked out some years ago. One of the salaried workers welcomes us. She was once a beneficiary of the association. She shows us around and apologises for the mess. They have been busy washing the party's curtains. "What party?" asks Neriman. "Our AK Party (Justice and Development Party, AKP)", says the woman with a big smile. Neriman is visibly disturbed, she snaps, "Can they not pay to wash their own curtains?" The smile freezes, the woman falls quiet. It is only the bathing women's chatter that interrupts the silence.

After the bath house, we stop by at the supermarket where Beyaz spends most of his days. Although it looks like a supermarket and is named so, it is actually a food bank where the registered poor spend their bi-monthly allowances on food and cleaning items. At this hour of the day, it is empty, clean, neat. I cannot imagine how it will be bursting with life in the year to come, when I will spend several days of the week there, filling shelves, talking with the beneficiaries, and observing their interactions with the workers.

By dusk we head to the graveyard and visit the modest grave of a leading figure in the city's beneficence scene, the late Nevin Akyurt. Her headstone is simple, engraved only with her name and dates of birth and death. It stands in contrast with the conspicuously large and well-decorated neighbouring headstones. Beyaz and Neriman do not comment. They crouch silently and recite the Quran. I send my silent prayers.

This is how my research on non-state welfare provision in the central Anatolian town of Kayseri began: with visits to several unlikely places, where people from different walks of life came together and orchestrated a seamless mixing of public and private resources, driven by religious, political, and civic motivations, to provide assistance to those in need. I assumed that we owed this intensity to Neriman and Beyaz's enthusiasm to give me a full tour in a few hours. I was wrong. It was how their days ordinarily unfolded. Every day, they were approached by people struck by poverty and its consequences, and they tried to solve their problems with a very personal approach. To do this they would connect people, collect donations, direct the flow of money and materials, remember and remind each other of their role models, and travel within and around the city. All in all, their work seemed to be primarily about connecting dots, mediating between people, and pulling things from wherever they could find them. What constituted their work was radically different from what they told me when I asked them about it – official criteria, existing institutional resources, well defined processes, and clear-cut goals. What they lived through and mastered was impromptu gift-exchange – in the form of favours, money, objects, phone calls, bodily labour, prayer, and care. Their gifts and the gifts they instigated had consequences that went beyond the alleviation of the immediate suffering of the poor. They created relations, which also carried ambivalent potentials.

In this book, I explore the potentials of gift-giving in the realm of non-state welfare provision at two levels, which together make up the notion of "welfare as gift". The first level employs "gift" as a conceptual and analytical tool to examine non-state welfare provision. Approaching beneficence as a gift makes it possible to trace the circulation of resources, meanings, affects, discourses, as well as worldly and other-worldly gains between spheres that are often approached as separate, if not juxtaposed: public and private, state and market, formal and informal. The gift as an analytical tool creates the rare capacity to look at the exchange of the material (money and goods) and the immaterial (discourse, affects, prayers) simultaneously and within the same framework. Welfare is thus analysed through the perspective of the gift in this work.

On the second level, I take up the political task of questioning the social powers that gifts carry in the context of poverty alleviation, when welfare provision is realised and/or presented as a gift. I illustrate the wide spectrum of these potentials, ranging from solidaristic to antagonistic actions, from embodied ethical transformations to massive state-level corruption. Building on these findings, I move back again to the theoretical level and reiterate Marcel Mauss: gift is a total social phenomenon.[2] We cannot understand poverty alleviation only by looking at redistributive mechanisms, nor would analysing the interplays between redistribution and commodity exchange – often understood as states and markets – be enough. We must take reciprocity, a primary mode of exchange, seriously and treat it not as a private, negligible phenomenon but as broad, far-reaching, powerful, multi-scalar, and multi-faceted as it is. As much as reciprocal relations are readily found in families, patronage networks, and between peers, they can also seep into market relations, political formations, and government schemes. They serve as the bedrock of intimacy in some of these spheres, all the while producing dangerous dynamics in others.

Within this framework, I do not approach reciprocity as a dyadic and circular phenomenon. As will be shown in detail throughout the book, reciprocity often involves more than two parties, either as active participants or by implication. It also resists closure – the completion of the give-and-take circle. Reciprocity

---

[2] Mauss 1990 [1925].

is temporally extended and resembles more a spiral than a circle, if sticking to geometrical metaphors. And here lies its various powers: the powers to transform people as well as political regimes, not always in similar directions.

This analysis is based on an ethnographic study of the local charitable organisations in the central Anatolian town of Kayseri, Turkey, conducted in 2008–2009. At the time, Kayseri was an exemplary case of the industrial boom in the rural Anatolian hinterland. The civic pride of its denizens was matched by their right-wing conservative politics, showcased by the 70 percent support the municipal and parliamentary candidates from the governing AKP gained in several elections. Informed by and equipped with historical and religious references, the wealthy of Kayseri was conspicuous in their endowments to the city; to such an extent, in fact, that they even used to hold a major event called the Philanthropists Summit with the participation of prime ministers, ministers, and religious leaders, on an irregular basis. They had also established a large number of local charitable organisations that served, albeit much less visibly, the urban poor. Their operations ranged from running foodbanks to providing shelter for travelling hospital patients, from coal distribution to helping young couples marry. During my fieldwork, I worked with three of these organisations and conducted intensive participant observation. I also joined coordination meetings at the city and district levels and met with representatives of several other organisations. To complement the ethnographic findings I interviewed these representatives, as well as charitable organisation workers, municipal employees, and philanthropists.

The findings of this research do not support an analysis of welfare that focuses solely on where the resources originate: public or private money. They also do not comfortably fit into the widely circulating critical narrative that sees a dismantling of the welfare state in favour of markets. Instead, they illustrate local underpinnings, societal context, and the language of a transformation that is taking place in Turkey, as well as in many other places around the globe: a transformation that involves, rather than a withdrawal of welfare states, a change in their focus from employment-based social security to social assistance; a mixing of public resources with private ones, rather than a decrease in public funding; and an expansion of poverty alleviation schemes, often through means-tested direct transfers, on a par with growing income inequality and urban precarity; and, finally, an increasing participation of non-state actors in welfare provision.

The Turkish welfare regime began to achieve a greater coverage and substantial effect on the lives of the most disadvantaged at a time when the welfare states of northern Europe had gone into a crisis under the attack of neoliberal policies. In the literature, neoliberal policies are often equated with the retreat of the state and a weakening of states' welfare facilities.[3] However, Turkey's growing welfare expenditures have gone against the expectations of many critical scholars,[4] similar to what has been happening in South Africa, Brazil, and China.[5] The change has not been a retreat but a transformation towards a "social assistance state"[6] – an outcome of efforts to contain grassroots political movements[7] and marking a particular moment in the history of the Polanyian double movement, which both entrenches and restricts the expansion of the power of capital over society.[8]

In Turkey, the main enactor of this change is the AKP, with its staunchly pro-market agenda and immense privatisation schemes. The AKP has been ruling the country single-handedly since 2002 and has radically changed the prevailing welfare regime.[9] Previously, Turkey was considered among the southern European welfare regimes, with its heavy reliance on family and kinship systems to provide a safety net for the most vulnerable, and with a corporatist social security system for the formally employed.[10] This social security system was very limited in its population coverage and highly hierarchical. In the 2000s, the system was changed in favour of the informal proletariat, while welfare expenditures have increased to unprecedented levels. The share of welfare expenditures amounted to 2.2 percent in 1980 and increased to 12.5 percent in 2016.[11] In 2011, about 14 percent of the population received healthcare through a means-tested government scheme, while access to this scheme also became the pre-condition for the allocation of several other welfare benefits – disability and carer benefits, education support, cash transfers, and in-kind support funded by the central budget as well as by municipalities and non-state organisations.

Rather than retreating from welfare provision, the Turkish state morphed into a "populist welfare state".[12] As much as there is no singular neoliberalism,[13] there is also not a singular route to market liberalisation and financialisation of

---

3 Goldberg and Rosenthal 2002.
4 Koray 2005; Dedeoğlu 2009, Çelik and Koray 2015; Elveren 2008.
5 Barrientos 2013; Ferguson 2007; Ferguson 2015; Lutz and Barrientos 2013.
6 Eder 2010.
7 Yörük 2012a, Yörük 2022.
8 Buğra 2020.
9 Buğra 2007; Buğra and Candaş 2011; Özdemir and Yücesan-Özdemir 2008; Aybars and Tsarouhas 2010.
10 Buğra and Keyder 2003.
11 Yörük 2022.
12 Yörük, Öker and Tafoya 2022.
13 Ferguson 2010.

public services.[14] Turkey's shift towards a social assistance state[15] goes hand in hand with massive privatisation, but not with a decrease in public expenditures on social protection and poverty alleviation.[16] While this book is situated within this context, its primary focus is not on welfare provision by the state. It also does not look into marketisation and privatisation trends. Its focus is on non-state, non-market agents, who, however, operate within a moral universe marked by a shared discourse with state and market actors, and cooperate with them. Within this language of benefaction, both non-state welfare provision and public services are framed in terms of care and gift-giving. While enlarging the realm of intervention and expanding its array of services and expenditures, the Turkish state under the rule of the AKP has refashioned social citizenship with a vocabulary of religious compassion and benevolence.[17] However, what is shared is not only a discourse. The non-state actors are so greatly entangled with state bureaucracy and commercial enterprises that they often share and re-direct resources between fields via formal and informal routes. In order to understand this phenomenon in its entirety, I propose not to limit the view to the agents, which are often (but not rightly) positioned in exclusive and binary opposition, but to rather focus on the modality of exchange that connects all these realms: reciprocity.

## Situating Reciprocity in Welfare Provision

Anthropological traditions delineate three distinct forms of circulation of goods: reciprocity, redistribution, and commodity exchange.[18] All three forms often co-exist in societies, serving different needs, and having distinct cultural significance. The predominance of one system or another in a particular society

---

**14** See Read and Thelen 2007 for a discussion of this process in the post-socialist eastern European countries in comparison to western European transformations.
**15** Eder 2010.
**16** Buğra and Adar 2008; Buğra 2020; Yörük 2022.
**17** In a sense, this is reminiscent of "compassionate conservatism" in the USA (Kutchins 2001; Carlson-Thies 2001; Cnaan and Boddie 2002; Morgan and Campbell 2011) and "moral neoliberalism" in Italy (Muehlebach 2019).
**18** Reciprocal relations include exchange of gifts, collective labour, household activities, and the like. Redistribution is the pooling of resources and their return to members of the society at different rates. It often goes together with a relative centralisation of power, whether in the form of bureaucratic states or less complex chiefdoms. Finally, commodity exchange is the exchange of goods or services with immediate return or with the promise of a definite return. See Polanyi 1957; Dalton 1965; Lomnitz 1988.

varies greatly; there are societies in which markets are mostly unimportant,[19] and there are others in which the accumulation of power through redistribution is kept under strict control.[20] In most contemporary societies around the globe, as in Turkey, markets have achieved unprecedented importance and reach, but the other two modalities still play vital roles. In the scholarly literature on advanced capitalist societies, there is a tendency to limit the analysis of redistribution to states and reciprocity to the private sphere, which, as will be illustrated throughout the book, does not reflect the reality on the ground.

Mature welfare states are a particular case in point on the problems associated with exclusively matching modes of exchange with certain social actors. While welfare states are primarily agents of redistribution, this function is both historically and empirically entangled with the expansion of the markets. Modern citizenship, as a system of political and social equality, and capitalism, as a system of inequality, have flourished simultaneously over the last 250 years of Western history, although they are seemingly in opposition. As capitalism was raging, social rights and the redistributive faculties of the state emerged as a means of protecting the social order from the threat of the working classes, while keeping the capitalist organisation of the economy intact.[21] Hence, in this context, redistributive states both controlled and enabled the expansion of markets.[22]

More important for the discussion here is the significance of reciprocity in welfare state formations. Reciprocity is based on mutual dependence and obligation among members of a group, rather than freely entered contractual agreements. Therefore, at the largest scale, it forms the basis of non-legalised obligations towards fellow citizens and the imagined community of the nation in modern societies.[23] Reciprocity makes possible the circulation of goods and services in patterns that are not solely determined by profit, but by social norms and values. Hence, a reciprocal mode of exchange potentially limits the brutal powers of market exchange, especially within capitalist constellations, with varying implications.[24] Yet, reciprocal relations may very well be incorporated into market relations, by way of shaping the decisions about whom to engage with in contractual exchange.

---

**19** Mauss 1990 [1925].
**20** Graeber 2004.
**21** Marshall 1992 [1950]; Karatani 2008.
**22** Polanyi 1957.
**23** Karatani 2008.
**24** Polanyi 1957; Sahlins 1972; Gouldner 1960; Komter 2005; Servet 2007.

Reciprocity is also imminent to welfare provision by states. Families lie at the heart of social reproduction and states rarely shy away from relying on the non-commercialised caring labour provided in family settings, especially by women.[25] Southern European welfare states and the welfare regimes of the Global South are particularly highly dependent on familial care,[26] as is also the case with Turkey. Yet, the role reciprocal relations play in welfare provision is not limited to family-provided care of children, the elderly, or the infirm. Non-state actors (dubbed as the voluntary sector, charitable sector, or the third sector in different policy approaches) hold a significant place in welfare provision around the world, through both transnational humanitarian organisations and more localised, even individualised and informal forms of giving to the needy.[27] There is also a strong trend towards bringing public resources together with private ones in relief efforts, as exemplified by the World Health Organization or UNICEF. In national contexts, government-voluntary sector cooperation is also hardly the exception.[28]

This phenomenon is most immediately observable in the realm of poverty alleviation. Unlike the premium-based social security regimes of western Europe, emerging welfare policies in the Global South prioritise poverty relief and social assistance, often in the form of conditional cash transfers that incorporate family relations.[29] The World Bank and International Labour Organization show strong support and preference for such schemes and now favour them over micro-credit and in-kind assistance. International development agencies, large philanthropic organisations, and local humanitarian agencies join forces with governments in creating resources and guaranteeing delivery. With these cash transfers, greater numbers of citizens are incorporated into welfare systems, and states are expanding their horizontal and vertical encompassing capacities.[30]

At a time when quite a significant portion of the world population is no longer needed in the workforce, life-long employment is not readily available even for the most educated. Production capacities now rely more on technological advancement than manpower, and the traditional northern European safety net type of welfare schemes have become unattainable for these growing redundant populations. The astounding increase in social assistance schemes attest to

---

**25** Katz 2001; Bhattacharya 2017; Read and Thelen 2007.
**26** Esping-Andersen 1990; Roumpakis 2020. Moreover Read and Thelen 2007 details how family and kinship relations became vital in social protection in the post-socialist states.
**27** Cammett and MacLean 2014.
**28** Jessop 1999; Bode 2006.
**29** Ferguson 2015.
**30** Ferguson and Gupta 2002.

states' recognition of the changing political economy and their attempt to find an answer to the pressing question of political legitimacy when full employment has become no more than a dream.[31]

Yet, within these general trends, each state has its own unique institutional history and cultural tools to build its claims to legitimacy through a reformulation of social citizenship. For some, this history involves the church-based logic of poor relief, for others it builds on religious gift-giving.[32] These logics, referring as they do to the histories of provision for needy members of society, involve mechanisms of reciprocity as much as redistribution of national wealth through bureaucratic formations. Therefore, both in its constitution as a historical continuity, as well as its current workings in the neoliberal era, social assistance is seen as a joint state-society endeavour, which brings reciprocal and redistributive modes of exchange together in a new constellation.

In Turkey, a similar trend has been observable. The increase in public social expenditure, especially in the realm of social assistance, has been paralleled by an increase in the span of beneficence and a valorisation of it. These two trends are not independent, either. Charitable giving and public social assistance coalesce both institutionally and at the imaginary level. For those operating in the field as providers, this coalescence takes shape as collaborations, either informally, as in the case of Neriman cooperating with state-employed social workers to provide support to young girls living in state custody, or formally, as in the case of the bath house receiving electricity and water free of charge thanks to cooperation agreements. At a larger scale, it means a massive redirection of state resources to government-friendly foundations for the provision of basic services. At the level of beneficiaries, differences between state-provided welfare and humanitarian/philanthropic aid are even more opaque. Receivers of support often do not know, and do not show interest in knowing, where the aid comes from.[33]

In the Turkish context, this non-differentiation is neither arbitrary nor inconsequential. It is indicative of a transformation from a premium-based corporatist welfare regime to a social assistance regime that deliberately incorporates civic elements of choice to further a particular political agenda. This incorporation has strong religious undertones. Islamic instruments of charity are positioned on the

---

31 Ferguson 2015.
32 See van Kersbergen and Manow 2009 for western Europe and North America; Bornstein 2012 for India; Jawad 2009 for Lebanon; Jawad and Yakut-Cakar 2010 for a Middle Eastern comparison.
33 Buğra 2015.

same plane as public assistance. Both are framed as beneficence.³⁴ This particular framing has two important effects. First, as Çağrı Yoltar convincingly argues, it works towards the making of the indebted citizen, who, having been invited into reciprocal exchange with the state or its civil partners, is expected to return the gifts received when the time comes.³⁵ Second, it legitimises a non-transparent and unregulated mixing of private and public resources, following the logic that, if the intentions and the deeds are "good", such distinctions can be withheld without any negative ethical consequences.

While reciprocity is universally inherent to modern welfare provision in various ways, these consequences are, if not unique, quite particular, and they refer to the institutional history of Turkey. The coalescence between public assistance and religious charitable giving is not only happening at the discursive level or in the form of ad-hoc collaborations between autonomous entities. It also has a strong institutional basis . In the next section, I will briefly introduce the institution of *waqf*, which provides this basis, and discuss its significance for contemporary welfare provision and poverty alleviation in Turkey.

## The *Waqf* and its Discontents

*Waqf* (*Vakıf* in Turkish) is an institution through which endowments have been channelled to specific civic purposes throughout the history of Islam. The institution is still alive and well in the Muslim world in a similar fashion to the Western institutions of trusts or foundations. In Turkey, the most peculiar characteristic of the growing state-provided social assistance system is that it is run almost completely by state-founded (and funded) *waqf*s as will be explained in more detail in Chapter 2. The *waqf* has been employed as the primary tool of welfare provision and social aid, and incorporated into the bureaucratic machinery since the late 1980s, but most significantly in the last two decades. However, the state founded *waqf* is a historical aberration.³⁶ What has been happening in Turkey is an incorporation of this private initiative into public welfare provision so as to benefit from its cultural resonance and structural features.

---

34 Buğra 2015; Yoltar 2020.
35 Yoltar 2020.
36 A *waqf* could only be established through endowments by real persons and had to be run by their appointed trustees. Therefore, it is in principle a fully civil institution. Despite the fact that, throughout its heterogeneous history, power holders have founded and used waqfs to provide public services and to generate legitimacy, they still acted as private persons and never in the name of an office. See Singer 2008.

While the *waqf* has been the primary mechanism to provide welfare, education, and health services in Muslim societies for more than a millennium, this complex system came under great pressure during the last decades of the Ottoman Empire and early Republican era in Turkey. In the 1930s, *waqf* assets were appropriated to finance state-run development projects, leading to a large-scale demolition of the welfare system that had been catered to by these institutions. Only in the 1960s did it become possible to establish new *waqf*s, but those focused mostly on arts and culture. However, from the 1980s, *waqf*s started to regain their earlier prominence in the realm of welfare provision, both as civil society organisations and public institutions.[37]

The 1980s also marked the time when Turkey's official secular nationalism was gradually replaced by the "Turkish-Islamic Synthesis", an ideology that proposes a mutual dependency of national and religious elements in Turkish culture and state-making. In this view, Islam is the sole religion that suits the Turks because of their ancient monotheistic beliefs and ways of life, and that the Turks contributed to the expansion of Islam so much that they should therefore be recognised as the natural leaders of the Muslim world.[38] While the earlier official secular nationalism of the Republic was oriented towards the ancient past of Turkic tribes and a future that would situate the Turks within a modern, Western community of nations, the Turkish-Islamic Synthesis has drawn references primarily from the Ottoman era as the golden age of the nation. The neo-Ottomanist nostalgia reached its peak during the AKP's reign from 2002 in the realm of cultural production, city-planning, architecture, history writing, and in foreign policy.[39] The resurrection of the *waqf* as an institution can be situated within this wave; however, as a paradigm of welfare provision, it had already occupied a significant place in the social imaginary even before this more recent adoption.

There has long been a tendency, especially among the more religious segments of society, to identify any kind of welfare work, disaster relief, education, and social assistance as *waqf* work. The *waqf* is also embedded in the self-perceptions of those who engage in individual and informal acts of generosity. Damla Isik's ethnographic research among the workers and volunteers of charitable organisations[40], as well as the findings I present in this book, attest to an association of the *waqf* with selfless, altruistic giving to strangers, whichever context it happens in and whatever institutional form it takes. In Kayseri, workers and

---

**37** See Zencirci 2015 for a detailed analysis of the historical process.
**38** Şen 2010.
**39** Yavuz 2020; Hecker, Furman and Akyıldız 2022.
**40** Isik 2014.

volunteers at charitable organisations, as well as municipal social workers, call themselves "*vakıfçı*" (*waqf* worker) and explain their work and devotion with the "*waqf* spirit".[41] For Beyaz, who is a salaried employee of an association, this goes without saying – he is a *vakıfçı*, and indeed a very devoted one. Anytime he recognises a potential for wrongdoing on the part of the administration of his organisation, he recites the final words of the 15th century *waqf* deed of Mehmed II, the Conqueror. The final section of every pre-republican *waqf* deed, just like Mehmet II's deed, lists fiery imprecations aimed at those who breach the articles of the deed. Contemporary *waqf* deeds, as secular documents, do not call for God's fury over those who misuse, appropriate, or sell *waqf* property; rather they refer to the laws that bind them. However, Beyaz's organisation – an association, not a *vakıf* – is not even bound by those laws. Yet, for him, what makes an organisation a *waqf* is not its legal title but its social function: welfare provision. It is quite striking to see that in Kayseri, and more generally in Turkey, distant fields like religious education and disaster relief fall into the same category and bring together people of different organisational affiliations (or of none at all) under the title of *vakıfçı*. Unsurprisingly, though, these activities all correspond to the historical range of *waqf* operations.

As will be discussed in more detail in Chapter 2, two particular features of the *waqf* are acted upon in this enlargement of the concept. The first is the *waqf*'s indifference to a differentiation between public and private in the liberal sense, as state vs market and civil society.[42] The *waqf* as an institution does not recognise clear-cut distinctions between self-interest and public benefit, or between the salvation of the soul and the well-being of the community. Better said, it interweaves these strands into an institutional and legal form. The second feature is its nature as a person's endowment. The *waqf* is built on personalistic relations that situate human beings not as anonymous individuals assembled as a population, but as persons with well-defined positions in society. The contemporary apparitions of the *waqf* on the welfare scene in Turkey illustrate how these characteristic features haunt the discourses and practices of those involved in welfare provision there. The current political scene in Turkey provides ample evidence for the political uses of these two features. The blurring of boundaries, while resonating among the public, opens new routes of corruption, and the personalistic dimension supports authoritarian paternalism,[43] which has gained new momentum in the past few years.

---

41 Alkan Zeybek 2012.
42 Weintraub 1997.
43 Kuran 2016.

The blurring of these assumed boundaries does not end with a political party's curtains being washed on the premises of a charitable organisation. Nor does it start there. It might potentially have begun with the allocation of a historic public bath to this organisation without any competition between similar charitable initiatives. However, the story goes even further back, to a dinner eaten at the family home of a prominent Kayseri businessman and to the personal relations between the mayor and the founders of that organisation, some of whom were classmates, others part of the same political movement in their youth. It starts with the ordinary gestures of care and hospitality; ordinary gifts changing hands, and eventually more substantial favours being done. Where it took us to in 2023 is a Turkey consistently dropping in corruption perception indexes,[44] with news items about the extraordinary growth of three *waqf*s, founded and run by the close relatives and friends of President Erdoğan, and the allocation of exorbitant amounts from the state budget, as well as massive real estate holdings around the country, to them.[45]

Personalisation also goes a long way. It neither starts nor ends with the need to make phone calls to the founder of a soup kitchen to make him properly hire an employee, instead of exploiting her labour under the guise of voluntary good deeds. It is reflected in the political language that presents municipal services as the charitable acts of a mayor, as in the case of the mayor of Kayseri, who later became a prominent minister in several Erdoğan governments and the vice-president of the AKP,[46] or state-provided welfare as the beneficence of a president, as in the case of Erdoğan himself.[47] Yet, it again starts with the well-intentioned, pious acts of generosity that take place between the poor and their benefactors.

Notwithstanding, there is no determinism implied in this analysis. A vast scholarship on the gift and the *waqf* provides countless historical and contemporary examples of other possibilities.[48] Cultivation and promotion of direct links between political leaders and their constituencies is a trademark of rising populism around the globe.[49] So is nostalgia.[50] The incorporation of the institution of the *waqf* into current Turkish authoritarian populism aligns with these global trends. Certain features of the *waqf* provide, if not legitimacy, then at least an

---

44 Transparency International 2023.
45 Ünker 2022.
46 Özhaseki n.d.
47 See Chapter 2 for examples and a larger discussion.
48 Graeber 2004; Eisenstein 2011; Vaughan 2007; Mauss 1990; Singer 2008; Gerber 2002; Baer 1997; Thelen 2023.
49 See, for example, Selçuk 2016; Brubaker 2017.
50 See, for example, Betz and Johnson 2004.

imaginary about how the poor and disadvantaged members of society should be aided during Turkey's transition to a social assistance state fuelled by concerns about containing social unrest.[51] I will come back to this discussion in Chapter 2. Here, before moving on, I narrate one last anecdote that illustrates the porousness of the boundaries and how welfare attains the outlook and structure of a gift within this porousness.

A *waqf* I worked with in Kayseri utilises another historic bath house. Just like the one I visited with Beyaz and Neriman, this bath house also belongs to the General Directorate of *Waqf* (*Vakıflar Genel Müdürlüğü*), i.e., the state. Once a *waqf* itself, it is now part of a greater pool of properties all around Turkey registered as cultural heritage. Behind it, there is a large plot of land. An elderly man rented this plot from the directorate to cultivate vegetables for sale at the market. As a condition of his rental contract, he also pays the rent of the bath house. In front of the bath house there is a large sign that flashes the name of a woman from a famous Kayseri family. According to the sign, the place is a soup kitchen run by an association, yet it now hosts a number of mentally ill, homeless men. Someone added "Shelter" to the inscription with non-matching letters, apparently later. However, it is not a registered shelter; it is neither monitored by the social services nor the Ministry of Health, though the police know that it exists, turn a blind eye to it, and bring anyone they find on the streets there. Its whole existence relies on favours and gifts: the favours made to the tenant and his reciprocity, the police, and the municipalities' willingness to cooperate or at least to act indifferently, and the donations that come from heterogeneous sources. Just next to the bath house, there is a make-shift hut. An Afghan family of four resides there. The daughter suffers from bipolar disorder. The organisation provides her medicine whenever they have the means, but it is irregular. Equally sporadically, they give the family food and coal. Thus, a paperless migrant family lives in plain sight in this shabby tin house built illegally on historical *waqf* property, which now belongs to the state but is rented by an individual for commercial purposes, yet supporting the mostly informal activities of a contemporary *waqf*. And this complexity is the most ordinary in Kayseri, not even to be noticed, let alone contested. It is also the crux of welfare as gift.

---

51 Yörük 2022.

## The Gift

Since Marcel Mauss published the *Essai sur le Don* in 1925 as the first comprehensive attempt to theorise the gift as a universal phenomenon, the anthropological discussion has evolved to illustrate that the concept can be used productively to understand modern complex societies, and that its value is not limited to societies without market economies and money.[52] The concept has also received attention from scholars of law and political science,[53] political economy,[54] and philosophy,[55] who discuss not only its empirical promises but also its ontological possibility.

This book employs a broad understanding of the gift, which roughly means any thing or service given without the expectation of an immediate and equal return, but always with the expectation of being accepted. This definition highlights a number of important features of the gift. First of all, for a gift to be a gift it should be received, accepted, and understood as such. Second, almost every gift creates an obligation of return. However, the return comes after an initially indeterminate amount of time. Finally, the relation between gift and counter-gift is not one of material equality but of unquantifiable equivalence.

The combination of these features gives gift relations their unique durability, extended time span, flexibility, and power to create bonds between people and groups. Because gifts create obligations – the obligation to accept and to return – they bind people together at least for the period of the gift cycle. However, the gift cycle is *never complete*, because counter gift-giving is itself an act of gift-giving, thereby multiplying the cycles of obligation to accept and return. Gifts rely on an accumulation of gratitude, indebtedness, and generosity; a reliance which makes them the fertiliser and catalyst of social ties.[56] Gifts invoke honour as much as shame; they may be a source of solidarity as well as of competition and rivalry.[57] They are tools of status or power-plays, and also a means for showing care and compassion. Tracing the circulation of gifts, observing the rituals that accompany acts of gift-giving, and investigating theory of the gift in any given society – i.e., why people give gifts – provide valuable opportunities to explore social relations, the task I undertake throughout the book starting with Chapter 3.

---

52 Carrier 1995; Godbout and Caille 1998; Parry 1986; Gregory 1982; Strathern 1990; Thomas 1991.
53 Cf. Fennell 2002; Titmuss 1997.
54 Polanyi 1957.
55 Derrida 1997; Jenkins 1998; O'Neill 2005; Hamington 2004.
56 Alkan 2021; Laidlaw 2000.
57 Werbner 1990; Shryock 2004.

In the narrowest understanding of the concept (as in the case of presents on special occasions, for example), gifts can be characterised as "redundant transactions in a moral economy." Yet, even then they make "possible the extended reproduction of social relations."[58] However, a broader understanding of the gift illuminates an existential human dependence on gifts. Every act of care, from breastfeeding to caring for a loved one during an illness, from donations to giving a friend a lift, is a gift. Every unpaid service, from volunteering at a retirement home to offering to help a neighbour, is a gift. In the same vein, anything voluntarily given to meet someone else's welfare needs is a gift. These gifts may well be the donations of wealthy benefactors, or the time spent by volunteers, and caring gestures by employees. They are called, understood, and framed as gifts by those who give them, sometimes explicitly, often by implication. They are given without the expectation of an immediate return, with uncertainty, and always in a neatly prescribed manner. These gifts oblige those involved to observe many social norms and are subject to ethical assessments. They are borne out of religious commitments as much as citizenly attitudes, and are part of the habitus of the people who give and take them.

In Mauss's conceptualisation, the obligation to give, receive, and reciprocate is the backbone of society. In reciprocal exchange, people stay in relationships and act out friendship, partnership, hostility, cooperation, honour, war, and diplomacy. Therefore, the obligatory nature of the gift relationships is an answer Mauss provided to his tutor and uncle Emile Durkheim's famous question of what makes society possible, what makes it stick together. For Mauss, one possible glue is the gift. According to him, the gift is a total social phenomenon, with its legal, economic, religious, kinship, moral, and aesthetic dimensions which then creates possibilities for thinking beyond the dichotomies of state versus market, individual versus society. By introducing the reciprocal voluntariness of subjects in the circulation of goods and services, the gift challenges the idea that distribution and redistribution in societies with money economies are regulated either by the market or the state. This is also a challenge to the prevailing conception of calculative, interest-run, selfish man: *homo economicus*. According to Mauss, although "it is our western societies who have recently made man an 'economic animal' … we are not yet all creatures of this genus".[59] This is revealed in the fact that nearly every aspect of our lives is still deeply involved in gift economies.[60]

---

[58] Cheal 1988, 19.
[59] Mauss 1990, 76.
[60] For this reason, for Mauss, a gift is what we can stick to in order to keep hope for a more humane world alive. This particular political agenda has found its way into many of the latter texts

## The Gift as a Conceptual Tool

The gift framework serves both theoretical and methodological purposes in this book. The theoretical contribution of the body of gift literature stems from its intervention into common understandings of political economy, as discussed earlier. The methodological benefits of this framework are related to the wide-angled lens it provides for viewing beneficence in a holistic manner, which includes simultaneously looking at the institutions, discourses, benefactors, beneficiaries, and intermediary actors and tracking cycles of exchange and modes of redistribution that go beyond the state and the market.[61]

Looking into these cycles is important because gift-giving and receiving is not primarily about providing goods and services but about establishing personal bonds. The establishment of bonds via gift relations is directly related to the workings of obligation within gift systems. Every gift is embedded with the obligation that it be accepted and returned, but the source of obligation is a question theoreticians of the gift have been seeking to answer for a long time.[62] The most common explanation for why people give is a rather economistic one: people give because they know that they will be given to in return; they give for future benefit and they, later, assess how profitable (or at least equitable) the transaction was. Against this simple logic, Bourdieu sharply states that, "[e]conomism is a form of ethnocentrism", because it does not recognise any interest other than those that

---

on the gift. See, for example, Bourdieu 1997a on disinterestedness; Godbout and Caille 1998 for a critique of utilitarianism; Graeber 2004 on self-regulating socio-economic systems; Cioux 1996, Vaughan 2007 and Gibson-Graham 1996 on the possibility of a feminist economy; Komter 2005 on solidarity and social cohesion in multi-racial contexts. See also Thelen 2023 for a review of the literature that approaches the gift as critique.

61 While I look at organised beneficence and civic gifts, I do not suggest that the gift economy managed by Kayseri organisations and local notables provides an absolute alternative to either side of the 'state-market dichotomy'. Indeed, I rely on historical examples that illustrate how gift economies almost always work simultaneously with market economies (Polanyi 1957; Mauss 1990; Godbout 1998), but assume an ethos that is carefully kept separate from the operational logic of the market (Mauss 1990; Titmuss 1997).

62 Mauss appreciates the explanation that was provided to him by a Maori wise man and explains that the Hau, or the spirit, of the object wants to go back to its original owner. See Mauss 1990. For Levi-Strauss the gift is a structural relation of exchange involving three inseparable components: giving, receiving, and reciprocating. Asking why reciprocity exists is dividing the indivisible and mistaking the part for the whole. A gift obligates its own acceptance and return because we are implicated in this structure of exchange and bound by its unconscious rules, which govern our social practices. Hau is just another 'magical name' that allows us to make sense of this structured social world. See Levi-Strauss 1987, 55.

capitalism has made known to us: the material interests of the money economy.[63] Economistic thinking informs the first question sceptics of beneficence ask: What kind of tax benefits do the donors get? The answer in the specific context I worked in at the time was "often none". However, they do receive other things in return: prayers, favours, a good reputation…etc. But, more significantly, they lose much more if they do not give, or give less than what is expected. Gifts are judged not only by their timeliness or quality but also in comparison to their "shadows" – the gifts that could have been given but were not given, which then "may come to haunt and unsettle" what was given.[64]

In gift relations, what is often at stake is the symbolic capital of the giver and the receiver.[65] Every gift poses a challenge to the receiver. Failing to reciprocate successfully is risking one's honour, dignity, and connections. Yet it is also a challenge to the giver, who is judged according to what they could have given but did not. Keeping one's gift relations in good shape is an immediate requirement of the field of power in which the relative accumulation of symbolic and material capital determines the position of an agent in that field. Borrowing Annette Weiner's expression "keeping while giving,"[66] there are things that are kept – even accumulated – while you are giving.

In Chapters 3 and 5, I will illustrate in detail that, with its paradoxical nature, gift-giving cannot be explained by "logical logic", only by "practical logic".[67] It does not necessarily require rationality, reflexivity, or even intentionality to be performed correctly. Gift-giving is part of a *habitus*, an aggregated disposition that is acquired (and inherited) over a lifetime. It is an important vehicle, carrying the symbolic capital of social actors in a field of power in which individuals strategise using the dimensions of time (when to return a gift) and resources (how and what to give). Yet, social actors are already implicated in that field through their *habitus*; and reciprocity – as well as gift giving – is a norm not in itself but always in relation to the systems of kinship, religion, economy, and morality that shape this *habitus*.[68] Religions provide meanings and rituals around giving, while the value ascribed to the objects of exchange is created in dialogue with the premises of the sphere of economic transactions. The delineations between moral and immoral ways of giving, such as donations vs. bribery, are as significant as how

---

[63] Bourdieu 1997b, 205.
[64] Copeman and Banerjee 2021.
[65] Bourdieu 1997a.
[66] Weiner 1992.
[67] Bourdieu 1997b.
[68] See, for example, Osella and Osella 2009; Parry 1986; Rozakou 2016; Shryock 2004; Stirrat and Henkel 1997.

the rules surrounding the properness of giving to and receiving from social superiors and inferiors are constructed. Only by inhabiting these norms does a person become a socially apt giver and receiver of gifts; and this habituation requires both deliberative negotiations and almost automatic, embodied responses. When welfare is framed and operates as a gift, the providers are required not only to give, but also to give properly – to the right receivers, in the right manner, and within a suiting code of conduct, while the receivers should accept the gifts properly, unless they want to be called ungrateful.

Yet, a code of conduct is different than the contracts that lie at the heart of market exchange and modern conceptions of citizenship – as in the notion of "the social contract". Reciprocal relations are non-contractual by definition. People who are engaged in reciprocal relations rely on the social bond created and sustained by the relation itself. The unboundedness and infiniteness of reciprocal relations make them a source of various social bonds ranging from indebtedness, patronage, affection, care, compassion, and congeniality to competition. The same thing may change hands, but its social effect may be drastically different depending on the occasion. While commodities have prices, gifts have ranks, and these ranks are determined by relations of closeness, power, and hierarchy.[69]

In Kayseri's beneficence field, entitlements and obligations emerge in reference to several registers. The poor claim their rightful share of the wealth of the rich, referring to the religious dictum. They also make demands based on the simple existential fact of being fellow human beings. Yet most often it is the intermediaries, the *vakıfçı*, who feel entitled to make such claims in the name of the poor. Their claims on other people's resources work through relations and the spirals of gift they have been embedded within. In order to understand this phenomenon, we should look for mechanisms of obligation that are not subject to formal laws, but which work through the intermingling of religious faith, honour, prestige, and family. This has drastic consequences for those who give, but more significantly for those who receive, leading to disciplining of their behaviour, bodies, and souls. This tells us that beneficence is not as arbitrary or voluntary as theorists of social citizenship tend to think; instead, as it is embedded in belief systems, social networks, the accumulation of capital and so on, it is institutionalised and well-orchestrated. In the following section, I explore the literature on religiously motivated gift-giving to illustrate one of the ways gifting is institutionalised, not the least for the significance of religion in the practices of the participants in this research project.

---

**69** Gregory 1982.

## Religiously Motivated Gifts

The Islamic faith and canon occupy a significant place in the initiation and maintenance of the gift-relations that are the subject matter of this book.[70] My interlocutors often explain and understand their gift-acts (whether giving, receiving, or reciprocating) as acts of piety, and they abundantly use religious terminology. Donations are often classified as *sadaqah* (*sadaka* in Turkish) or *zakat* (*zekat*), falling under different regulatory regimes that determine the legitimate beneficiaries, the timespan within which the gift has to reach its final recipient, and the protocol that has to be followed. While *sadaqah*, the Islamic alms, is much more flexibly regulated and can be freely given to almost anybody, at any time, and to serve any need, *zakat*, the annual obligatory alms calculated as a percentage of wealth, is subject to several rules. If a donation comes from a person's *zakat*, it is made known to the intermediaries so that they can observe the religious regulations. Unlike *zakat*, *sadaqah* is not always spelled out and framed as a religious donation. Religious signification is generally achieved through more subtle, colloquial, and softer measures with off-hand references to God. In that regard, although it is certainly important in shaping motivations, the prominence of religion in this field most significantly stems from the vocabulary and discourse it readily provides, which makes people immediately recognisable to each other as members of a shared moral universe, a "semiotic community".[71]

While giving to others without the expectation of immediate return is a universal trait (not even only of humans), considering the practices shaped by traditional and religious precepts is a teaching exercise in understanding a particular sociality. Amy Singer's decades-long work on Islamic charitable giving builds on this premise and suggests that giving in world religions, and in this context Islamic giving, points to a shift from "the ancient morality of the gift" to a "principle of justice".[72] According to Singer, *sadaqah*, *zakat*, and *waqf* are mediums to address the question of social justice in Muslim societies. This notion of justice does not only concern itself with the redistribution of material riches between human beings in this world. It also refers to the afterlife – the location of ultimate justice. In other words, it is an understanding of justice that transcends secular social justice both temporally and in terms of the actors involved.

The religious semiotics of my interlocutors in Kayseri point to the presence of God in every act of gift-giving and receiving. While being handed to the poor,

---

70 Cf. Rudner 1987; Kochuyt 2009; Osella and Osella 2009; Silber 1995; Silber 1998.
71 Elyachar 2010, 460.
72 Singer 2008, 10.

gifts are given to God and only truly emanate from God. God is the ultimate giver and receiver of gifts and the true judge of their value and purity. People give, among other reasons, because God has told them to do so, because the poor have a rightful share in the wealth of the rich, but also because God has given them the capacity. As I will discuss in detail in Chapter 3, being able to give is a gift in itself – the gift of God to the fortunate believer. This triadic understanding of the gift relation[73] has several implications. First, as Amira Mittermaier succinctly identifies, giving to God defies the necessity of having compassion or good intentions to engage in the act of gift-giving.[74] One gives because it is a duty, and if it is a duty then there is no moral superiority to be gained from it, no conscience cleansing, as critiques of charity and liberal humanitarianism would argue.[75] Second, because reciprocity is mediated, its disciplining power over the receiver is limited and the recipients are protected from the hurt that charity causes.[76]

According to Mittermaier, by defying the necessity of having pity, empathy, or compassion as the precondition of giving, a necessity that has been much critiqued by the students of modern humanitarianism,[77] Islamic "nonhumanitarian ethics" carry the potential to disrupt the "humanitarian reason".[78] It displaces the wounding character of charity, as well as the selectiveness of compassion and neoliberal notions of developmentalist self-help. Yet, it is also not interested in social justice or structurally improving the conditions that led to the poverty.[79] The primary concern lies with one's relationship with God.

However, this analysis is too narrow to explicate the workings of charitable giving because religion is hardly the sole point of reference and frame of action in pious people's lives. My observations in Kayseri occasionally resonate with Mittermaier's conclusions; however, they also contradict them even within a single person's practice and discourse. Giving is multi-referential, polyphonic, and hardly stabilised within one paradigm. My interlocutors shift seamlessly between different "gift theories",[80] from Islamic to neoliberal, from developmentalist to humanitarian. These frames are not mutually exclusive within a person's practical orientation. Contradictory explanations, motivations, reasonings, and drives stand side-by-side and exist in multitude without paralysing consequences. In

---

73 Kochuyt 2009.
74 Mittermaier 2019.
75 Cf. Rozakou 2016.
76 Mittermaier 2019, 4, with reference to Mary Douglas's Foreword to *The Gift*, 1990.
77 Cf. Ticktin 2011; Berlant 2004; Malkki 2015; Bornstein and Redfield 2011; Redfield 2008.
78 Fassin 2012.
79 Mittermaier 2019, 45.
80 Silber 1995; Silber 1998.

the following chapters, especially in Chapters 3 and 4 and 5, I unpack them in detail. However, understanding the multitude of reasons behind giving – the "theory of the gift" – is not in itself enough. What is more relevant from a social science perspective is to inquire into what "the impulse to give"[81] does, what gifts achieve in a society, as well as how they circulate – the "gift circuits".[82]

By bringing people together in temporally extended chains of reciprocity, non-state welfare provision is often seen as significant in strengthening the vertical ties between donors and organisations, and beneficiaries.[83] Yet how important these ties are in serving particular political agendas is a matter of debate.[84] What is more readily observable is the strengthening of horizontal ties. Janine Clark, in her work on Jordanian, Egyptian, and Yemeni Islamic social institutions, illustrates that the social role of these organisations is not so much one of recruiting the lower classes than of creating a sense of solidarity among the middle classes.[85] In that sense, religious welfare organisations exhibit the characteristics of social movements with their high impact on horizontal ties and relatively low impact on vertical ties. In Kayseri, both philanthropy and volunteering in charitable organisations bring people of similar social strata closer together.[86] While these people share religious beliefs and cultural codes, the gift circuits they become embedded in create tangible connections, lasting relationships, and social networks. In these circuits, it is not only donations that travel, but also competition, prestige, social value, and respect. What brings people to give is often the requests that come from others in their social circles, rather than those that come from beneficiaries. Hence, contrary to common-sense assumptions, the gifts with the greatest social power are not directed from the wealthy to the poor but are exchanged between people from similar social classes.

Remember the shop owner's donations, which we carried around in the car in my first day with Neriman and Beyaz. They were his *sadaqah*, given in response to a sacred call. Yet, practically, they were given because Beyaz asked for them so he could distribute them to beneficiaries he was working with. They were gifts: to God, to the poor, and to Beyaz, to be reciprocated with other-worldly rewards, with gratitude and prayers, and finally with a long-lasting friendship. During the

---

[81] Bornstein 2009; Bornstein 2012.
[82] Silber 1995.
[83] Benthall and Bellion-Jordan 2009; Harmsen 2008.
[84] Zubaida 2001; Flanigan 2010; Göçmen 2011; Brooke 2019.
[85] Clark 2004.
[86] People of lower classes, particularly the beneficiaries of these organizations, entering into such networks is rare but not extraordinary. When they do, their gifts are often gifts of labor, not of objects or money.

months I spent in Kayseri, I accompanied Beyaz or Neriman to Murat's shop many times and witnessed their talks on the phone about what to do for one or another person in need. I saw solicited and unsolicited gifts change hands between them, always wrapped in a religious discourse that signalled trustworthiness, shared values, and a deep sense of solidarity. In their joint efforts they found civic pride, personal humility, connection to God, and a sense of belonging to a community.

In the following chapters, readers will come across gifts in many different modalities: as materials, money, care, prayers, gestures, touch, and favours. They will also find "the gift" to be the founding premise of institutions, a levelling gesture, a vital aid, a measure of discipline, and the keystone in ethical and moral progress. These will unfold in daily encounters and mundane occasions, as my primary focus always rested on the intermediary work performed by the workers and volunteers of the local welfare organisations. It is there, I believe, and not in the conspicuous endowments marking the city, that the empirical richness can be found that allows us to explore the refashioning of welfare as a gift, and its various consequences.

## A Reader's Guide

This book has different offers to those with different intellectual interests. The first chapter is an introduction to Kayseri, the central Anatolian town where I conducted this research, and the research methodology I employed. Because Kayseri's religious outlook and capitalist success have attracted attention, both nationally and internationally, and positioned the city at the focal point of discussions on the relationship between Islam and capitalism, the chapter also presents those debates. The second half of the chapter, however, is devoted to a more self-reflective analysis of methodology; my own position (seen as a daughter, a spy, and an eager-to-learn stranger), gender, and the role of embodied learning in ethnography.

Chapter 2 is more for the historically minded. It gives a brief introduction to the institution of *waqf* and its various meanings and functions throughout the history of Islam. After this introductory section, I describe the particular trajectory that led to its dismantlement, and, later, resurrection in Turkey. Because the institution has always persisted as an imaginary shaping welfare provision in Turkey, I then move to an account of the contemporary Turkish welfare regime. This is also the chapter in which I trace back and explicate the emergence of "welfare as gift" as a savvy political discourse, which builds upon two fundamental features of the *waqf*.

With its ethnographic material and close-up view of intimate daily relations and encounters, Chapter 3 would be the most interesting to those who study contemporary instantiations and significance of the gift. This chapter is built around the concept of *hizmet*, which literally means "service", but has broader religious and civic connotations. It is an umbrella term that refers to any act that involves caring for strangers, whether done in public institutions or by private initiative. *Hizmet* provides actors in the Kayseri beneficence field with a theory of gift, and thus gives their acts their meaning and spirit. It provides the discursive tools for creating collaborations which would otherwise seem suspect. And, finally, it allows them to frame their daily activities as gift acts. Throughout the chapter, I investigate how labour, donations, prayers, and the formation of networks turn into gifts.

Any attempt at poverty alleviation begins with a definition of poverty and tries to differentiate the deserving poor from the undeserving (or the not-enough) poor. In Chapter 4, I engage with these debates, which historically inform charitable giving and give shape to current humanitarianism. Yet, while explaining the selection criteria and their governmental effects, my primary focus rests on the understanding and enactment of justice in applying these criteria. The chapter is woven around the theme of how certain needs are viewed to be worthy of entitlements, and how the criteria are used flexibly and relationally to justify decisions. Invocations of justice, not as normative phenomena but as part of a person's ethical standing (in terms of being a just person), create the possibility to circumvent these criteria, however well entrenched they may first appear to be.

The last chapter takes inspiration from current scholarly debates on positive ethics and piety, focusing on the gendered subjective formations of the workers and volunteers at the charitable organisations, especially of women, similar to what Rebecca Allahyari calls "moral selving".[87] While doing beneficence work, women experience a transformation that starts with their embodied dispositions towards poverty. With rich ethnographic accounts, I illustrate that their boundaries shift over repeated encounters, and that this shift makes up the core of their ethical formations. Although the point of departure of their engagement is often formulated in religious terms, it includes a broader commitment to an ethics of care. This ethics is necessarily built on the practice of care and is intersubjective. In the final part of the chapter, I consider the affinity between the feminist ethics of care and the gift, and investigate how gift mechanisms are masterfully used to constitute mutual respect.

The book ends with an epilogue, which juxtaposes the anthropological inquiry with the current political shifts and developments in the Turkish welfare regime.

---

[87] Allahyari 2000.

# 1 Fields and Methods

Turkey's transformation under the AKP (Justice and Development Party) government has received growing interest from academics as well as the international media since 2002, when the party came to power. Discussions soon revolved around whether the AKP, as the heir to a lineage of Islamist parties, aimed to turn Turkey into an Islamic state, or if it sought to represent moderate Islam, and further, whether it had the potential to successfully wed Islam and capitalism.[1] Within the first ten years of its reign, as the AKP proved to be more and more market oriented, "pro-progress", and an ally to Western powers, the moderate Islam view predominated. Proponents of this view suggested that the AKP experience illustrated an example of how democracy, economic growth, and modernisation could be embraced by practising Muslims without any major tensions. For most, the indicators of this peaceful, if surprising, co-existence was economic growth in Turkey and the changing lifestyles of its visibly Muslim citizens, often finding expression in the urban landscape. In that sense, the strengthening of capitalism in the production of commodities, landscapes, and lifestyles was often taken as proof of successful modernisation, or at least as a proof of the possibility for Islam and modernity to co-exist.

The central Anatolian city of Kayseri (population 1 million), with its flourishing industry, rapid capital accumulation, and conservative outlook, occupied a special place in these accounts. It was one of the so-called Anatolian Tigers, out of the way from Turkey's established business centres, but a booming industrial success and an AKP stronghold, with the party's candidate winning 70 percent of all votes in the 2009 municipal elections and those that followed it since then. Kayseri has thus been showcased as a prime example in many narratives about Turkey's transformation under AKP rule. In this chapter, I will first introduce the field site of my research, Kayseri, and review how scholars and policy institutions approach the city. I will then introduce the ethnographic method I used to conduct this research and address some key challenges.

## Kayseri

Kayseri strikes the first-time visitor with its large boulevards, tall buildings, and vast squares. Situated on the northern plains of an inactive volcano, Kayseri looks as if it has all the space it needs to expand. It is a city that adores greatness, vast-

---

[1] Nasr 2005; Turam 2007; Gümüşcü and Sert 2009; Tuğal 2009.

ness, and visibility. Apartments are advertised by their spaciousness: an ordinary middle-class flat is 180 square metres, twice the size of a comparable one in Istanbul. Offices are even more conspicuous, furnished with desks larger than family dinner tables and sofas you cannot sit back in without your feet being lifted off the ground. It takes quite an effort to cross the boulevards that cut across the city in all directions. Except in the historical heart of the city and in the few shanty neighbourhoods on its outskirts, Kayseri, in its greatness, makes the lonely pedestrian feel like Gulliver in Brobdingnag.

In this land of greatness, the signboards on public schools are equally huge. Each of these signboards, which are too large to be nameplates, has a person's name written on it. And it is not only the schools; the same names, or at least the same family names, can be read on hospitals, student residences, health centres, mosques, Qur'an schools, and day care centres, from quite afar. These are the names of people who donated to the construction and furnishing of these buildings. After spending some time in the city, one feels a sense of acquaintance with them from seeing their names so often in such huge letters. Kayseri's wealthy are proud of their gifts to their hometown and want to make it known. They like the notion of leaving something behind, and they also like commemorating their ancestors with public buildings.

This custom becomes even more prominent on the campus of the town's only public university. There, every faculty building has a sign almost as wide as the building itself displaying the name of a city notable. Only one building was built with public funds and hence has remained anonymous: the president's office. All other faculty buildings, cultural arenas, meeting halls, and sports facilities have proper names–first and family names of people. It is widely known within the city that, once the decision to build a second university campus had been made, the prime minister of the day called Kayseri's rich one by one and assigned each the construction of a building. The notables' enthusiasm for building schools is not limited to higher education. Nearly every primary and secondary school in the city centre built within the last 20 years has a philanthropist's name engraved on it. People from Kayseri business circles proudly told me this anecdote more than once: according to them, on his visit to Kayseri, the minister of education congratulated Kayseri's wealthy, because they had made endowments to schools to such an extent that the ministry subsequently needed to allocate no further funds.

In addition to these very visible endowments to public projects, Kayseri is the home of quite a large variety of *vakıf*s involved in an array of social services and assistance provision. These associations and *vakıf*s are much less visible than the endowed public buildings, and they certainly receive less funding from the business community. Still, there is a significantly higher number of such organisations in Kayseri than in neighbouring cities.

Kayseri businesspeople put forward a deliberate effort to construct and represent themselves as benevolent and responsible citizens by investing in civic gifts and founding *vakıf*s. They proudly call themselves *hayırsever*s – literally meaning those who love doing good deeds. This self-representation finds its utmost expression in the Kayseri Philanthropists Summit (*Kayseri Hayırseverler Zirvesi*). Until 2013, four summits took place, with the Turkish president in attendance as an honoured guest at the last two. The attendance of President Gül, who is also a Kayseri native, gave the summits airtime on national TV, thus entrenching the reputations of city notables as philanthropists. The Kayseri municipality encourages the aspirations and self-representations of its wealthy by hosting these events and actively bringing matters up for discussion and resolution during these summits. At the closing ceremony of every summit, those who have made the greatest endowments receive plaques expressing gratitude for their contributions to the city.

The Kayseri Chamber of Commerce has published a book to commemorate those who have made endowments to the city, titled *A Story of Distinction: Our Philanthropists*.[2] This heavy volume includes names, short life stories, achievements, and endowments of the Kayseri rich. Some of those who are included in the book give advice, tell stories, and share their experiences about their careers and philanthropy. Others express their pride through photographs submitted to the editor that depict them with their families or in front of the buildings they donated.

Summits, books and, most importantly, those buildings that carry the names of their respective benefactors, help generate and sustain a local identity for Kayseri that celebrates beneficence and creates a competition among the rich. As one of my interlocutors – a wealthy businessman who lived in Istanbul but owed his fortune to Kayseri-based industry – remarked, "Kayseri rich compete not only to earn more but also to donate to the city. However, for this to happen, there has to be wealth first." Certainly Kayseri has wealth. Business-mindedness is another adjective proudly claimed by the *hayırsevers of Kayseri* and known nationwide as an attribute of the city's natives – although not always with positive appreciation. Kayseri claims a legacy of excelling in commerce that dates back four thousand years, referring to the famed clay tablets of the Kültepe-Kanesh mound, a major Assyrian trade hub, in the northern outskirts of the city. These tablets attest to a dynamic and well organized trade of goods coming from different parts of the Fertile Crescent, which, since their discovery in mid-twentieth century, provided Kayseri businesspeople a historical explanation of their shrewdness.

---

2 Şeker 2008.

Yet, despite these proudly claimed early histories and some state investments during the early Republican era, Kayseri has grown from an agricultural and trades-oriented small town to a major manufacturing site only over the last three decades. As of 2009, when I conducted my research, Kayseri had a designated industrial zone occupying 2350 hectares on the western outskirts of the town, with approximately 800 factories and large workshops employing about 45,000 workers. Outside the borders of the industrial zone were some other industrial compounds hosting a major textile factory, a sugar producer, and a giant electronics manufacturer.

An early and influential study on Kayseri was conducted in 2005 by the Berlin-based European Stability Initiative (ESI). The ESI's report was tellingly titled *Islamist Calvinists*.³ With their observations regarding the booming economy of Kayseri as a major furniture and textile exporter, they aimed to challenge views of Central Anatolia as a heartland of religious conservatism, backwardness, and stagnation. In order to account for the economic development of the city, ESI reporters followed Weber's analysis of the Protestant ethic being what led to the emergence of capitalism in the West, and argued that Islam, as it was lived and experienced in Kayseri, might well be understood as providing fertile soil for entrepreneurship and economic progress. Weber, in his seminal work *The Protestant Ethic and the Spirit of Capitalism*, approaches capitalism not only as a product of material conditions, such as a change in property ownership, but as a social phenomenon with cultural and religious origins.⁴ Trying to build a causal explanation for the historical and geographic specificity of the emergence of capitalism, Weber directs his interest to the Christian Reformation and to the radical changes it caused in the psyches of European Christians. Weber argues that Protestantism, especially Calvinism, provided an answer to the question of how believers could be assured of their salvation when the authority of the church and clerics was deeply undermined. In Calvin's teachings, worldly material success and gains could well be interpreted as an indication of salvation. Therefore, it was almost a religious duty, a calling, to have a profession and make worldly gains. These gains could not be spent conspicuously or for leisure, so they had to be accumulated. This accounts for the necessity of capital accumulation, which allowed for the emergence of capitalism and its related work ethic.

Although the ESI reporters cautiously stated that it was "hard to say whether the rise of 'Islamic Calvinism' among Kayseri's entrepreneurs is a cause of their commercial success (as per Max Weber), or whether increasing prosperity has led

---

3 European Stability Initiative (ESI) 2005.
4 Weber 1985 [1930].

them to embrace interpretations of Islam that emphasise its compatibility with the modern world"[5], they argued that in Kayseri religion and economic prosperity had reinforced each other. Authors of the report went on to note that "economic success has created a social milieu in which Islam and modernity coexist comfortably"[6] in the heartland of conservatism in Turkey.

The report has been applauded for the challenge it posed to accounts that argue for an incompatibility between Islam and capitalism. Similar accounts produced by the Western media followed. A New York Times article argued that "the case of Kayseri presents one of the strongest arguments that Islam, capitalism and globalisation can be compatible",[7] so Turkey's EU membership might be nothing to fear. Similarly, the US broadcaster PBS produced a documentary called "Turkey's Tigers" and emphasised how Islam did not present an obstacle to capitalist development in the town, featuring clichéd shots of women with headscarves on the streets and businessmen in smart suits being interviewed in their spacious offices.

Following in ESI's footsteps, other scholars looked at similar Anatolian cities to find out whether Kayseri was unique in character or representative of a trend.[8] The conclusion was that the processes of globalisation and Europeanisation had affected Turkish cities in similar ways, but cities' reactions to these processes varied significantly depending on local capacities. Prevalent Islamic values in Kayseri, as much as they advise prudence, protection of family ties, and hard work, were seen as inducers of economic growth, although they might also become impediments to urban development by supporting conservative and introverted tendencies.

In both the ESI report and the studies that followed it Kayseri is depicted as a city of business people whose Islamic values and practices support their business aspirations and give them a competitive advantage within a globalising market economy. One of the most important of these advantages is benefiting from Islam as a resource that nurtures a communal bond of mutual trust. Within the world economic trends which requires production to become increasingly flexible this has important functions.[9] Flexible production brings about the increased need for outsourcing, subcontracting, informality, and flexible working hours. The needs

---

5 ESI 2005, 25.
6 Ibid., 34.
7 Bilefski 2006.
8 Keyman and Koyuncu Lorasdağı 2010.
9 Buğra 1999.

of these firms can be met more easily within networks of reciprocal exchange, mutual trust, and shared values.

In that sense situating "Islamic capital" against a notion of "secular capital" can be a fruitless attempt.[10] The rise of a capitalist class in religious Anatolian towns can be better understood by looking at processes of internationalisation rather than attempting to craft unsustainable distinctions between Anatolian capital and Istanbul-based capital, or Islamic capital and secular capital. Yet there is also a "dialectical process wherein capitalism and Islamic culture interpenetrate and transform each other" and capitalism is made part of the local culture.[11] This incorporation requires creative work, involving going back to primary resources (like the Qur'an and *hadith*) and interpreting them anew in communication with the actualities of the market and economic order. It also involves investing in bodacious material signifiers of "morally" acquired wealth through endowed buildings in public spaces.[12] Philanthropy is an integral part of the transformation that has been happening in Kayseri.

## Research

Kayseri became the field site for this research project because of its non-apologetic self-identification as the "city of philanthropists" and its dynamic non-governmental welfare provision and poverty alleviation landscape. As will be described in detail in the next chapter, the Kayseri cityscape is conspicuously saturated with philanthropic donations to the city: mosques, schools, student housing, hospitals, university buildings, cultural centres, and public baths. And behind this glittering façade, which very much matches the general partiality of the Kayseri elite for the grandiose, is an array of welfare services provided much less visibly and with the involvement of larger segments of society than the wealthy few. In 2008–2009, when I conducted this research, Kayseri had a relatively confined and introverted charity scene. Most of its organisations were strictly local. Well-known national and international aid NGOs were either absent or were running very small operations in the city. Kayseri's local organizations had additionally expressed no aspirations to operate on national or global scales.

---

**10** Hoşgör 2011.
**11** Adaş 2006, 115.
**12** Critical of the outcomes of this dialectical process, Marxist urban scholars approach the outcomes of this incorporation with suspicion, especially in terms of its effects on the public space. See, for example, Doğan 2007.

Even the operations of religious groups that otherwise organise at national and international levels were very much localised. Because of these features, Kayseri provided good research conditions for this study, which seeks to trace gift cycles from large donors down to humble volunteers.

With this focus on the circulation of money, materials, and care within non-state welfare provision, I conducted extensive ethnographic research at three aid organisations in Kayseri. I spent a total of ten months in two phases between August 2008 and August 2009, working in these organisations and joining their workers both in their work environment and outside of it. My aim was to be as close as possible to the actors who play the intermediary role between donors and beneficiaries in order to be able to observe the minute details of decision-making, registering, giving, and receiving. However, I also developed strategies to reach the founders of organisations, their donors, and executive bodies, as well as the beneficiaries. The latter strategy to work with the beneficiaries failed for reasons I will explain later, but ethnographic methods, particularly participant observation, otherwise gave me an intimate understanding of the field. Before discussing methodological issues, a brief description of the three organisations I worked with is necessary.

All three organisations distribute aid (usually in kind) and provide defined welfare services to their registered beneficiaries. Their legal statuses differ. Two of them are actual foundations (*vakıf*s) and one is an association. Yet, colloquially they are all called *vakıf*s.[13] Their activities are limited to Kayseri, although they occasionally send needed items to organisations elsewhere. Their founders are self-confessed Muslims with varying degrees of observance. None of the organisations have direct ties to a particular sect or religious order, but a few of the founders and workers are active members of one religious order or another. The organisations' beneficiaries have different ethnicities, religious orientations, and lifestyles and the organisations claim to be blind to these differences. Islamic discourse and terminology is widely used as a common repertoire to communicate ideas of justice, to initiate and reciprocate gift-giving, and to discuss ethical problems. However, I did not observe any systematic attempts to Islamicise the lifestyles of beneficiaries or educate them in religious matters. Some of the volunteers and founders have personal or familial ties to the ruling AKP, but the organisations have no direct affiliations with the party.

---

13 I discuss how the concept of *vakıf* transcends these legal distinctions in the coming chapter.

**Kayseri Derneği**

At the time of the research, Kayseri Derneği[14] was one of the largest aid-providing organisation in the city. They had around a thousand households registered for regular (almost monthly) aid. The association runs a supermarket that is not open to the public. Registered beneficiaries have bi-monthly allowances to spend in the market on their allocated days, on items like standard brands of food, detergent, nappies, tableware, etc. Beneficiaries also receive clothing two or three times a year and are provided with furniture and carpets if needed. All clothing, furniture, and carpets are donations in kind, but most of the food items and detergents are bought by the association from suppliers that have agreed to a considerable discount on wholesale prices. In 2009, monthly purchases amounted to 50,000 TL (equal to around €25,000).

Kayseri Derneği also runs a public women's bath for those without access to hot water. Every day, approximately 50 women and children bathe in this facility and have their laundry done by the employees. Most of the clients are impoverished widows and their children, but the organisation also accepts women who are known to be in need, in exchange for a symbolic payment that amounts to €1. The bath house is exempt from water and electricity bills. Kayseri Derneği only covers the cost of the coal used to boil water and the salaries of three workers.

Another significant activity of the association is running a soup kitchen for fast-breaking (*iftar*) during the month of Ramadan. Every year, an unused floor of a multi-storey car park is rearranged as a refectory and hosts 700–800 people per evening. The *iftar* visitors include poor families, working men and women who cannot make it home to break their fasts, and anyone outside at dusk for one reason or another. Because the car park is located at a busy junction where people change buses and trams, this last category makes up a significant share. Every evening, a three-course meal and beverages are served to these diners. There is a fixed sponsorship rate that covers approximately one evening's expenses. Every *iftar* is paid for by someone from the Kayseri business community. Kayseri Derneği covers evenings that are not sponsored.

In total, Kayseri Derneği has 10 full-time employees (four women and six men) and around 20 active female volunteers. The association does not have a salaried director; the head of the executive board attends to all administrative work, as well as to purchasing and employment decisions. The bulk of Kayseri Derneği's expenses are covered by this businessman, a spice trader from a prominent family, and six others who make up the board. Miscellaneous donations

---

[14] All the names of the institutions and the people involved are pseudonyms.

make up a minimal share of the budget. Yet, in-kind donations come from other sources, mostly via the director and board members' networks. Additional fundraising activities are mostly organised by female volunteers. I will discuss one particular fundraising event, the charity fair, in Chapter 3.

## Sinan Vakfı

Sinan Vakfı owns a private hospital serving the healthcare needs of patients with private or public insurance, or with the financial means to pay. Unlike other private hospitals, they also accept patients who have neither the means nor any kind of insurance. These patients, who fall outside the public health insurance scheme, are treated for free. The hospital was built exclusively with donations and then leased to a company. The tenant company pays an agreed upon amount of rent and also guarantees the free treatment of a given number of patients each month. These patients also either receive their medications directly from the foundation or are reimbursed for their prescriptions.

Sinan's second major undertaking is a shelter for patients of the state-run hospitals and their attendants who come from neighbouring towns and do not have the means to pay for a stay in Kayseri. Kayseri has two very large public hospitals and a university research hospital. It thus serves as the healthcare hub for the region and attracts patients from surrounding cities. Sinan's shelter provides these patients and their relatives with rooms/beds, hot water, laundry services, breakfast, dinner, and shuttle services to hospitals while they complete their treatment. It works in cooperation with the hospitals' social services departments. Patients and their attendants who declare they have no place to spend the night are transferred to the shelter via shuttle buses. There are 85 beds in the shelter, often in rooms of four. There are also futons in the corridors and in common rooms, which are used to accommodate patients' relatives if the demand for the night is higher than the capacity.

The shelter building was actually constructed by a well-known industrialist family and was endowed to the university to be used as a local health clinic. It was far too large for this purpose; the university had only utilised the entrance floor of the three-story building and left the rest untended. Noticing this, Sinan proposed using the vacant space as a shelter. They refurbished the building with donations and continue to receive donations of sheets and mattresses. The same sponsor, a large furniture manufacturer, provides breakfast and dinner from his own soup kitchen.

The founders of Sinan include the chair of the Industrial Region and the metropolitan mayor, alongside many notable Kayseri businessmen. There are 11 employees working at Sinan, and only the director, who also has close ties with other *vakıf*s of the city, is a woman. As will be detailed in the upcoming chapters, her activities go well beyond her formal work at Sinan, which is indeed indicative of the structures and mechanisms that uphold the beneficence field in the city.

**Yardımlaşma Vakfı**

Yardımlaşma Vakfı was founded with the aim of building a care home for the elderly. It indeed managed to quickly build a large compound to serve this function, thanks to large donations. However, after the care home was built, its administration was transferred to the municipality. The foundation itself then became partly obsolete. At the time of my research the beneficiaries of Yardımlaşma Vakfı were mental health patients and their families, but the *vakıf* was functioning with very limited resources and only three part-time employees. Yardımlaşma Vakfı uses a former public bath as a shelter for ten to twelve homeless men with cognitive disabilities and diagnosed psychological illnesses. This shelter is not as well supported as Sinan's patients' shelter, so both the living conditions and the services provided to their guests are limited.

Besides running this shelter, Yardımlaşma Vakfı assists families with mental health patients. It distributes basic food packages consisting of pasta, cooking oil, flour, and tomato paste, and occasionally pays electricity and water bills for these families. In the winter some of these families are given sawdust to burn in their stoves.

In order to generate some income, the *vakıf* collects paper and plastic from factories and sells it to recycling facilities. They also accept donations in cash and in kind, including second-hand clothes and furniture. These donations are then sorted at the shelter and used for the patients themselves or families included in the outreach scheme.

Throughout the entirety of my fieldwork, I conducted participant observation at these *vakıf*s, meaning that I worked on their premises 5–6 days a week, participated in their staff and board meetings, and joined their employees and volunteers in their work routines. While my participant observation involved holding back at times and taking hasty notes, it often meant active physical labour, traveling for deliveries, and taking part in discussions. I became an accessory to some workers and volunteers whom I identified as having the largest networks and joined their rounds in the city. I visited other organisations, city notables and dozens of beneficiary homes with them, witnessing the negotiations that went on, as well as the unfolding of intimacy and care. I also joined volunteers when they hosted their private guests, some of whom were volunteers themselves, and befriended some workers to a degree that I would stay over with them regularly. These occasions created a space for initiating conversations with a more critical tone than those which took place on the premises of the organisations.

## A Troubling Access

I am a Turkish woman, who was born and grew up in a pious Muslim family of Balkan migrant origins that has been living in the country for about three generations. I am native to the language and have command over religious and cultural vocabulary. Or so I assumed, before I began my fieldwork in Kayseri and faced the well reported troubles of the "native anthropologist".[15] When I went to Kayseri, my initial contacts were acquaintances of my mother, who had visited the town to give a talk in 2002. She was invited by an acquaintance of hers, the late Nevin Akyurt, who had been a very prominent figure in the field of beneficence in Kayseri, and who will be introduced in detail later in the book. To these early contacts, I was my mother's daughter and by implication Akyurt's bequest. But for the great majority of the people I met I was simply a young woman who had come from London with the vaguely defined task of "research", for which she had left her husband and home behind. Kayseri had hosted researchers from European countries before, such as journalists and employees of think-tanks, but I did not belong to either of these categories, and the way I wanted to conduct my research was unlike the way journalists prepared their stories. Namely, I was not particularly interested in meeting town notables or learning the secrets to the city's industrial success. So, who was I?

As in many other settings, it is very common in Turkey to believe foreigners to be spies.[16] The fact that I was not a foreigner did not actually make a big difference (so much for being a native). Some state officials I met with were confident enough to ask openly whether it was the British government that had asked me to conduct this research. "I am funded by a British university, but I chose my own topic and this is my project," I replied. They were so unsatisfied with this answer that they did not even bother to discuss it any further. My name appeared in the phone book of the middle-aged director of an aid organisation as "the British Spy", only half ironically. He had a particular talent for figuring out people's insecurities and playing on them; mine was easy to guess, and he kept pushing that button. I remember one particularly embarrassing incident: His organisa-

---

15 Narayan 1993.
16 See, for example, Owens 2003.

tion had been invited to a collaboration meeting at the governor's office, along with some others. He kindly invited me to join them and observe the meeting, and I happily accepted. Yet, when we arrived, he introduced me to the director of another organisation in the most undermining way: "This blonde lady came from England to research us." I rushed to get hold of the conversation and started to explain what I was doing there, but as I was mumbling about my research topic my contact went on with his witty comments, "See how good her Turkish is! She is really well trained!" I was now a British spy who spoke the language as good as the natives! I gave up and laughed the situation off, hoping to find another chance to meet with this other director. It never happened. Although most of it was mockery, there was certainly an element of sincere distrust embedded in this and other more subtle incidents.

I thus found myself in a setting in which everyone approached me politely, but always with reservation. At the extreme I was seen as a spy, but most often I was simply a stranger and as a result, a source of suspicion. My attempts to overcome this by talking about my project and describing myself and my life were usually received with polite nods, which did little for my peace of mind. Yet, I eventually established solid, reliable, and enriching relationships with many of the people working and volunteering at *vakıfs*. Retrospectively, I figure that if half of this accomplishment was owed to long-term contact, the other half at least had to do with my own readiness to viscerally learn the subtle codes of their behaviour.

## The Body as a Research Tool

In the final chapter of this book, I explore the ethical transformation of the women and men taking part in the activities of charitable organisations in Kayseri. I argue that this ethical transformation has an intrinsic bodily aspect and, in some instances, it is actually this aspect that precedes *the intention* to change. This embodied transformation requires a level of docility that gives subjects' bodies plasticity and malleability. Docility and ethical self-formation, as such, do not only have theoretical and empirical implications for this project. They also signify important research processes. In Kayseri I experienced a transformation, a very particular self-formation, one certainly resembling that of the people about whom I write.

Looking back now, I can see the docility with which I rendered myself to the people I admired and respected there. I let them affect me, shape my posture, voice, and gestures, and teach me by example. I also disciplined myself by trying, sometimes very hard, to act like the person I wanted to become, but this came a little later. This was not to pass as a native; for me, just like them, working in these organisations was part of an ethical self-formation. And just like them, again, I got tired, I had regrets, I developed conflicting attitudes and thought about my reactions over and over again. I pushed myself to be more patient – to practice *sabr* – when I felt the urge to argue. I personally experienced the hardships of sustaining a desired behaviour when in a hurry, tired, or distressed. I struggled to keep my smile intact and my attitude genial towards the shoppers at the charity fair after ten hours of standing on my feet. I had to act with humility in order to gain humility – not the other way around.

This attitude was my response to a combination of my co-workers' expectations and, in part, my own feminist research agenda. The expectations were there for those who knew my mother, even if barely. She was a good reference for me at the beginning; but, at the same time, she set the standard for my moral and societal standing in their eyes. It took a while for me to be known by my own name, not just as her daughter, and with my own values, which sometimes very much contradicted theirs. But more importantly, as I said, I was eager to walk the way they led me, to be as perceptive as a child and as responsive as a disciple. While I was doing ethnography, I figured that my research tools were not limited to my sound recorder, notebook, and cognitive skills. My body could be a tool, too, and its capacities were not limited to seeing and listening. It could teach me a great deal if I chose to be adaptive and step back from my privileged yet cramped observer position, all the while reclaiming and maintaining an analytical distance.

When Clifford Geertz compared culture with a drama to be read over the native's shoulder, he emphasised the role of the ethnographer as the reader who has the privilege of being close enough but still outside the text, such that it can be impartially read as it unfolds before her own eyes.[17] While this perception was generally criticised for ignoring the role of the ethnographer in actually "writing culture",[18] feminist anthropologists carried the critique further by questioning the sufficiency of the metaphorical act of "reading", which gives primacy to seeing and listening, as a research tool.[19] Ethnography, in its intense form as participant observation, demands bodily immersion. Understanding what this entails, reflecting on the embodied attunement, and using this awareness as a deliberate research tool opens new realms of knowledge.

Lila Abu-Lughod recounts an illuminating incident from her fieldwork among the Bedouins of Egypt, which then showed her how much she had internalised

---

[17] Geertz 1972.
[18] See Clifford 1986.
[19] Altorki 1988; Abu-Lughod 1999; Mahmood 2005.

the values of her hosts and how this internalisation had helped her develop a fruitful analysis afterwards.[20] During the two years she spent with the Awlad Ali Bedouins, she was hosted by a prominent figure of the tribe and eventually became accepted as a member of his household. As a woman with Arab roots, she eventually found it more comforting and also more strategically feasible to be the "dutiful daughter" of her host family, welcoming the boundaries such a role imposed on her as much as the opportunities it created. She even sincerely wanted to become like the persons she admired during her stay there. One day while they were preparing a feast and she was cleaning rice for cooking, she accidentally found herself in a position of embarrassment: "face to face with a dignified old man, not a relative" her face uncovered. She blushed deeply and ran into the nearest doorway. After describing this incident, she comments:

> It was at this moment, when I felt naked before an Arab elder because I could not veil, that I understood viscerally that women veil not because anyone tells them to or because they would be punished if they did not, but because they feel extremely uncomfortable in the presence of certain categories of men. Veiling becomes an automatic response to embarrassment, both a sign of it and a way of coping with it. This and my other experiences trying to live as a modest daughter were... essential to the development of my analysis of modesty and women's veiling.[21]

Similar to Abu-Lughod's experience, my docility improved my understanding of the practices common at Kayseri *vakıf*s. The last three chapters of this book benefited very much from the perspectives such embodied learning made possible. This particular readiness led to a gradual improvement in my relationships with the people I worked with in the field and significantly bridged the social distance created by where I came from, my vocation, and my class origins. Changes in my attitude, posture, and boundaries, as well as my vocabulary, both facilitated my research and contributed to the knowledge I acquired in the process. Yet my embodied presence had to be negotiated for one more, and certainly significant, aspect of research: gender.

## Gender Matters (as Always)

While I was planning this research project, I noticed a particular emphasis in the news items and literature on the semi-formal in-home gatherings for which

---

20 Abu-Lughod 1988.
21 Ibid., 155.

Kayseri was famous. In the limited social scientific writing on Kayseri, these semi-formal home visits (*oturma*, literally "sitting", as they call it in Kayseri) were identified as an important site of politics and decision-making processes.[22] This scholarship describes an *oturma* as a private gathering in which public matters are debated between the elites of the town, especially among men. In my preliminary visit to Kayseri, I was told that even the decision to establish another university had been taken at one of these gatherings.

Given the importance of these visits and my aspiration to access charitable networks in the city, I initially planned to attend several of these *oturma*s and to conduct participant observation within the circles in which beneficence was organised. I was aware that *oturma*s were strictly gender segregated get-togethers, and I was intrigued by the fact that none of the publications mentioned the other room where women gathered. I was therefore hoping to grasp this missing part of the story in depth, but also to be accepted into the men's room as a researcher, which already bracketed my gender in our daily interactions. Both of these assumptions and expectations proved non-realistic after spending some time in Kayseri and learning more about the culture of *oturma*. As reported, all *oturma*s were gender segregated, but, to my surprise, this segregation was not only spatial but also temporal. During a men's gathering, which always took place in the evenings, the women of that household were solely responsible for serving their male guests. The wives of the men they were entertaining would not accompany their husbands as guests of the host's wife, nor as her helpers. Women's *oturma*s would always take place during the day and were strictly bound by time regulations imposed on the women by their husbands' working hours, such that no men would be present where and when a women's gathering was taking place. As a result of this system, it turned out to be impossible for me to be invited to men's *oturma*s where decisions important for my research were taken.

Unaware of the nature of the meetings, I assumed for a while that I had not been invited due to issues of trust or rapport. Only later did I figure out that a structural obstacle existed that I could not possibly overcome, or even attempt to overcome. A young Turkish woman who is overly interested in men's gatherings would only arouse further suspicion, which could in turn harm my access to women's activities as well. I had to accept these norms and change my research strategy accordingly.

Making such gender-based alterations to research strategies is common. Similar examples of how gender played both a limiting and an enhancing role in research experiences can be found in contributions to Altorki and El-Solh's

---

22 ESI 2005; Doğan 2007.

collection *Arab Women in the Field*.²³ For example, Shami details how she gained access to the impoverished slum neighbourhood of el-Wadi in Amman, Jordan through the special care she paid to operating within the moral boundaries of the locality.²⁴ This required limiting her interaction with the male residents, but allowed her an in-depth comprehension of the women's world. Similar accounts are provided by Altorki and Abu-Lughod regarding their experiences in Saudi Arabia and Egypt, respectively.²⁵

The gendered boundaries that I came across during my research kept me away from the private sphere of men but allowed me access to that of women, which made it possible to collect a considerable amount of material. I also experienced no difficulty accessing the public part of the men's world. In the organisational environments of the *vakıfs* I studied, men and women worked together, so I was welcome to follow men on their daily tasks, take long rides with them, join their home visits, and to load and unload vans, sort clothing, and distribute coal with them. I also attended many meetings that took place during the day or after work hours in offices. The reason I was the only woman in most of these meetings was not an issue of segregation but rather of the limited presence of women in decision-making positions (which also indicates gender disparity but in a different way). I also conducted interviews with male directors in their offices, warehouses, or workshops. Some of these men were public figures, for whom my research was a confirmation of the significance of their hometown, and they were thus eager to meet me, provide me with contacts, and answer my questions. Ultimately, my access to men as research participants was only restricted when they moved into the private spaces of their homes.

My interactions with women were more intimate. I regularly attended the weekly meetings of the female volunteers at Kayseri Derneği. I worked with them at fundraising lunches and charity fairs. We had opportunities to spend time together outside of the *vakıfs*. I was also invited to their fortnightly *oturma*s, each time in a different person's house. The female director of Sinan Vakfı was one of my initial contacts. I travelled with her to nearby towns, joined her at weddings, and kept her company during her hectic workdays. However, I was never invited to her home, where she lived with her parents and brother. I later became the welcome house guest of some of the women I met, staying over in their homes for many nights. But it was always single or widowed women who invited me for

---

23 Altorki and El-Solh 1988.
24 Shami 1988.
25 Altorki 1988; Abu-Lughod 1988.

dinner or to spend the night. All other women made sure that I left before their husbands came home and their family was reunited.

In these more intimate settings, I became part of women's daily housework and chatter. I witnessed the conflicts that arose between them, heard their comments about each other's behaviour, and therefore had opportunities to observe how subjectivities were worked on in the quotidian. Hence, gender made a big difference to the final content of this book. Had I been a man I would have had different access limitations and different opportunities. I would have had to be closer to the world of the *hayırsevers* (philanthropists) than that of the *vakıfçıs* (*vakıf* workers) and would have produced a different account.

## Methodological Limitations and Complementary Strategies

Another structural limitation born out of my position presented itself when I tried to gain levelled access to all actors in the beneficence field. Roughly categorised, there are three types of actors in the field of beneficence in Kayseri: a) *hayırsevers*, the *vakıf* benefactors, b) *vakıfçıs*, the intermediaries who work at *vakıf*s either voluntarily or on salary, and c) the beneficiaries who receive aid and services from these *vakıf*s. The following chapters will complicate this categorisation; however, it is beneficial to stick with it in this section for analytical purposes. Beneficence is often understood as the straightforward process of donating for the well-being of the needy members of a society. However, these donations rarely reach those who need them directly. There are often institutions, processes, and people who pass the donation on, though not without affecting it. Beneficiaries of these institutions only interact with these mediators – employees or volunteers. Therefore, beneficence is not a singular process in which goods and services flow unidirectionally, but rather is a web in which a multitude of services and goods are carried between nodes.

In this web, in Kayseri, *vakıfçıs* occupy significant nodes where the power to decide who-receives-what resides. This position deeply embeds *vakıfçıs* in a variety of gift relationships with both the benefactors and the beneficiaries. At the same time, they devote their time, energy, connections, and sometimes financial resources to the *vakıf* work and therefore actively give gifts themselves. In both situations, they are far from being simple vessels; their discourse sets the limits of possibility in the field, their decisions affect the livelihood of beneficiaries, and their practices have both ethical and material consequences.

I designed this research project to gain maximum access to this day-to-day work of mediation. Participant observation proved to be highly effective for reaching this goal. By living and working with *vakıfçıs* I have acquired an intimate knowledge of their practices, language, relations, fields of influence, interactions, networks, and transformations. However, for the overall comprehension of the gift circuits and the web of beneficence, the research had to be complemented with data about the benefactors and beneficiaries, as well. I have had ample chances to observe these two groups in their interactions with *vakıf* people and at the moments of gift exchange. I was able to take note of the variety of ways they responded to *vakıf* workers: most of the time, they were amenable to joining the *vakıfçıs'* game and playing according to the rules. Yet occasionally, there were some who defied the unspoken rules, challenged the decisions, refused to give or accept gifts. Moments of contact were rife with possibilities.

These observations gave me insights into the perspectives of the benefactors and the beneficiaries but my observations remained limited to the moment of the encounter. In order to overcome this anticipated limitation, I developed a number of complementary strategies. These included participant observation among the benefactors in the form of attending their informal but regular meetings in each other's homes, however, as I explained above, gender boundaries left these gatherings beyond my reach. As initially planned, however, I conducted interviews with the benefactors and founders of *vakıf*s and asked about their motivations, as well as their self-reflections (more details below).

My relationship with the beneficiaries was more complicated. I had initially planned to conduct interviews with them. However, I was already sceptical about this strategy, and it proved to be of very little use. I conducted seven preliminary interviews with the beneficiaries of one of the organisations I worked with, and had countless opportunities to chat informally with them as they waited their turn to apply for or receive provisions. I told them openly about what I was doing there, then enquired about their lives in general and listened to their stories of hardship. But as soon as the conversation reached the point at which I asked them about the experience of receiving aid, my interviewees turned timid. In their eyes, I was closely connected with these organisations, and regardless of how hard I tried, I couldn't successfully distance myself from the *vakıf*s. My questions intimidated them because they had already been subject to serious questioning before their applications were approved. Their responses were not addressed to me but to the organisation to which they were registered, such that even as they voiced criticism, they always also expressed gratitude. I was unable to get them to speak candidly to me and me alone.

In any case, as a believer in the strengths of ethnographic methods, I would not have considered interviews sufficient to meet the goals of this research project. Participant observation would be necessary, which would mean observing the beneficiaries' daily survival strategies, tactical moves to improve their own conditions, decision-making processes leading to preferences for one organisation over another, as well as listening to their comments about *vakıfçı*s, their encounters with them, the *vakıf* admission criteria, and so on. And such a task could only be accomplished if I had not begun my research by working with the *vakıf*s. I would have needed to start over, in a place no one (falsely, but justifiably) associated me with a *vakıf*. But the time available for the project was insufficient to attempt to conduct these two separate but intimately related ethnographies. Still, it would be ideal, and that side of the story deserves to be told in a future project.

Participant observation at the three *vakıf*s gave me a substantive understanding of practices and discourses, as well as an insight into the processes of ethical transformation that take place among *vakıfçı*s. Yet, I developed some complementary strategies to gain a better apprehension of the context in which these are embedded. These strategies included interviews with an array of *vakıf*-related people, selective study of the media, and general attention paid to public life in Kayseri.

I conducted 21 interviews and one focus group study. These interviews included the Director of Social Services of Kayseri Municipality; the wife of the mayor of Kayseri, who is also active in arranging coordination meetings with the women working and volunteering in almost all of the charitable organisations in the city; other municipal officers working in welfare provision; some donors and founders of these organisations; and the chairman of the Industrial Zone. I also attended several coordination meetings at the municipality and the local governor's office. At the final months of my research, I formally talked to some of the people, whom I worked with on a daily basis – the *hayırsever*s and *vakıfçı*s – to give them an opportunity to reflect on what they saw as the core issues regarding their work and to create a platform allowing them to enquire about my research findings. Finally, I conducted a focus group study with the Kayseri Derneği volunteers. Eight women accepted my invitation and found time to participate in this study, where we discussed what it meant for them to be active in such a context, as well as their own evaluation of the work done and the impact of gender in this work.

Aside from participant observation and interviews, I also paid attention to public life in Kayseri, and some of the interviews were part of this effort. With public life I refer rather ambiguously both to the state and the people, who in their interactions and intermingling act out the public life of a town.[26] I deliberately refrain from using the term "public sphere" in order to avoid a clear-cut distinction between the domains of "power" and "resistance", state and civil society. Thinking along this vein, I did not approach public life categorically but

---

[26] Navaro-Yashin 2002.

instead thematically. Any event, person, news item, organisation, book, or film that related to the concerns of this research was therefore identified as a potential source of data.

In order to learn about the resources that people make use of in constructing the discourse and practices of *vakıf* work, I attended some talks and a stage show about charitable giving, followed news items and columnists writing on the issue, borrowed commonly read books, and followed the national media in general. This part of the research helped me to connect all that is happening in Kayseri to the wider transformation of state discourse in Turkey. Especially by paying attention to mass media, which is equally consumed nationwide, I aimed to shift the scale of the research.

# 2 *Waqf* as Institution and Imaginary

This chapter introduces institutional forms of gift-giving in Turkey and the imaginary that has developed around these forms. The discussion revolves around the institution of the *waqf*. I do not examine this institution merely as a historical example but instead as a living legal formation that shapes and affects current welfare provision in Turkey, whether by civic actors or the state. I also illustrate how the *waqf* can and should be understood simultaneously as a religious and secular institution, by emphasising its civic aspects in relation to its religious features.

I begin with a detailed description of the *waqf* and its features. I then discuss the historical roles *waqf* institutions have played in societies: as social policy tools, building blocks of the public sphere, and instantiations of citizenship. The final section of the chapter is devoted to illustrating how the *waqf* as an institution affects and informs current beneficence activities and the welfare scene in Turkey. In order to do so, I give a brief overview of the historical development of welfare services since the foundation of the Turkish Republic.

## The Institution of *Waqf*

In Turkey, conducting registered charitable activities is only possible under two legal titles. The first of these is the title *dernek* (association), the generic name for any civil society organisation. Any seven people who come together around a cause can establish a *dernek*, register it with the Ministry of the Interior, and start functioning immediately. The second legal title is *vakıf*, which brings with it some special tax privileges but is harder to establish. The founding of a *vakıf* requires a considerable initial endowment and a guarantee for its perpetuity. The number of existing *vakıf*s in Turkey is therefore much smaller.

But in Kayseri, the founders, workers, and volunteers of charitable organisations almost always refer to their respective organisations as *vakıf*s, regardless of their actual legal status. These organisations may be associations, or they may even lack any legal status, but in the vernacular, they are all called *vakıf*s. There are also derivations of the word in wide circulation, such as *vakıfçılık*, signifying the activity of being involved with these organisations or charitable activities in general, or *vakıfçı*, identifying those who actively work for such causes. Although there exist a variety of terms that could be used to define the work that *vakıfçı*s do, as well as their institutional affiliations, the strong preference for these neologisms points to a significant element of these people's self-understanding and identification, as well as the historical path we can trace back in order to develop a fuller understanding of these acts and their social meaning.

*Vakıf* is the Turkish variant of the Arabic word, whose common transliteration in English is *waqf*. Throughout this book I use "*vakıf*" when I refer to the organisations I worked with or focused on, and I employ "*waqf*" to denote the institution itself, with its social, economic, and civic implications. The *waqf* is a legal institution that has regulated religious endowments throughout the history of Islam. Despite many changes in the details of *waqf* law over this lengthy history, the term *waqf* has usually designated a particular endowment made by a person for the benefit of well-defined beneficiaries. The endowment might consist of movables and immovables that would either generate revenues to sustain the *waqf*, such as land or an estate, or that would be beneficial on their own, such as books or scientific equipment. The beneficiaries of these endowments could be mosques, schools, hospitals, aqueducts, fountains, roads, or inns; they might also be their administrators, personnel, students, patients, guests, and patrons, or even the family members of their founders, as well as various categories of the poor. A complete list of endowments, beneficiaries, and plans for distribution of revenue from these endowments is compiled for every *waqf* in its founding document, the *vakıfname*, or *waqfiyyah* (*waqf* deed). Before the founding of the republic in Turkey, *waqf* deeds were written in the presence of a judge (*qadi/kadı*) and two witnesses, then signed by the founder, witnesses and the judge. The established *waqf* was then administered by a trustee (*mutawalli/mütevelli*) or a board of trustees, who were responsible for keeping the promises made in the deed; therefore, their performance was not a private matter but subject to checks and balances by local judges and the community in order to keep the legal, religious and societal implications of the *waqf* intact. In contemporary Turkey, *waqf*s are established at a state office (*Vakıflar Müdürlüğü*) and are periodically audited by state officials, so their system of oversight has been moved from the purview of local judges and communities to a centralised state agency. The significance of this shift will be discussed later in the chapter, but first I want to introduce some basic features of the *waqf*.

Historically, founding a *waqf* was a civic act that gave the founders prestige. Yet *waqf* founders did not always belong to the ruling or upper classes of their respective societies; they were men and women from all walks of life. All these founders were individuals who made endowments from their own property, not in the name of an office. Among such founders were sultans, sultanas, high ranking government officials, local notables, traders, and owners of small property or even a booklet. Women actively founded *waqf*s too and in no small numbers.[1] Suraiya Faroqhi notes that by the mid-sixteenth century in Istanbul, 37 percent of all *waqf* founders were women.[2]

Founding a *waqf* was not a right/obligation restricted to Muslims, either. In the Ottoman Empire, Jews and Christians were equally qualified to make endowments. Initially, these endowments could not be made to benefit a Jewish or Christian religious institution, like a church or a synagogue, but this prohibition was later lifted on the premise that these too would benefit travellers and the poor.[3] Thus, having come into being as a Muslim institution, the *waqf*'s civic features soon overshadowed any religious content, and the idea was adopted by members of different faiths. Through various adoptions, the institution travelled as far as England and gave rise to the institution of the trust.[4]

Over the course of the institution's history, *waqf* institutions have become an integral and essential element of urban environments in Muslim geographies. Mosques, hospitals, schools, soup kitchens, roads, infrastructure, caravansaries, Sufi lodges, libraries, observatories, scientific laboratories, student inns, scholars' quarters, public baths, fountains, marketplaces, bazaars... in short, nearly all public places were built via *waqf* and financed by endowments. While in Tabriz in the thirteenth century a complete neighbourhood housing 30,000 people was built as the *waqf* of the chemist-statesman Rashid el-Din, Ottomans used the *waqf* as an urban development tool to transform the landscape of newly conquered towns.[5] Various studies have documented in detail the impact of the *waqf* on the built environment, but the urban function of the *waqf* was not limited to architecture.[6]

*Waqf* institutions were an integral part of daily life in Muslim towns. *Waqf*s provided a steady supply of public goods by effectively financing public welfare services.[7] A range of professions were sustained by endowments, including scholars, teachers, doctors, Qur'an reciters, imams, the administrative personnel of all these establishments, their cleaners, porters, drivers and so on. Moreover, *waqf* institutions were an integral part of commercial and productive life in cities as well as in rural areas, since shops in marketplaces, workshops for industry, and the arable land in villages, in most cases, belonged to *waqf* institutions. Therefore, *waqf* laws and practices directly affected leases, production, and trades.

---

1 Isin and Üstündağ 2008; Gerber 1980; Merriwether 1997.
2 Faroqhi 2000.
3 Singer 2008, 99.
4 Makdisi 1981; Verbit 2002.
5 Arjomand 1998.
6 See, for example, Ergin 1953; Pinon 1987; Haneda and Miura 1994; Demirel 2000.
7 Çizakça 2000.

The *waqf* system acted as the main welfare provider in a vast geography for more than a millennium. Hospitals, soup kitchens, lodges, shelters, orphanages, and schools were all run by *waqf* institutions.[8] Moreover, these institutions provided the poor and destitute allowances of food, clothing, and money. It will be evident later in the chapter that, at the moment, it is this dimension of the *waqf* that effectively shapes the imaginary regarding the well-being of society and poverty alleviation in Turkey. However, the eminence of the *waqf* is not limited to its vital importance in welfare provision. The *waqf* is a civic institution with implications for urban space, performances of statehood, and polity formation. In other words, the *waqf* is a social policy tool, a public sphere agent, and an instantiation of citizenship. Scholarship on the history of *waqf* institutions abound with examples. In Iran, successive states and their rulers used *waqf*s to shape the denominational composition of their subjects, and delicately balanced possible tensions between various groups by favouring one Sufi sect over the other, or supporting education in one subject or the other.[9] In this context, the institution of the *waqf* provided the legal and social basis for a civil society that cannot be thought of as exclusively separate from the state.[10]

There is also a vein of scholarship that approaches the *waqf* as a testament to the existence of a public sphere in Islamic states throughout history.[11] Here the notion of the public sphere is understood as "a zone of autonomous social activity between the family and the ruling authorities"[12], in a way broader than Western conceptions of civil society. Within the specific constellation of power in Islamic political history, *waqf* institutions have created a realm for the communication of discourse between the rulers, the community of believers, and the Islamic scholars, wherein each party acted in accordance with a shared understanding of rights and duties. Because the rulers were as bound by *waqf* law as any other citizen, members of the public could rightfully and openly make claims to rights and entitlements. The same principle also initiated a participatory cooperation between the rulers and local communities on issues such as welfare provision and urban development. In short, the *waqf* thus functioned as an integrative institution in which shared values were established and maintained between the people and their rulers.[13]

---

**8** Bonner, Ener, and Singer 2003; Dallal 2004.
**9** Arjomand 1998.
**10** Ibid.
**11** Hoexter 2002.
**12** Ibid., 119.
**13** Ibid.

In a similar vein, Engin Isin and Alexandre Lefebvre approach the *waqf* as an institutionalised form of "gift giving [that] instantiates and organises legal rights and obligations, legal subjectivity, and legal legitimation".[14] As such, they see it as a legitimate source of citizenship, to be understood beyond Orientalist and Occidentalist conceptualisations. Building on Derrida, they argue that subjects are implicated in gift-giving practices, that "they do not pre-exist but are constituted through them".[15] Hence, the *waqf* as a civic gift-giving practice creates the subjects that enact and fulfil it.

With all these facets, the *waqf* is not solely a religious organisation. The discourse that surrounds it is interwoven with religious imagery and vocabulary, but at the same time it is a governmental tool, a citizenship act, and a building block of civil society. The reasons behind both its establishment and its social functions attest to an intermeshing of secular and religious values and operatives. It is also a significant institution of welfare provision and fulfils this function through civic gift-giving.

### The *Waqf* Between Public and Private

The institution of the *waqf* poses challenges to our modern understanding of the public-private binary, as well as of self-interest and altruism. This challenge owes to the foundational principles of the waqf, which I will recount in detail because these principles have strong relevance to the provision of welfare as gift in contemporary Turkey. From the first establishment of *waqf*s until the twentieth century, there were two rules that bound all *waqf* operations:

1 Perpetuity:
A) of the endowment: the Arabic word "waqf" literally means "to stop" or "to immobilise", pointing to the fact that endowed goods and properties were, once and for all, removed from market transactions and made absolute. They were then seen as belonging to God, upon whom humans had no claim. In that sense, at least in principle in premodern law, *waqf* property was protected against state confiscation, taxation, inheritance laws (to varying degrees), and market transactions. This rule was fervently explained in every *waqf* deed and those who impeached it were declared eternally cursed.

---

14 Isin and Lefebvre 2005, 6.
15 Derrida 1997, 8.

B) of the deed: In premodern *waqf* law, a *waqf* deed was a document that was irrevocable and unalterable. Even the caretaker/trustee who was appointed by the founder was only entitled to oversee the daily operations and make sure that these operations conformed to the *waqf* deed. So, not only were the revenue-generating endowments sheltered in perpetuity, but so too were the *waqf* founder's wishes regarding the function of the *waqf*, where the revenues would be directed to, whom the beneficiaries would be, and who would be employed. In that sense, a *waqf* was a rigid organisation in which the founder's desires and wishes were held sacrosanct, with no room for flexibility or transformation over time.[16] This particular feature, however, also endowed *waqf*s with the powers of a "decentralising institution, gaining mandate and legal force by specification of [their] founder".[17]

2. Personal endowment: A *waqf* could only be founded with the endowment of personal wealth. It could not be established in the name of an office or by a legal entity. Moreover, premodern *waqf* law did not recognise *waqf* institutions as legal entities on their own. Every *waqf* was known with the name of its founder, and sole liability fell on the founder or the trustee. Hence, founding a *waqf* has always been a very personal act. In the Ottoman Empire, it was common for members of the dynasty and ruling elite to establish *waqfs* that provided significant public services. However, none of these *waqfs* were established in the name of an office or by the treasury, although one can argue that the endowment came from public resources in the modern sense.

These principles make it hard to situate the institution within contemporary Western notions of public and private, and therefore have been a matter of heated debate among scholars for over a century. Often questioned is the genuineness of the charitable intentions of the *waqf* founders. According to Timur Kuran, for example, the primary aim in founding a *waqf* was to protect one's property against confiscation.[18] He argues that *waqf* law privileged Muslim landowners, who mostly belonged to ruling classes, allowing them to shelter their property from expropriation and taxation. Amy Singer and Haim Gerber, on the other hand, counter this view and illustrate with numbers that *waqfs* predominantly had charitable objectives and were established with benevolent and communitarian motivations.[19]

---

[16] Kuran 2001; Kuran 2016.
[17] Isin and Lefevre 2005, 11.
[18] Kuran 2001.
[19] Singer 2008; Gerber 2002.

The discussion on whether the founders abused the perpetuity principle for their private interests or acted out of genuine generosity actually falls on the fault line created by the modern understanding of public and private as dichotomous categories. The institution of the *waqf* challenges both this construction of the public/private binary and the opposition of self-interest versus altruism in the context of aid and welfare provision. An influential strand of this debate appears in the distinction made between family *waqf*s and charitable *waqf*s. As suggested by the name, the *waqf ahli* (family *waqf*) was intended to shelter family property and to make sure that it was transferred to future generations. The *waqf* law did not, in principle, allow for ownership to stay in the family; however, by carefully crafting the *waqf* deed, it was possible to allocate revenues and rights of usage to family members and, by appointing a family member as the caretaker/trustee, to guarantee that the control over the *waqf* property stays in the family. On the other hand, *waqf khayri* (charitable *waqf*) were established to benefit not a single family but a larger community, if not the public in general. Yet in legal terms, a family *waqf* was no different than a charitable *waqf*, so the classification was made not on a legal but on a moral basis.

In the lived reality of *waqf*s, this distinction was not possible to uphold in many circumstances. Only very few family *waqf*s solely benefited family members. Even the most exclusive *waqf* deed would still end by listing the poor as the final beneficiaries in the event that the original beneficiaries had died.[20] Hence, some of the *waqf*s that had initially been founded as family *waqf*s were gradually transformed into charitable *waqf*s over their centuries-long existences. Moreover, almost all *waqf* institutions (even the most "charitable" ones) benefited family members, freed slaves, servants or relatives by assigning them to trustee or staff positions, or by listing them as recipients of revenue, despite the fact that the main aim of the *waqf* was to serve public causes.[21] So, in the end, even enthusiastic embracers of the distinction note that all *waqf*s have elements of both to different degrees and the distinction is not absolute in any sense.

However, the attempt to make a classification that is based on opposing familial motives with public ones says something about the modern liberal desire to establish an absolute separation of public and private interests and functions, as well as about colonial legacies. In Egypt, India and the French colonial territories in Northern Africa, the distinction was formalised, and used to dismantle the *waqf* system.[22] Colonial regimes aimed to access land endowed through *waqf*s

---

**20** Çizakça 2011, 80.
**21** Baer 1997.
**22** Pioppi 2004; Singer 2008, 107; Kozlowski 1985.

for settlements and to liberate these properties for commercial transactions. The *waqf* system was inimical to these goals because it had created a considerable amount of inalienable property. Proving that some *waqf*s served no public function created legitimate grounds for a shift to a private property regime.

Yet such pragmatic concerns are hardly the sole driving force behind this categorization. The public-private dichotomy is one of two premises that serve as ground rules for contemporary humanitarianism and charitable work, and which force themselves on *waqf* studies. It is one of the most debated and challenged dichotomies in modern thinking, yet is equally influential and effective as a boundary drawing tool. Jeff Weintraub provides a non-exhaustive yet illustrative list of how the distinction operates in different disciplines and schools of thought.[23] The first way the binary is used appears in the liberal-economistic model. In this model, public corresponds to the state and private to the market. In the republican virtue model, on the other hand, public means the political community and it is positioned both against the market and the family. In the discipline of economic history, private corresponds to the sphere of family, while public is where waged employment is found. Feminist critical analysis adds a new layer and successfully illustrates how these models effectively assign women to the private and men to the public, whichever distinction is used.[24]

Looking through the lens of each of these distinctions, the *waqf* poses a serious challenge to the binary, always resisting being boxed in on either side of the line. According to Ahmad Dallal, "[w]aqf systems duplicate many of the roles played in the modern states by public, non-trading corporations, religious and charitable foundations and trusts, religious offices and family settlements".[25] Thus *waqf* institutions were public agents providing social services using the private funds of individual persons to generate income through market operations, with a special role assigned to family. Therefore they did not fit into the Euro-American legal lexicons.

The intentions of *waqf* founders as recorded in *waqf* deeds also attest to the simultaneity of disinterest and self-interest in the acts of gift-giving. They complicate the matter further, however, by introducing one more agent to the scene: God. In their *waqf* deeds, Ottoman *waqf* founders systematically elaborate two sources of motivation for their acts: spiritual development and guaranteeing a good afterlife by being close to God and contributing to the well-being of the

---

23 Weintraub 1997.
24 Pateman and Philips 1987; Gavison 1992.
25 Dallal 2004, 28.

community.²⁶ Although the first motivation is oriented towards the salvation of the self, the second is directed towards public well-being and relief; these two are neither conflictual nor incompatible. Instead, they complement each other because they reflect the conception of the community of believers "not as an antithesis to the private individual but as an integral or synthetic component of [an individual's] life as a Muslim".²⁷ Therefore, the well-being of the community of believers, the maintenance of its order according to Islamic principles and morals, and the well-being of each and every individual who is part of it contribute to the spiritual progress of the individual as much as they contribute to the community.

This deduction is a natural outcome of thinking with the concept of *maslaha*. *Maslaha*, a guiding principle in Islamic approaches to public policy and governance, is sometimes translated as benefit²⁸ but more often as welfare²⁹. *The Encyclopedia of Islam* prefers welfare too, but also notes that the concept has been used by jurists to mean "general good" or "public interest".³⁰ Hence it is often transferred from the level of the individual to the broader scale of society and comes to mean "social benefit".³¹ In fact, these two levels were never thought to be divisible. According to Al-Ghazali, *maslaha* "is the ultimate purpose of the *Shari'a*, consisting of the maintenance of religion, life, offspring, reason and property".³²

Yet, there are limits to studying the personal benefits of *waqf* endowments by focusing on manifest aims. The material heritage left by *waqf* institutions all around the predominantly Muslim world attest to the prestige these buildings once delivered to their endowers. Those buildings were public (and sometimes grandiose) expressions of power, piety, and social commitment.³³ In particular, monumental *waqf* works like huge mosque complexes that include soup kitchens, schools, public baths, and accommodation facilities for students and staff were vital in communicating the rulers' virtues to the public, and this communication was an essential way of gaining legitimacy. If power was necessary to gain

---

26 Singer 2008, 100.
27 Hoexter 2002, 122.
28 Tripp 2006.
29 Khan 1995.
30 Khadduri 2012, 738.
31 For further discussion, see Tripp 2006, 68–76.
32 Khadduri 2012, 739.
33 Kayaalp-Aktan 2007.

sovereignty over people, then piety, and hence prestige, were required for a ruler to establish him- or herself not only as powerful and capable but also as "just".[34]

This brings us back to the second principle of *waqf*: the principle of *personal endowments*. The creation of a *waqf* was necessarily the act of an individual, and how it would be run was also determined in detail by that individual. It was the same for the rulers of Islamic states as for lay people. As explained above, sultans, governors, and high officials only established *waqf*s as individuals, never in the name of an office or a realm. As Miriam Hoexter observes, this would be a practice "simply unknown to Islam and unacceptable according to the terms of the law of *waqf*".[35] The *waqf* is essentially a person's gift to his or her community, city, and eventually to God (although the endowments may be financed from the state treasury in the case of sultans). Despite being a public act that carries legal, moral, and social obligations, this personal starting point should not be taken lightly, as it provides a clue about the power regime that the social order of the *waqf* symbolises. This power, however institutionalised, remains a personal one, enacted within relations of gift-giving. Hence, it is neither abstracted nor impersonalised, unlike the bureaucratic workings of modern welfare states. I will come back to this notion of personalisation of power in the second half of the chapter, and illustrate its significance in the making of welfare as gift in contemporary Turkey. Here I should also emphasise that, this personal nature of endowments also implies belonging to a polity, having a status within it, and acknowledging an obligation to contribute to that polity as a virtuous member. The religious articulation of such an act only adds strength to its personal aspects.

In short, the *waqf* as a welfare institution is hard to locate within the modern lexicon that tries to establish a clear-cut distinction between public and private (in terms of rights, liability, and interests), and between personal and bureaucratic power. Although modern *waqf* laws try to overcome these difficulties with varying measures, the historical imagination cannot simply be disconnected from the institution itself and continues to inform *waqf* operations today.

**The Decline of the *Waqf***

During the nineteenth century the complex welfare system that had been upheld and maintained by *waqf* institutions became a target of detrimental policies. Western powers persistently asked for the abolition of the *waqf* system and the

---

34 Mardin 1991.
35 Hoexter 2002, 121.

liberation of *waqf* properties in the Ottoman Empire.[36] According to Isin, they had a double motivation in doing so. The first was the capitalist drive. At the time, almost one-third of all land across the empire was withdrawn from market transactions as *waqf* property. Liberating this land and making it accessible to market actors in order to transform modes of production and circulation in the empire became a priority of the colonial powers. Second, the project of abolishment was driven by ideas and ideologies about nation-state building and citizenship. Intermediary institutions, such as guilds in Europe and *waqf*s in Muslim societies, were then seen as impediments because they were presumed to come between states and individuals. Citizenship in centralised nation-states ties every individual directly to the state, and more importantly, is expected to tear apart all other belongings, identifications, sources of rights, and loyalties. On the contrary, *waqf*s were themselves sources of multiple legal subjectivities, local connections, and lasting relations of gratefulness and reciprocity.

Colonial regimes, as a general trend, are marked by such dislocations. Colonialism was never only about extracting resources and transferring wealth, but also transforming the institutions of the colonised in the mirror image of the colonisers' institutions at home.[37] As a consequence these local systems and institutions were labelled backward, non-modern, and impediments to progress. Although the Ottoman Empire occupies an ambiguous place in the history of colonisation, its encounter with colonisers included similar efforts. The Ottoman property regime, taxation system, and the *waqf* institution became targets of these policies that were eventually taken up by the bureaucrats of the empire.[38]

Still, the abolishment of the *waqf* system did not happen instantaneously, given its entrenchment in society and its sacred status. In Anatolia, it took almost a century for the nationalist and secularist modernisers to tear the system down. First came centralisation, which deprived the *waqf*s of their financial and administrative autonomy. All *waqf*s in the empire were placed under the rule of the newly established *Waqf* Ministry in 1836.[39] The ministry was charged with collecting all *waqf* revenue and redistributing a designated portion back to *waqf*s. Centralisation caused an immediate decline in the establishment of new *waqf*s and crippled the existing ones by causing a shortage of resources.

The second measure resulting in the dismantling of the *waqf* system came in the form of taxation. *Waqf* institutions had enjoyed tax exemptions due to the

---

**36** Isin 2007.
**37** De Landa 1997.
**38** Pamuk 1987.
**39** Çizakça 2000.

Islamic legal basis that recognised them as property endowed to and owned by God. In 1860, after the Crimean War, the British government posed the condition of abolishment of the *waqf* system in response to the Ottoman government's request for a loan.⁴⁰ It was not possible to abolish the system completely but, in 1867, for the first time in history, *waqf* institutions were made to pay taxes to the state. According to Isin, this was not simply a financial decision aimed at reducing the budget deficit and contributing to the payment of foreign debt, but also an important move towards secularising the state and its framework of citizenship.⁴¹ He argues,

> ... the secularisation of *waqf* administration practically displaced *waqfs* as an institution of virtue, a gift to the city and God, and thus exempt from taxation, and dissolved it into a state service. With the 1867 tax law, the ground on which the massive secularisation of the early republic would be built on was established.⁴²

During the second part of the nineteenth century, the *waqf* system continued to lose power and importance. The empire's loss of territories had a catastrophic effect on *waqf* institutions, as it also meant the loss of revenue-regenerating *waqf* land. During the chaotic years of World War I and the subsequent Independence War, the abolishment project was put aside for a period. The new Turkish Republican government then made a last move to eliminate all traces of the previous welfare regime by confiscating the great majority of *waqf* properties.⁴³ With this move, the perpetuity principle was irretrievably damaged and most *waqf* property was sold or nationalised. In 1926, the Civil Law introduced the term "*tesis*", simply meaning *establishment*, in order to designate endowments for a specific purpose, and wiped the legal system of the term *waqf* considerably *Waqf* then became a term used to refer to the remnants of Ottoman *waqfs* that had been centralised and confiscated, and also to *waqf* institutions belonging to non-Muslim minorities protected by international agreements. Only after 1967, with a change to the Civil Law, was the legal concept of *vakıf* brought back into legislation, replacing *tesis*, and the foundation of new *vakıfs* became possible, albeit without the institution's religious character and the principle of perpetuity, due to the secularist foundations of the republic.

Yet, despite all attempts to secularise and centralise it, the *waqf* as a regulative ideal and an important element of the social imaginary has survived. With

---

**40** Çizakça 2000.
**41** Isin 2007.
**42** Ibid., 10.
**43** Zencirci 2015.

its religious, personalistic, and public undertones, it is this ideal that still resonates between the discourse of politicians and the acts of civic benefactors in the contested realm of welfare provision in Turkey. It is also this ideal that feeds into the vernacular vocabulary developed by Kayseri charity workers, such as the neologism *vakıfçı* as a term of self-identification denoting anyone who personally and systematically aides and cares for others. The idea of the *waqf* is also alive in the state discourse about providing for its poor citizens, to such a degree that the state inserts itself into this arena by founding *waqf* institutions of an interesting sort. Understanding the creation of these state *vakıf*s requires a brief introduction to the Turkish welfare system.

## A Brief Overview of the Turkish Welfare Regime

The first three decades of the Turkish Republic were a period of authoritarian, single-party rule, during which the state tried to consolidate itself. Within its newly drawn borders lived a mostly agrarian, war-ridden and poverty-stricken population, only 24.4 percent of which resided in urban environments.[44] With the exception of the industrial workers, villagers had no health insurance or social citizenship rights. During the 1940s, the last decade of single-party rule, employment and premium-based social security institutions began to be formed. First, the Social Security Organisation for formal sector workers (*SSK*) was established in 1945, and second, various retirement schemes for civil servants were gathered under the roof of the Retirement Chest (*Emekli Sandığı*) in 1949. These two organisations, along with another scheme established in 1971 for the self-employed, including agricultural workers, *Bağ-Kur,* would then form the corporatist three-tier social security system of the second half of the century.

Corporatism is a hierarchical welfare system that treats various elements of the working population differently under an assortment of welfare schemes.[45] The trademark of this system is the special privileges civil servants have. In Turkey, too, the three-tier social security system consisting of the Retirement Chest for state employees, SSK for workers, and Bağ-Kur for the self-employed favoured civil servants in terms of benefits, pensions, and health care.[46] Also, all of these

---

[44] Buğra 2007, footnote number 25
[45] Esping-Andersen 1990.
[46] Buğra and Keyder 2006.

schemes were premium-based and left more than 50 percent of the working population (i.e. informal workers), and those who are not eligible to work, uncovered.[47]

The Turkish welfare regime can best be understood in comparison with the regimes of southern European countries.[48] These regimes are characterised by a labour market structure in which self-employment and family workers are prevalent; a large portion of labour and other economic activity goes undocumented; the social security system is corporatist; there is an almost total absence of formal policies against poverty; and the role played by the family, local governments, and networks in increasing the livelihood of individuals at social risk is significant.[49]

Both in other southern European countries and in Turkey a significant transformation along more universalistic and egalitarian lines began at the end of the last century. In Turkey, one of these recent developments was the introduction of the unemployment wage in 1999 for those who have accumulated a certain amount of premiums in the system. The three-tier system was then abolished and all schemes were brought under the umbrella of the Social Security Institution (*SGK*) in 2006. The establishment of the SGK first eliminated inequalities in the realm of healthcare provision to different scheme members: all hospitals, including participating private ones, opened to the working population, pensioners, and their dependents. Moreover, all children under the age of 18 were granted universal healthcare access.

Welfare provision to those who are not covered by the social security system is a different story. Until the 1990s there were only local first level clinics and a few hospitals that would serve the healthcare needs of the population excluded by the formal insurance schemes. The greatest social assistance scheme of the Republican era, the Green Card, introduced in 1992, gave the poorest portions of this large population access to healthcare services, based on income tests.[50] Gradually the number of Green Card holders reached almost 20 percent of the population and exceeded the number of SGK members in some impoverished provinces. When the Green Card scheme was terminated and all cardholders were transferred to the General Health Insurance system by the end of 2011, 9.5 million cardholders' medical needs were being met by public funds.[51] Direct monetary assistance also

---

47 Buğra and Keyder 2003.
48 Ibid.
49 Saraceno 2002; Buğra and Keyder 2003.
50 For an overview of the transformation in the early 2000s see the edited collection by Keyder et al. 2007.
51 SGK 2011.

came very late. Although minimal cash benefits to "poor and needy" citizens over 65 years of age began in 1976, their span was very narrow. A much larger disability and carer benefit scheme only began in 2005. All these benefits are financed by the Social Security Institution (SGK), but the eligibility of individual beneficiaries is at the discretion of Social Solidarity *Vakıf*s in every province and district. These *vakıf*s sit at the centre of state provided social assistance and give us the connection between a modern welfare regime and a historical institution.

## Social Solidarity *Vakıf*s

In Turkey, state financed social assistance has been provided through the Fund for the Encouragement of Social Cooperation and Solidarity (*Sosyal Yardımlaşma ve Dayanışmayı Teşvik Fonu*), which, since the 1980s, reported directly to the prime minister and later to the president. Social Solidarity *Vakıf*s (*Sosyal Yardımlaşma ve Dayanışma Vakıfları, SYDVs)* function as local branches of the fund and as local level decision-making bodies. As of 2009, when this research was conducted there were 931 SYDVs located in town halls all around Turkey. The trustees of each *vakıf* consist of the provincial governor or the district governor, the mayor, the highest Ministry of Health and Ministry of Education officials, the chair of the Social Services and Child Welfare Directorate, and three citizens. This board of trustees is responsible for assessing and selecting those who are in need of assistance and managing the funds they regularly receive from the Fund. They also determine who will receive old age or disability benefits. Established in 1986, the Fund became involved in systematic poverty alleviation during the 1990s, yet it was only at the beginning of the 2000s that its budget and reach became significant. In 2001, the Solidarity Fund's budget was 486 million Turkish Lira (€373 million), and it has provided support and relief to over 9 million citizens.[52] By 2009, the Fund's expenditures reached to 2.365 billion TL (€1.110 billion), of which 500 million TL (€234 million) was used for transfers made to the Ministries of Education and Health for their own social assistance schemes (like free meals for students at rural schools or the Green Card scheme), while the rest was spent on its own social assistance schemes.[53] The assistance activities of the SYDVs include provision of cash allowances; food, clothing, and coal; coverage of extraordinary medical costs that fall outside the Green Card scheme; running soup kitchens; and providing disaster relief.

---

[52] Buğra and Keyder 2003.
[53] SYDGM 2010.

Initially, SYDVs were expected to receive donations from individuals and the private sector alongside their public funding. This way, they would have had autonomy and fulfilled the function of creating solidarity, as the name suggests. Yet the plan proved unsuccessful and the SYDVs are currently almost solely dependent on public resources.[54] There was one significant donor to the fund, though: the World Bank. After the catastrophic financial crisis of 2001, the World Bank began allocating resources for conditional cash transfers to be distributed through SYDVs. Transfers were tied to school attendance and regular health checks for pregnant women and their new-borns, in accordance with World Bank policies; the responsibilities of the *vakıfs* were only procedural.

Local SYDVs have relative control over their resources, which are not earmarked for such strict schemes, but they do not have the autonomy to invest their income in revenue-generating activities, as ordinary *vakıfs* can lawfully do. The majority of their boards of trustees consist of appointed bureaucrats, and these bureaucrats act like agents of distribution for centrally allocated funds. Boards have a few members from the civil sector – local notables reputed to have expertise in the needs of the poor – yet, at least in Kayseri, these members act only as advisers to be heard from once in a while. The real decision-making powers lie in the hands of the governor, who determines the allocations and the criteria for assistance. But again, given their official positions, governors lack the autonomy to shape the *vakıfs* as a *waqf* founder would be able to do. Practically, SYDVs are no different from local Social Services or Healthcare Directorates, spending centrally allocated resources on centrally determined causes.

As discussed earlier, *waqf* institutions are by definition founded by persons. In that sense, SYDVs, as state-founded, impersonal redistribution tools, are an aberration. Given their current operations, it is also hard to suggest that they function like a *waqf* at all. So, this choice of designation and legal status for an institution of this type is truly striking. Why would a modern welfare state choose a civic gift-giving institution to regulate its welfare provision activities, even though it does not want to relegate it any autonomy in practice? The answer to this question is hidden in the social imaginary that defines legitimate and socially appreciated ways of providing aid and welfare in Turkey. These state *vakıfs* show us how entrenched the institution is and how strong is the imaginary of caring for needy members of society through civic initiatives. It is rather ironically telling that, in its first large-scale attempt at being an inclusive social welfare state, the Turkish Republic resorted to the very social citizenship institution it had aimed to abolish.

---

54 Açar 2009.

## Welfare Provision as a Personal Act

The case of SYDVs illustrates how the institution of the *waqf* and its social significance haunt the Turkish state in matters of social citizenship. When the welfare of its citizens became an issue to be tackled, the social and institutional memory of the state came up with the same system that had fulfilled similar needs for centuries. Even though the contemporary apparition is far from loyal to the essential features of the *waqf*, this institutional choice is still indicative that it is alive in the imaginary. In this final section I will delve into the matter a little more and try to trace a certain characteristic of the *waqf* in today's welfare politics. I will also briefly describe a historical period with which we can draw some parallels and which exhibits the same characteristics at work.

In his speech on 25 December 2007 on the distribution of coal to families in need, then Prime Minister Recep Tayyip Erdoğan said, "My esteemed governors, you need to get on the truck, take the driver's seat, and go there if need be. You ring the doorbell and hand out the coal and the stove yourself. The day you do that, Turkey shall fly high".[55] He has then repeated the same sentences in various contexts, sometimes in criticism of the self-conception of the state and bureaucracy, other times when introducing new policies, but always to point out a populist transformation of the state structure, as well as the image of the state in Turkey. The figure of the centrally appointed governor who does not hesitate to enter the house of a poor family, who serves people personally, who shows up in the most deprived parts of cities as the representative of the benevolent state and as a person with compassion for the inhabitants of those neighbourhoods has been positioned, in Erdoğan's speeches, in direct contrast with the faceless bureaucrat who feels no personal responsibility to the people, who does not leave, as he puts it, "his ivory tower" to see the extent of the poverty all around; a representative of a state which is itself distant, detached, oppressive, and even hostile.

Erdoğan's populist discourse not only reveals an acknowledgement of the state's responsibility towards maintaining the welfare of its citizens, it also prescribes a very specific way of performing this duty: personalised gift-giving. The coal to be distributed by the local governors is actually among the holdings of the SYDVs in every town and the governors are the heads of these *vakıf*s. However, the personalistic aspect of the *waqf* as an institution of civic gift-giving allows and informs governors to be personally involved in their operations.

---

55 CNN Türk 2007.

Erdoğan is not the first political figure in Turkish history to employ this language when presenting a welfare provision, nor is he the only one criticised for it. Among others, there is one historical figure much appreciated by Erdoğan, who also employed a similar language and invested in welfare provision as a personalistic act in the final years of the empire: Sultan Abdulhamid II. Nadir Özbek's illuminating analysis of welfare and social state policies in the Abdulhamid II era (1876–1908) gives a detailed account of how Abdulhamid was personally engaged in a variety of welfare activities.[56] During his reign, schools were built in the remotest villages, the first poor house/shelter of the empire was founded, as was a well-equipped, modern children's hospital. Charities of all sorts that were affiliated with various ethnic and religious groups flourished with the support of the sultan. Mass circumcision ceremonies were held in Istanbul for the sons of the urban poor, while Abdulhamid himself sent presents to new graduates of primary schools in provincial towns. A welfare benefit/income support wage (*Maaş-ı Fukara*) was issued to help the poor. This complicated system of welfare effectively bypassed any impersonal bureaucracy and borrowed from the former *waqf* system its personalistic element, establishing Abdulhamid himself as the benefactor of the poor and the needy. Özbek convincingly argues that this particular strategy of power "resulted in the 'over-personalization' of rulership in the Ottoman Empire" and added further paternalistic motives.[57] Abdulhamid's particular brand of gift-giving was also a communication strategy that allowed him to reach the remotest parts of the empire with a language that resonated well among the public, helping to sustain his 32-year reign.

In his influential article "The Just and the Unjust", historical sociologist Şerif Mardin argues that the success of the Ottoman rulers in consolidating the society and legitimating their rule for centuries laid in the moral language they effectively shared with the heterogeneous population of the empire.[58] This language, made up of common idioms and "root paradigms", as Victor Turner calls them, tied the two tiers of the society (i.e. the rulers and the ruled) together and created a basis for sovereignty.[59] The main idea that crosscut these two otherwise distant (and sometimes hostile) sections of society was the idea of justness. A ruler was considered legitimate only if he was perceived as just. And justness was not only a matter of acts but was also the product of successful communication with the ruled population through the use of resonating moral language. Abdulhamid's

---

56 Özbek 2002.
57 Özbek 2003, 206.
58 Mardin 1991.
59 Turner 1980.

example illustrates that the vocabulary that surrounds charitable giving had a particular appeal within this moral language. Through this moral language, *waqf* institutions created a realm for the communication of discourse between the rulers, the community of believers, and the Islamic scholars, wherein each party acted in accordance with a shared understanding of rights and duties. Therefore, the *waqf* functioned as an integrative institution in which shared values were established and maintained between the people and their rulers.[60]

The political realm as a whole, and the configuration of institutions in Turkey, have drastically changed since the heyday of the *waqf* institutions. Within the current state of state-society relations in Turkey, the *waqf* is not the sole institution that functions as an interface between the two, nor is it the only available civil society mechanism. However, the *waqf* still plays a significant role, not simply as the stage and space of interaction but as a constitutive idiom that makes similar sense to the rulers and the majority of the population in contemporary Turkey. And still, despite the fact that it contains much more than the *waqf*s in terms of institutions and tools, welfare provision is the realm in which this powerful moral language is shared, disseminated, and articulated.

Coming back to Erdoğan, we can observe a reference to this notion of rulers and citizens in which gift-giving is a primary mechanism of legitimation, and being a "just" ruler is an important criterion of this legitimacy. Erdoğan and "his governors" provide welfare services within terms of gift relations and revitalise certain aspects of the *waqf* as institutionalised civic gift-giving. Erdoğan operates in a terrain of terms and solutions that are readily available to him while reinforcing a populist authoritarianism with neo-Ottomanist references. The imaginary that has developed around the institution of the *waqf*, which is itself a form of gift-giving, haunts available discourses, vocabulary, and horizons of the imagination; and proves handy in the consolidation of this regime.

## Conclusion

As an institutional way of showing the responsibilities of citizenship and endowing to the polity, the *waqf* tells us about ways of understanding welfare provision that is not necessarily limited to the market or the state. The *waqf* is better understood through the lens of gift-giving, and in this institutionalised form the *waqf* interpellates the givers.[61] It therefore outlines the framework for legitimate and

---

60 Hoexter 2002.
61 Isin 2005.

socially appropriate ways of giving and creates legal and socially recognisable subjects. *Waqf* founders, workers, benefactors, and beneficiaries are all situated within this framework and thus have certain accompanying entitlements and responsibilities. In this sense, the *waqf* is both a source of social citizenship and a tool of welfare provision.

In this chapter I have focused my interest on two features of the *waqf* in particular. The first is its indifference to distinctions made between public and private. I have argued that the institution blurs the boundaries between self-interest and the public benefit, salvation of the soul and the well-being of the community; or better said, it interweaves these strands into an institutional and legal form. The second feature emphasised in this chapter is the *waqf*'s nature as a personal endowment. It is built on personalistic relations that situate human beings not as anonymous individuals assembled as a population, but as persons with well-defined positions in society. The importance of this feature will once again come to the surface when I discuss the significance of networks in Chapter 3.

In the second half of this chapter, I focused my interest on contemporary apparitions of the *waqf* in the welfare scene of Turkey. I suggested that the *waqf*'s characteristic features haunt the discourses and practices of those who are involved in welfare provision in Turkey.[62] The *waqf*'s significance stems from the challenge it poses to the all-or-nothing approaches that dominate recent welfare discussions. It introduces the concept of the gift back into contemporary political economy. In the coming chapters, I will direct my interest to the daily practices of contemporary *vakıf*s, which will give us a greater opportunity to see how the gift marks and shapes these practices.

---

[62] However, this account is specific to the Turkish case. For other contemporary repercussions of *waqf* see Jawad 2009b for Arab countries; Sadeq 2002 for Bangladesh; Aburaiya 2009 for Palestine.

# 3 *Hizmet*: A Contested Ethos of Service

This chapter illustrates how gift-giving operates in the beneficence field and how it is enacted in religiously informed vernacular terms. In order to achieve this end, I borrow Ilana Silber's conceptualisation of gift-giving within a religious imaginary. In her work on donations to medieval European monasteries, Silber approaches this particular form of religious giving as a "total phenomenon" in the Maussian sense, which means that giving has political, economic, moral, spiritual, social, and individual dimensions that affect and shape social relations in a plurality of ways.[1] In order to grasp this total phenomenon, she suggests making an analytical distinction between the theory and circuit of gifts, but without overlooking either, which is common practice in the study of religion. She convincingly argues against such contrasting approaches to religion, which are known for "dismissing religious beliefs and values as mere ideological varnish covering up the underlying social and economic interests actually furthered (the actual gift 'circuit'), or on the contrary, giving central weight to religious beliefs (or gift 'theory') and taking these pretty much at face value."[2] Silber develops a more composite approach and focuses on the mutual interaction between these two dimensions of gift-giving.

This chapter follows Silber's insightful conceptualisation and focuses on the mutual interaction between religious beliefs and social practices that surround beneficence in Kayseri. The Kayseri beneficence field exhibits an intermeshing of public and private funds, NGO and municipal involvement, and efforts by individuals who are not necessarily related to any of the parties mentioned. This intricate circuit, which is upheld by volunteers, benefactors, and paid employees alike, is maintained by a shared ethos that makes such intermeshing possible. This ethos is signified by a common repertoire of concepts, the most important of which is *hizmet*. This chapter will focus on the unfoldings of this particular concept and the ways in which it signifies and shapes acts of beneficence.

In colloquial Turkish, *hizmet* (from Arabic *khidma*) loosely means service. In this broader, secular sense it is used to denote municipal services (*belediye hizmetleri*), for example, or social services (*sosyal hizmetler*). Yet depending on the context it gains a religious emphasis, and the meaning covers all human services with the ultimate aim of serving God. Therefore, building a school, helping an old lady with hospital procedures, preaching Islam, or working in a municipal office may all be valued as *hizmet*. Regardless of whether it is done voluntarily or

---

1 Silber 1995
2 Ibid., 225.

 Open Access. © 2023 the author(s), published by De Gruyter.  This work is licensed under the Creative Commons Attribution-NonCommercial-NoDerivatives 4.0 International License.
https://doi.org/10.1515/9783111156552-004

as paid work, in this context, *hizmet* is identified with its direction towards God. Besides bringing together a variety of meanings, like charity, beneficence, good deeds, paid service, and duty, *hizmet* also brings a range of actors, resources, materials, and acts together, serving both as an encompassing paradigm and as a shortcut to all the meanings it connotes.

This chapter elaborates on *hizmet* in its various aspects: as labour, as donations and as networking. All of these aspects are explored in relation to the main argument that *hizmet* provides Kayseri beneficence actors with a "theory" of gift-giving – its meaning and spirit. As the chapter proceeds, it will become clear that *hizmet* as gift resists immediate returns, calculation, anonymity, and neutrality. Therefore, it is also an important resource of network formation and peer relations, both of which rely on personal ties. In the final section of the chapter, I question the intentionality in *hizmet* and end by asking if giving is a gift in itself; in other words, if there is a gift of giving.

## Labouring for *Hizmet*

In the charitable field of Kayseri, doing *hizmet* is most often understood as labouring in one way or another. Any act, in any sector, whether performed by salaried workers, volunteers, or entrepreneurs, can be broadly described as *hizmet*, as long as it is service for the public good, for somebody in need, or for the overall welfare of society. For example, businesspeople claim that they do *hizmet* by creating jobs, just as schoolteachers argue that they do *hizmet* by teaching morals alongside their official curricula. But most significantly and without dispute, *hizmet* labourers are those who work for *vakıf*s. These workers may be paid or volunteers. However, my observations suggest that this difference is not reflected in the self-conceptions of workers or the general treatment of their work.

Whether paid or unpaid, *hizmet* is *hizmet*, because this particular qualification does not stem from the material returns of the job but rather from its direction and nature. Both volunteers and salaried workers claim that they do not expect anything in return for their *hizmet*. This phrase is not a simple misrepresentation of the truth for those who receive monthly salaries for their work. It is indeed indicative of how they approach their labour, how they want it to be presented – as gifts. By suggesting that they are labouring not for the sake of money, not for any immediate return, but "to help other people", "for the sake of God", and "for it is our duty", even those who are paid try to refrain from having an expectation of return. What they are doing, and their intentions for doing so, exceed any immediate return. This is their way of framing their acts as acts of gift-giving.

However, as in any gift act, there is always the question that silently lingers in these claims of altruism and selflessness: Am I going to receive anything back? One day? From somebody? Or at least eventually from God? Beyaz, an exemplary figure in the Kayseri beneficence field, whispered the question with the help of a proverb, "Who serves in the dervish lodge drinks the soup. Would any of those (pointing to the beneficiaries in the waiting room) offer us a bowl of soup when the day comes?" When I asked him what he meant, he clarified, "You know, on Judgement Day, are they going to testify for us?" Beyaz's contemplation is indicative of the paradoxical nature of gift-giving. The first rule is not to expect a return, but at the same time the gift itself obligates return. As I will illustrate, the paradox is resolved by the lapse of time between giving and reciprocating and the indeterminability of the return-gift.[3]

All *vakıf*s in Kayseri heavily rely on volunteer labour. This is in accordance with the national situation. A study covering approximately 500 foundations operating throughout Turkey found that, on average, foundations employ four volunteers for every salaried worker.[4] In Kayseri, because the volunteer numbers change drastically over time, often with no record of the tasks, people, and working hours, it is not possible to produce exact numbers. But my observations support these findings about reliance on volunteers, in fact to a greater extent.

All Kayseri *vakıf*s have a few employees on salary, and it is these people who do most of the routine work. Volunteers are not expected to work regular hours or perform well-defined tasks. Rather, they are used as an emergency workforce, meeting up for extraordinary events like fundraisers, mass distributions, and assisting with Ramadan meals and health check-ups. In most of the *vakıf*s, directors also work voluntarily. Volunteers, whether they do the washing up or run the organisations, have a self-conception of doing *hizmet* and devoting their time to a sacred cause. Most volunteers describe what salaried staff do in identical terms and do not differentiate between themselves and the employees based on pay under normal conditions, though may question their *hizmet* at moments of crisis.

One such incident occurred during a clothing distribution drive held by Kayseri Derneği. Tension was simmering between the volunteers and staff from the start, as the staff were unhappy taking orders from the volunteers. The volunteers had already been advised about uneasiness among the employees, but a few senior volunteer women did not seem to heed the warnings. Just a few days after the distribution began, an argument broke out between an employee and a volunteer over a pair of shoes to be given to a beneficiary. Soon, the argument became

---

3 Bourdieu 1997a.
4 Çarkoğlu 2006.

so heated that other volunteers had to interfere and walk their friend to another room. Once the door was shut, the woman involved in the quarrel burst into tears. Others tried to calm her down, and the leader of the volunteers reassured her of the value of her labour, telling her not to mind the employees because they simply worked for money, while she, like all other volunteers, worked for God. Therefore, she had to maintain her composure, knowing that what she was doing was superior.

However, during lunch with the staff I observed similar reasoning from the employee who had been in the argument. According to him, what they, the workers, did at Kayseri Derneği day-and-night was *hizmet*, while these women who came in once in a while and acted as if they owned the place were only there to reaffirm their self-worth. What is striking about this rather ordinary organisational problem and crisis of hierarchy is the similarity between the moral claims of both parties. *Hizmet* in this sense is not only something performed but also something to be competitively claimed as an indicator of moral value. However, it was also the moral denominator, as it appeared in the reconciliatory intervention of the director later that day, "We are all here for *hizmet*, for doing good, for God's sake; you better remember this when you have problems with each other."

The line between volunteering and paid work is not only blurred in the self-understandings of actors. There are also material reasons that reinforce this ambiguity. As I said, *vakıf*s in Kayseri usually employ a few full-time employees to make sure that operations are not slowed by the constant influx and outflow of volunteers. Yet it is common practice to pay wages to those in need and let others volunteer. In most cases, it is the need of the employee and the financial resources of the institution that determine the nature of employment, not the position itself. Work requirements are almost never clearly defined. Most of the salaried workers regularly work unpaid overtime, or handle tasks that are not in their job descriptions. Their self-conception of doing *hizmet*, not simply work, is reinforced by these practices. Despite the low wages and extra work in some *vakıf*s bordering on exploitation, employees conceptualise it as their gift to the beneficiaries of their respective organisations. Most express gratitude for having such a job, like Emre from Kayseri Derneği, who worked the first nine months of his employment without social security, "Not everybody is as lucky workwise as I am. Here you get both money and blessings."

Men and women often work together at Kayseri *vakıf*s. There are only a few gender-segregated *vakıf*s, yet even they require the mixing of genders at important events. However, at all mixed-gender *vakıf*s, most of the paid employees are men. Women, if they are given paid employment, usually do secretarial and cleaning jobs. The only exception is the female director of Sinan Vakfı, who is the only woman in a high-level position. Although both men and women volunteer in *vakıf*s in general, the amount of time they are able to spare for *hizmet*, as well as when and where they do volunteer work, varies greatly according to gender and age. For *vakıf*s that are not intimately connected to a religious order, it is harder to attract volunteers in general, especially men. With the exception of a few retired middle-aged or elderly men, the only male volunteers in such organisations are found at the managerial level. They either work on the board of trustees, away from daily operations but still with a say in bigger decisions, or they contribute through their managerial skills by working as directors. Outside of this, it is women who do most of the volunteering. However, the more organisations are bureaucratised and salaried workers take on full-time jobs to handle routine work, the less space volunteer women find to contribute. Still, there are some occasions when women's contributions become vital for the organisations, like in clothing distribution drives, where intimate negotiations about the body take place, and at charity fairs, during which labour becomes crystallised as *hizmet*.

## Charity Fairs

Every year, all Kayseri *vakıf*s organise charity fairs to raise funds and make themselves known to the public. During the charity fair season between early May and mid-September there are a number of fairs going on in the city at any given time. Organisations compete for access to venues, applying as early as possible for permits so they can be among the first to open a fair in order to attract more enthusiastic shoppers. Although charity fairs are not the main, or even a significant source of income for *vakıf*s, they are afforded great importance by workers and volunteers alike.

More than one hundred people are mobilised for at least one month to organise each fair. Most volunteers are inactive throughout much of the year and consider the fairs a chance to contribute. Charity fair preparations and their day-to-day management usually rely on women's involvement and labour. During the charity fair season, ordinary *vakıf* operations are often suspended and women, both temporally and spatially, take over the institutions. At the fairs, the nature and gender of charity work changes, different meanings of money become observable, and the vocabulary of *hizmet* crystallises in innumerable encounters and iterations every day.

During my stay in Kayseri, I visited several charity fairs and volunteered at one of them for two weeks. Although these fairs differ in scale and take place at different venues, they all have common defining characteristics. Goods on sale are either handmade, like hand-knit vests and jumpers, embroidered tablecloths and bedcovers, and hand-sewn bags and clothing, or they are donated by their producers. Donated items range from furniture to plastic flowers, from trainers to toys. Materials for the handmade items are often given to women who do not have the means to financially support *vakıf*s but are willing to contribute. These women produce marketable items all year round, to be sold either at the charity fairs or at other fundraising activities. Both handmade goods and donations are sold below market price; charity fairs thus attract not only the wealthy of the community but also lower- and middle-class shoppers who find many bargains at the stalls.

In addition to the variety of consumer goods, all charity fairs also sell food. Homemade cakes, biscuits, snacks, pasta, tarts, puddings, baklava, and local specialities are prepared and served daily. Most of the fairs offer special hot dishes that are very labour-intensive and hard to find at ordinary restaurants. Some of these dishes, like *mantı* (an Anatolian ravioli particularly associated with Kayseri), are prepared by scores of women before the charity fairs, kept in freezers, and then cooked and served on the day of purchase. Others are prepared daily by a large group of female volunteers and workers backstage while the fair is going on. With women's labour free-flowing, these dishes are also extraordinarily cheap, making them a preferred alternative to restaurant lunches for students and working people.

Most of the *vakıf*s in Kayseri are legalised branches of some religious orders. These *vakıf*s have well-established and expansive labour pools that allow them to easily mobilise a great many people when hands are needed for charity fairs. For independent *vakıf*s like Kayseri Derneği or Yardımlaşma Vakfı, however, recruiting this much-needed labour force is a new challenge every year. This task is exclusively taken up by *vakıfçı* women, who make use of their social capital to organise teams in their neighbourhoods, among their circles of friends, and sometimes even among the beneficiaries of their respective *vakıf*s. The only beneficiaries whose help is elicited, however, are the rare women who either explicitly express a wish to help with *vakıf* work, or those who are well-known by or have been befriended by *vakıfçı* women.

Volunteer women do not only work *during* the charity fairs. They build these fairs from scratch and manage them to the end. It is the women who decide on the assignment of tasks to people, the prices of items on sale, and the supplies needed for production and maintenance. They actively produce, sell, and compete with each other to generate more income for their institutions. The role of men is limited to finding the venue and transporting large items like stalls, ovens, cookers, and the furniture to be sold. They then sit by the entrance and wait for orders from women to run errands. They do not enter the kitchen/backstage without permission, because women express the desire to be more comfortable and relaxed in their outfits. Nor do they intervene in decision-making processes, however troubled they may become. Charity fairs are unequivocally recognised as the women's realm, even though most of these women hold no official positions at the vakıfs.

Women volunteers at charity fairs express an "addiction" to these events. Every year, they start planning for the occasion months ahead of time. As the scheduled date approaches, they become more and more enthusiastic, claiming to derive pleasure from the hard work. Meryem, a middle-aged volunteer, used to repeat, "Nothing can compare with the charity fair," as if a mantra. When I asked what made it so special, she would tell me to come and see for myself because "it has such a different feel." During and after the fair, women exhibit pride in the visible traces of their exhaustion, like swollen ankles or sunken eyes, but always emphasise that they do not feel exhausted at all, that they surpass their normal physical limits. To make this point, Remziye, another seasoned volunteer, once told me, "You should see the fair, Hilal, you should see the fair. You get tired, you're worn out, you're wasted, and still you go home and cook for the next day." Apparently, charity fairs are an event to look forward to for women. A similar enthusiasm is visible in the pages of other ethnographic books on voluntary welfare provision. Lara Deeb relates how Lebanese Shi'i women working for orphanages and aid centres derive pleasure and joy from what they do, allowing them to work extraordinarily long hours without complaint. One of her research participants even suggested that "this work is morphine."[5] Egbert Harmsen hints at a parallel source of motivation in Jordanian voluntary welfare organisations.[6]

However, the value of charity fairs is not unequivocally established among all interested parties in Kayseri. Instead, it is occasionally challenged by male vakıf employees and becomes a source of tension between men and women. The director of Kayseri Derneği, who is a wealthy trader of spices and herbs, described this tension from the point of view of male directors, "Women, you know, make everything overly complicated. They make such a big fuss, which then makes you question whether it's really worth it. I can collect the amount of money they make with months of effort from my industrialist friends in just a couple of days." When this comment was discussed in a women's meeting, it sparked outrage. Women not only protested the derogatory characterisation of their working style, but were especially furious at the possibility they might lose the chance to organise another charity fair on the basis of low productivity and profitability. The women of Kayseri Derneği protested that there was more to charity fairs than simply making money and raising funds. There was, indeed, a lot more.

---

5 Deeb 2008, 194.
6 Harmsen 2008.

## The Gift of Labour

Viewed through the lens of business principles that overvalue productivity, efficiency, and profitability, women's charity work may seem incongruous and out of place. The women of the Kayseri *vakıf*s do not make detailed cost analyses of their sales items. Their selected profit margin is so narrow that they make almost no money, especially from food. Only those items that they receive completely free result in a financially meaningful return. In 2009, after a month of constant production and two weeks of sales at the Kayseri Derneği charity fair, net profits barely covered the organisation's expenses for one month. For Yardımlaşma Vakfı, the return was much lower. So, as a tradesman himself, the director of Kayseri Derneği has a point. Yet, what is more interesting and important to the discussion in this chapter is the women volunteers' point, which eventually convinced the director, too: that there is something more to charity fairs than making money.

Why these women do not make neat calculations as expected by the director cannot be explained by inexperience or lack of knowledge. Rather, some of the women have been working in similar organisations for almost a decade and others run their own businesses. The reason they exhibit so little interest in cost-benefit analyses should be sought elsewhere: outside the realm of economic calculations and market transactions, and within the realm of the gift. Everything that goes into and comes out of charity fairs is a gift. This applies to the labour of the volunteers as much as it does to the donated items. Women consider their labour to be gifts, and this understanding is the reason behind the silent and sometimes unconscious resistance to making calculations. Volunteers find it incomprehensible to attach any monetary value to labour spent on *hizmet* and often donate their labour to charity fairs without accounting for it.

While women do not openly count their hours and measure their contribution, this particular kind of disinterestedness is not only a matter of work etiquette. It further implies that labour is not considered a factor in determining the monetary value of charity fair goods. Labour is not added to the prices, which would otherwise increase profit margins considerably. On the contrary, it is deducted from the price, in a manner of speaking. Therefore, instead of creating a greater return for the organisation – and thus a greater gift to the organisation and its beneficiaries – women's labour, embedded in these products, most significantly becomes a gift to the buyers.

This does not mean that the women do not keep track of what they do. They track whatever they produce, for example, "Today I cooked six pots of *mantı*", or talk about how swollen their feet are or how severe their headache has become.

Nuran, who had a life-threatening health condition before she started volunteering at Kayseri Derneği, once told me about this in detail:

> I used to bake delicious cakes. So I thought, "Why do I make these cakes for my woman friends? I should better make them for the poor." Next year I stood behind the cake counter from early in the morning till evening, every single day. I emptied the trays and cake stands. Then went home and baked cakes with a 10-kilo bucket of flour... I couldn't stand on my feet because they were so swollen. But, because I did all of this without accounting for it, a goodness occurred in my body. I healed because of the prayers and good wishes I had received. I believe I am alive because of this.

Nuran then gave me an account of what type of cakes she used to bake and how sleepless she was during the fair. A vivid memory recounted so many years later. Just like Nuran, charity fair workers keep track of the effects of their labour, but this is not an equation of labour with time, and of time with money. Their labour is inseparable from the production, intentions, and meanings involved in the activity. This takes us to one of the most significant features of the gift: inalienability.[7] Unlike commodities, gifts are not easily alienable from the person who gives them (or in this case, who makes them). By refusing to alienate their labour from the product, the women volunteers at charity fairs mark what they produce as personal gifts, not as generic commodities.

The conception of charity fair goods as gifts rather than commodities becomes especially observable when a shopper protests that what they wanted to buy is overpriced. Although volunteers at the stalls often offer discounts and even give away some items when they believe the shopper needs them, a customer grumbling about the value of their goods causes consternation. Most of the women refuse to discuss the value of their labour and take a defensive stance, blaming their correspondents for confusing charity and business, and failing to understand the meaning of *hizmet*. They sometimes openly confront these customers, like Servet, a volunteer responsible for the sweets stall once did, "We are working here for God's sake, we are not salaried labourers! If you cannot appreciate the *hayır* (beneficence) you perform by buying these items, then go shop on the street!"

The idea of labour as embedded gift also crystallises with certain shoppers – those considered to be appropriate subjects of the generalised reciprocity involved in volunteering. The poor, the elderly, and students are seen as perfect recipients of these gifts. Women who work at the fairs become especially welcoming to these groups of people, as they are seen as natural and deserving recipients of charity. They are worthy of the gift embedded in under-priced goods, and the additional

---

7 Mauss 1990; Weiner 1992.

gift of price reduction and free items. The regular distribution of food and drastic discounts to needy customers and students is a common practice at charity fairs.

**The Gift of Prayer**

Charity fair volunteers make a deliberate effort to signify and further enhance what they produce as gifts with rituals. These rituals most commonly find expression in overflowing and indefinitely circulating good wishes like "may God be pleased" (*Allah razı olsun*). This phrase is evidently important with its reference to God as the receiver of the gift: the gift of the customer that is instantiated through their shopping at the fair, and the gift of the labourer who works to make it happen. It is a wish for God to accept the gift. This prayer is so naturalised that it often replaces an ordinary "thank you" altogether, coming out by habit of tongue. Still, it reminds everyone involved that this is not a commercial transaction. Instead, it is a gift transaction with God as the ultimate giver and receiver of gifts and is therefore sacrosanct.

There are also some less naturalised ways to further enchant the goods sold at charity fairs. Almost all fairs in Kayseri are launched with a ceremony that involves a short recitation from the Qur'an and a prayer/appeal by an important religious figure. This ceremony is then repeated every day in a more informal fashion by the person who unlocks the door of the venue early in the morning, and by volunteers and workers before they begin their workday. At the Kayseri Derneği charity fair, the daily ritual of collective prayer was directed by the leader of the female volunteers. This woman, who was a renowned religious preacher, would gather all the volunteers around her and improvise a prayer in Turkish, interspersed with verses from the Qur'an in Arabic. The prayer mostly consisted of an appeal for bounty; for well-wishes, peace, and harmony among the volunteers; and for the health and well-being of the customers. She would conclude with a further appeal to God asking for the acceptance of both the volunteers' and the shoppers' deeds and gifts.

While working in the production and sales of goods, some women have their own rituals to accompany their actions. Some pray with beads while sitting behind the stalls, others repeat a short prayer for every vine leaf they roll. Turning on and off the hobs and ovens, lifting the lid of a pot or beginning to chop spring greens become occasions for little prayers for the well-being of those who will eat the dishes and for acceptance of the good deeds of those who prepare them. Usually, this constant enchantment of production and the materials that result from it takes place in a silent and naturalised way. Women do not emphasise the symbolic and spiritual labour they imbue these items with so as to increase their value. Yet, there was at least one occasion when the way in which these rituals affect the products' quality was put on the table.

Every day during the Kayseri Derneği charity fair, a man came to have an early dinner in the company of a couple of women. He always ordered the women's food by coming to the food stalls while the women sat and waited at their table. One evening, the man spoke of how glad they were for the fair, as they were finally having freshly cooked hot dishes for dinner. I asked him if they worked until late. The man grinned and replied, "We don't have a house to go, you know, we are in the estate business." As I tried to make sense of this utterly meaningless sentence, one of the volunteer women interrupted, took the man's order and thanked him goodbye. After he walked away, this volunteer woman, Nuran, told me in a hushed voice that she had been observing the man for some time, and that she had become certain that he was "selling those girls". It appeared that I was the only one who had not "figured it out". All the women near us expressed their agreement with this assessment and said they hoped their food, on which they had prayed, would help them to have remorse and change their paths. Seyhan added that she was praying in particular for the deliverance and salvation of those young women. Nothing was said or implied to the customers; they were politely served and left unaware of the prayers, judgements, and wishes hidden in the food they were eating. But the gift was there, no matter if the receivers knew it or not. In that sense, this may be the closest that a gift, in the context of beneficence, can get to Derrida's impossible gift.[8]

## The Gift as Exchange

I thus contend that shopping at charity fairs can better be understood as gift exchange than as market transaction. Goods and products put on sale carry an inalienable personal, social, and moral value embedded within them which far exceeds their financial value and importance. By producing and selling these goods, charity workers are actively giving gifts, whereas by buying these items in the proper manner and by recognising the gift aspect of the goods, customers identify and accept these gifts. In the eyes of charity fair volunteers, those who try to bargain cannot recognise the gift and thus refuse it. Refusal of a gift enacts the worst possible scenario in a gift exchange. First and foremost, gift obligates acceptance.[9] Rejection creates a shared negative feeling in those who laboured

---

8 Derrida 1997.
9 Mauss 1990.

for that gift and becomes a subject of hours of blatter. On the other hand, those who recognise and accept the gift then pay the sum due. Yet the payment neither annuls the gift, nor does it complete the cycle of reciprocity. Signification as gift is, once again, marked by utterances of recognition.

As mentioned earlier, the moments when things change hands are always highlighted with the phrase "may God be pleased" (*Allah razı olsun*). Customers recognise the gift as one primarily given to God, and say so. Charity fair workers reciprocate with the same phrase when they receive payment for their sales. This time it is the seller's turn to appreciate this monetary transaction as a gift, again with the ultimate recipient being God.[10] Charity fair volunteers explicitly express a desire for their gifts to be recognised; but their faith in the final recipient gives them a tool to overcome their disappointment when events do not unfold as they expected. A dialogue that took place between two volunteers, in a focus group meeting with a number of women, shows this point:

> Remziye: So, dear Hilal, we work for two months, just as much as we work for our own households. We put that much effort, that much labour in. But whether this effort is appreciated or not, is only known by God.
>
> Nuray: We are doing it for God, already. So who else is to appreciate it?

What Remziye said here implies that, at least at certain times, she does not get enough recognition and appreciation for her gifts. However, expressing this disappointment is not a welcome part of their public rhetoric about what they do. Nuray therefore reminds her of that, by pointing to the final recipient of all gifts and thus the ultimate determiner of the value of deeds. This idea certainly gives women solace in moments of crisis. However, that being said, what most ratifies volunteer women's sense of accomplishment in gift-giving is the willingness of charity fair shoppers to enter into this enchanted exchange of things and words. These customers are active subjects in this symbolic and moral meaning creation, with the acts recognised as gift-giving. At first sight, charity fairs are not so different from any commercial enterprise, and their customers seem no different from high street shoppers. But a closer look reveals that those exchanges are closer to gift exchanges than market transactions. As detailed in the Introduction, market transactions are contractual and tend to have closure when payment is made and goods are delivered. Customers know what they are going to receive what they pay for. In short, the transactions have no strings attached except those explicitly spelled out in the contract. For shoppers at charity fairs, the act of buying is

---

**10** For similar examples from Egypt, see Mittermaier 2019

itself an act of gift-giving; a gift that is to be delivered to the beneficiaries of the host organisation. Therefore, the transaction does not have closure when they are handed the goods they have paid for. They are, rather, entering into open-ended gift flows. In that sense, neither the volunteers nor the shoppers see shopping at charity fairs as a structurally or fundamentally different kind of transaction than making donations. Although customers "buy" something, they know that, in the last instance, their payment will be used for charitable purposes and will be accepted by beneficiaries as a gift sponsored by a shopper.

I have thus far tried to illustrate how labouring for *hizmet* is an instantiation of gift-giving by focusing on different aspects of this labour as it appears during charity fairs. Certainly, labouring for *hizmet* is not limited to charity fair work. On the contrary, *vakıf* workers and volunteers identify all related work with *hizmet* and therefore give their labour as gifts to beneficiaries on innumerable occasions. Charity fairs are only one example of these occasions, but certainly a condensed one. I touch upon some other forms of labouring for *hizmet* in the coming chapters, but it is time to move on to another form of doing *hizmet*: donating.

## Donating for *Hizmet*

In Kayseri, although most of the vakıfs organise charity fairs and fund-raising luncheons, the greatest source of income for these charitable organisations are donations. Donations are made either in kind or in cash. Some organisations receive regular sums from their donors, especially from their board members, while others give more sporadically and spontaneously. At certain times of the year, like at Ramadan or Eid al-Adha, donations increase dramatically; still, the flow of donations continues year-round. This section will first focus on the donors and their motivations, then move to the qualities of the money that is donated: how money is differentiated according to the intentions of the donors and the sources of the earning, and how it is directed towards different uses.

Kayseri *vakıf*s receive donations from a wide range of people with different financial means: from the wealthy who either founded these *vakıf*s or serve in their boards; the shopkeepers and business owners who are visited regularly to request donations; and the middle-income salary earners who donate sporadically but especially during Ramadan or before the religious fests. Those who donate regularly and more substantially are colloquially called *hayırsever*s, and they are also the people whose names appear on the schools, mosques or public buildings they endowed to the city. Many of the *hayırsever*s I talked to present these donations and endowments as a response to a calling coming from the city itself, similar to ancient Greek euergerism.[11] For some, donating to the city is, as I explained above, the payment of a debt. For others, it is seen as a tradition they proudly continue. There are also more mystical ways of explaining how the city demands endowments. Such arguments assert that beneficence is an attribute of the city, that there is something impalpable about Kayseri that urges them to give. For example, according to Beyaz, Kayseri was home to many saintly figures who still watch over the city. Beneficence was their legacy, their particular way of extending care over centuries. Similarly, Ahmet H., a renowned industrialist, resorts to a more biological discourse, only to disclose that the source of obligation is as obscure to him as to Beyaz: "You know turtles. Their babies crack their eggs and immediately start walking towards the sea. How do they know that they have to reach the sea? How do they know, even, what sea is? It is in their genes. Just like this, Kayseri people have this [benefaction] in their genes."

Aside from these mystical explanations about how the city exacts endowments, most Kayseri donors have more concrete reasons to donate. The first of these is the humanitarian responsibility, which comes close to religious precepts for some and remains fully secular for others. One of the founders of Yardımlaşma Vakfı posited in a conversation with me that loving humankind was a religious dictate: "The basis of our charity should be the love of humanity. This is what we have learnt from the prophet and from Qur'an... In Islam, the basic tenet is being beneficial to human beings, so you have to do good. This is the sole objective of Muslims." However, for many of my interlocutors humanitarianism is an intrinsic virtue all human beings share, and cannot be attributed to a religion or a particular group. For example, opposing the subscription of charitable giving to Islam, Nihat B., a medical doctor and a founder of several *vakıf*s, suggested: "Human nature is based on charity. I mean, one of our most beautiful natural qualities as humans is this feeling of charity. Whether you are a Muslim or a non-Muslim, it doesn't matter. Everybody has this inborn quality."

A similar challenge to ascribing acts of beneficence to Islam came from Ahmet H. when our conversation was overheard by another person in the room, who volunteered a religious explanation for the endowments. Ahmet H. counter-argued:

> Let's not explain everything with religion. For example, if I pay my due *zekat*, should I still be engaged in *vakıf* work? Not necessarily. But on the other side, there is a humanitarian responsibility... If you come across an old man who fell and broke his leg, you take care of him. Or if you come across a crying child, isn't it my duty [to help her]? There are all sorts of institutions to take care of them. But you cannot think that way, at that moment. You have a humanitarian responsibility.

---

11 See Isin and Lefebvre 2005 for a detailed discussion.

In this second more secular explanation, there is a reference to a calling that these individuals experience and cannot completely attribute to their religious standing as devout Sunni Muslims. It is a call that directly addresses the inborn qualities of human beings, with immediacy.[12] In this understanding, love for humanity has to be universal, both at the level of subjects and at the level of its objects. In contrast, humanitarianism attributed to religion is universal only in terms of inclusiveness. Kayseri *hayırsever*s discursively switch between these two levels of universality whenever they mention love for humankind. However, in both cases, *hayırsever*s explain their acts of beneficence with reference to an obligation that is somehow ingrained in them, rather than being a product of free will or desire. They are constituted as benefactors while complying with an obligation to give, "the need to help".[13] In a rather contradictory way, they argue that they respond willingly and voluntarily to this obligation. In this sense, benefaction precedes the benefactors, and the obligation to give creates the gift giver.

Not always associated with universal humanitarianism, religious dictates themselves are another source of obligation. Without exception, all of the *hayırsever*s I talked with cited a famous *hadith* from Prophet Muhammad: "He who sleeps contented while his neighbour sleeps hungry is not one us." For them this meant more than a neighbourly responsibility; it was a test of their faith and belonging to the community of Muslims. It therefore required solutions that address the community as a whole, or at least all Kayseri citizens. Because as Ahmet H. said, the wealthy of the city "do not have the chance to check on neighbours regularly, enter their homes or ask if they have food in the cellar." To be able to adhere to this principle and remain "one of us", which according to him means living "in accordance with our faith, traditions and Islamic manners", one should establish "soup kitchens and serve everybody."

Yet there is one more reasoning behind donations that comes closer to upholding society as a whole – and one's privileges in it – than individual salvation. However, as discussed in the last chapter around the concept of *maslaha*, these two can be complementary. Here are the words of a private hospital owner and a food manufacturer, respectively, who also referred very much to the religious dictum at other moments in our conversations:

> Consider this: Somebody is suffering from hunger on the street. This is a major weakness for society. Or, for example, a student has to give up school because he cannot pay the tuition fee. This would lead him to revolt against society. Maybe this is the reason behind rebellious

---

**12** Cf. P. Singer 2009.
**13** Malkki 2015.

anarchist youth. When society does not care for these people, it leads them to insurgency and you end up with people who do harm to society.

I mean, of course, may God's bounty be on everyone, but this is the balance of the world. Some people are rich, others are poor. May God uphold this balance. When all this [the economic crises] happened in Argentina, Turkey was in a crisis too. We were in an even worse situation. Why wasn't there any lootings? It is thanks to hayırsevers. This is a very good thing.

Unlike the other reasons to donate, this discourse is limited to a few – a very particular group of people, in fact. The more involved with *vakıf*s a *hayırsever* is, the more frequently references to personal responsibility are found in their discourse. As engagement decreases, as is the case with second interlocutor, whom I met at a *vakıf iftar* he sponsored and who donates to the *vakıf* only once a year, the manifest motivation behind endowments becomes the abstract notion of upholding society and social cohesion. They are the ones who see a threat to their class positions in extreme poverty and desperation; they therefore approach beneficence as a societal "safety valve" that absorbs the threat of radicalisation of the poor. However, for *vakıfçı*s and those *hayırsever*s with more direct contact with *vakıf*s, the act of extending a hand to someone in need is an aim in itself, as Ahmet H.'s emphasis on immediacy illustrates. It is not approached explicitly as an instrument for sustaining society as it is, or for defending class interests, but as the act of saving a person – just that one person – and in that moment only. It is a very presentist concern in this world and infinitely unbound in the after-life. There is hardly a middle level between these two radically different time-scales for the gift that urges to be given. In the second part of this section I will look into the characteristics of these donations and how they become de-neutralized by processes of religious earmarking.

**Religious Money**

Richard Titmuss argues that donating for the welfare and well-being of strangers is a modern phenomenon that runs counter to the mechanisms of gift as formulated by Mauss.[14] What makes it inexplicable in the Maussian approach is that, because the gift object is money, it becomes fully alienable. What Titmuss says about money is, indeed, very much shared in contemporary literature, but I will go against the grain to argue and illustrate that money, at least in the context of

---

**14** Titmuss 1997; Mauss 1990.

donations, is not as alienable from its donor as expected. Money goes through various processes on its way to becoming a gift. This section is about the meanings, symbols, and spells that strip money of its neutral and colourless disguise and make it a means for *hizmet*.

One day at Kayseri Derneği, Beyaz was busy finding household furniture for a recently graduated female schoolteacher who had no family or support in Kayseri. After gathering some things from here and there, he made a phone call to a workshop to ask for a desk. Later, when we went to the shop to collect the desk, the shop owner, who was an acquaintance of Beyaz asked, "Is this desk for someone in need or are you going to use it in the *vakıf* office? I wanted to make sure, in order to decide whether to count it for my *zekat* or for my *sadaka*." Beyaz told him that the young girl who was going to use the desk was really in need and added, "It is as pure as *zekat* can be."

In the charitable environment of Kayseri, donations have these clearly Islamic markings – *zekat (zakat)* and *sadaka (sadaqah)* – distinguishing them from each other has practical implications. A complex set of regulations based on scripture, exegeses, and the deliberations of religious scholars are applied to these different but closely related types of donations and their usage.

Paying *zakat* is compulsory for every Muslim whose wealth rises above a minimum level, and it is considered equal in importance to faith in God or observation of prayers. Those to whom *zakat* can be given are listed in the Qur'an.[15] *Zakat* cannot be given to non-Muslims, to one's close kin or, according to convention in Turkey, to institutions like hospitals, schools, mosques, and the like.[16] Only *vakıf*s that distribute what they are given are seen as eligible for *zakat*. *Zakat* is also bound by time; it should reach its destination before the completion of the year in which the *zakat* is due. This point is a source of serious concern, as the director of Kayseri Derneği notes:

> It is not good for us to have too many donations. There is a limit to what we can righteously distribute and spend in a short period of time. It is people's *zekat*, so it has to reach its destination as quickly as possible. You cannot wrap yourself in money; you have to transfer it. So, neither too little nor too much money is good for us.

---

**15** 1- The poor; 2- The destitute; 3- *Zakat* collection officials (where *zakat* is collected by the state); 4- Prospective converts to Islam (this is the only exception to the rule that *zakat* must be given to Muslims); 5- Slaves (in order to help them gain/buy their freedom); 6- Debtors; 7- Those who are on God's path (like those receiving religious education, those on their way to pilgrimage, those fighting a just *Jihad*); 8- Wayfarers, travellers (given that they are in need). See *The Qur'an*, 9:60.

**16** Topbaş 2006.

In contrast to *zakat*, *sadaqah* is a voluntary, yet strongly encouraged, act of Islamic charity that has a wider meaning and coverage. It can be given to anyone under any circumstances of temporary or permanent need. It can also be donated to civic welfare institutions in order to serve a broader spectrum of needs. Because of its non-obligatory nature, *sadaqah* is often highly praised and is believed to lead to accrued merits with God. Alongside the aim of helping someone out, *sadaqah* may well be given with a variety of intentions: as penance with the hope of paying off some small sins, to show thankfulness for some gains or good news, in order to protect loved ones from accidents, and so on. Moreover, *sadaqah* does not even have to be something material. A caring gesture, an attempt to help somebody, or even a congenial smile to a stranger count as *sadaqah*; although normally only money is meant when *sadaqah* is mentioned.

The boundlessness of *sadaqah* and the highly regulated notion of *zakat* often create practical complications for *vakıf*s. Money and goods that are marked as *zakat* require different treatment than ordinary donations that come in the form of *sadaqah*. It is controversial to use *zakat* money for administrative expenses, so some *vakıf*s handle this situation by working mostly with volunteers and therefore avoiding any overhead costs, while others keep different accounts for *zekat* and for donations of all other sorts. Showing his own discomfort with the situation, the director of Kayseri Derneği told me how he covered the operational expenses of the *vakıf* by setting aside the income generated at the charity fairs for this use only. Yet sometimes this money is not enough, so he attempted to find a religious justification for occasions to mix resources and had consulted a religious scholar, who told him a story about the Prophet, "One day somebody asked the Prophet, peace be upon him, if they could pay for their camels' feed from the *zekat* they collected. The Prophet approved, saying, because these animals were working in the collection of *zekat*, of course they should be fed by *zekat*. Nowadays our animals' feed is gas, so we may cover such expenses with *zekat*."

Yet, this reasoning and permission are often seen as a last resort among the *vakıfçı*s of Kayseri. Paying attention to benefactors' intentions and the characteristics of their donations is seen as a requirement of becoming a just, trustworthy, and pious person, and hence a better *vakıfçı*. In order to maintain this, charity workers often make daily adjustments. For example, Beyaz uses various jacket pockets to store different sorts of donations, while Neriman, the director of Sinan Vakfı, has separate envelopes in her handbag, each with a designated purpose. These mundane and practical technologies allow them to observe the meaning and quality even of individual banknotes entrusted to them. In their hands, goods and banknotes carry the intentions, prayers, and beliefs of their previous owners. They remain enchanted, individualised, and marked with an otherworldly stamp. This lets us question the alleged neutrality of money.

## Tainted Money

Not only is money circulating in charitable gift networks marked with its purpose, but quite commonly the source of money also contributes to its character. How particular monies are earned directly affects how they can be legitimately and rightfully spent. Some types of money are seen as dirty in origin and should be spent carefully. Among the charity networks in Kayseri, earned interest is openly considered to be dirty money. As both charging and paying interest are forbidden in Islam, while also being impossible to avoid in contemporary banking, how one handles interest without doing harm is a matter of serious discussion among the Muslim public.[17] Among the *vakıfçı*s and beneficiaries, I have come across many creative ways to treat this "dirty money", all of which had to do with cleaning, food, and immediacy.

One day during Ramadan 2008, Kayseri Derneği Market was crowded with shoppers carrying gift vouchers. These had been sold by Kayseri Derneği to businesspeople, who in turn gave them away as their own *sadaqah*, to be spent at the market. It was a particularly busy time of the year, and I was helping out in the market. While bagging customers' acquisitions, I spotted a man who had filled his shopping cart with fourteen packs of washing powder, eight packs of wet wipes, and nothing else. After he paid with his voucher, I helped him load his bags onto his bicycle and expressed my curiosity about all the detergent. The young man politely smiled and told me that he was working as a porter in an upmarket highrise. One of the landlords had given him the voucher, but he knew this landlord was not a pious man and that he was receiving interest. Since he could not be sure of the purity of the "money" (the voucher) he had been given, he and his wife considered the situation and decided not to use it on food, but on something else. They had three young kids and lots of washing to do, so the young man bought bags of washing powder. "I do not know if this is the right thing to do", he said, "but you know, this is somebody's *sadaka*, you cannot throw it away. But I wouldn't want to feed my children with forbidden (*haram*) money either."

In this young man's story, two characteristics of the same money create a conflict requiring a creative solution. First of all, what this man was given is gift money, which necessitates recognition and acceptance. The existing relationship between the young man and the landlord makes rejecting the gift impossible, and as gift money, the landlord's dubious earnings make their way into the pious porter's pocket. But the second characteristic of the money, that it might have been earned in religiously forbidden (*haram*) ways, stains it, keeping him from

---

17 Siddiqi 1981; Naqvi 1994; Kuran 2004; Kabir and Aliyu 2018.

spending it on even basic necessities. He comes up with a strategy that permitted him minimum contact with the money, but that did not risk tainting the insides of his children.[18] This conflict over cleanliness and purity is resolved in its most metaphoric way: with soap. The young man was attempting to wash away the stain on the gift money with 28 kilograms of washing powder.

Viviana Zelizer starts *The Social Meaning of Money* with the statement, "It is a powerful ideology of our time that money is a single, interchangeable, absolutely impersonal instrument – the very essence of our rationalising modern civilisation,"[19] and as the book progresses, she illustrates how this ideology has become so widespread and convincing, as well as how it is mistaken. Starting with the early theorists of modernity, Marx, Veblen, Simmel and Weber, money has been attributed certain characteristics, such as infinite divisibility, homogeneity, impersonality, and liquidity, that make it an effective agent of social change, a determinant of the impersonalised, mechanised, and disenchanted modern experience. In the social science literature, money invariably appears as a neutral yet powerful source of change in social relations – both their symbol and their cause. This attribute of having the power to shape the social atmosphere finds its perfect example in Georg Simmel's writing.

In his famed essay "The Metropolis and Mental Life", Simmel positions money in a close and mutually enforcing relationship with the modern psyche, namely apathetic blasé attitudes, as they share a certain "erasing" effect.

> To the extent that money, with its colourlessness and its indifferent quality, can become a common denominator of all values, it becomes the frightful leveller – it hollows out the core of things, their peculiarities, their specific values and their uniqueness and incomparability in a way which is beyond repair.[20]

In short, money makes things similar to itself, imbuing its qualities onto every aspect of life that it touches. Zelizer illustrates how "colour blind" Simmel's otherwise detailed and attentive analysis is by showing how money itself is far from being homogeneous, impersonal, and colourless. Instead, people steadily earmark money, treat it differentially, categorise it and embed it in their social relations. Therefore, as much as money has transformative power over social relations, it is deeply affected and constantly reshaped by social ties and institutions themselves.[21]

---

**18** One immediately remembers Mary Douglas's *Purity and Danger*. Douglas 1966.
**19** Zelizer 1994, 1.
**20** Simmel 1964, 414.
**21** Ibid.

As I have illustrated with the examples above, money that circulates in the charitable networks of Kayseri is loaded with meanings, values, and qualities that far exceed its quantitative importance in the eyes of both receivers and donors. Money is unneutral, one way or another, and it is almost always earmarked. It is categorised according to the way it is earned and the way it is spent. It is further categorised according to the processes it goes through, especially the process of purification through charitable giving. Doing *hizmet* with donations has the function of transforming money from wealth to the sacred *sadaqah* and *zakat*.

An elderly *vakıfçı* man I met in Kayseri told me that "genuine Muslims" should be grateful to the recipients of their *zakat* and *sadaqah*, because it was the only way for them to clean their money from its inherent stain. Hence, *zakat*, *sadaqah*, and any other kind of donation are ways of purifying one's earnings and wealth. This idea is shared by religious scholars too.[22] However, the same feature of religiously motivated donations is also the target of cynical criticism.[23] Muslim industrialists are accused of veiling the exploitative nature of their means of making money by giving a tiny portion of it as *zakat* and *sadaqah*, or of attempting to wipe their consciences clean of the burdens of this dubiously earned wealth.

Whether approached positively or with criticism, it is clear that the transforming and enchanting logic of *hizmet* extends beyond interpersonal relations and one's labour to the realm of materialities, even if that material is the seemingly colourless money. Within the framework of *hizmet*, money is earmarked by the means of its generation and intentions for its expenditure. Therefore, donating for *hizmet* is, at the same time, an act of meaning creation and social signification that challenges the alienability of the most alienated and disenchanted of material objects – money – thus transforming it into a gift with proper gift qualities.

## Networking for *Hizmet*

On an ordinary day at work, Neriman, spends a significant share of her time talking on the phone. She receives calls from the manager of the Industrial Zone, who is also the head of the executive board of Sinan Vakfı; from the mayor's wife; the regional director of education; the superintendent of the university hospital; and from school principals. She herself makes calls to municipal officers, other

---

22 See, for example, Maududi 1984; Topbaş 2006; Şentürk 2007 as well as Islamic economists Choudhury 1983; H. Dean and Khan 1997.
23 See, for example, Çınar 1997.

members of the board, some wealthy townswomen, the director of social services, other *vakıfs*' employees and volunteers, friends in the health sector, police officers, pharmacists, and the governor's secretary. Her mobile phone seems to be her most immediate and valuable instrument, almost the sole facilitator of her vocation, as she spends barely a few hours per day in her office. She is always on the go, handling some task somewhere in the city. Without her mobile phone, she would not be able to maintain her connections, and without these connections she herself would not be of so much value.

In Kayseri's charitable field, carrying out most ordinary tasks involves plenty of informal networking, outsourcing, and cooperation between various institutions and persons of power and authority. These actors have positions in the public services, in *vakıfs*, or in the business community. They mix and match efforts and resources, which may again be public or private, at the request of others in their personal networks. Whether the resources are public or private is not a matter of concern for any of the people involved. Nobody cares when Sinan's patient shelter is cleaned by municipal sanitation workers before the governor's visit, or when Kayseri Derneği rents a municipal building for a symbolic amount, without any competition from other organisations or a public bid. In situations like these, what is problematised is not the source but *the use* of resources. Are they used appropriately for *hizmet* or for private transactions? If they are used for the public interest or for providing to someone in need, resources, either public or private, are understood to have achieved their aim. If they come from a private donor, "may God be pleased with her"; if they are public resources, then this is what public resources are for (still, "may God be pleased with the person who handled the allocation").

The reason behind this indifference relates to the structure of organisations, as well as to a paradigmatic imaginary signification that sustains the ethos surrounding this structure. It is the features of the *waqf* as an institution, that affect the contemporary beneficence field in Kayseri. As discussed in detail in Chapter 2, the *waqf* can be intimated as a *personal* act with *public* aims and consequences. It, therefore, resists anonymity. On the most primary level, in Kayseri, *vakıf* networks are based on personal relations. Individuals acting within these networks may owe their social standing to their institutional positions, yet in the field of civic gift-giving they are primarily seen as persons with very *personal* characteristics: they may be trustworthy, benevolent, hardworking, pious, as well as unreliable, selfish, lazy, etc. They may have power over resources through their connections, wealth, family names, or vocations. Whoever they are, they are called into these networks primarily as persons, through personal ties. As a result of these personalistic processes, bureaucratic red tape is often put aside, record-keeping is taken loosely, and the speed with which a request is responded to takes primary importance. Thus, at the request of the superintendent of a public hospital, for example, a patient's debt to the social security system can be covered by a *vakıf* immediately and the patient can be operated on the same day. Or, the prime minister could assign each of his wealthy friends the construction of a building on a university campus and they would be obligated to undertake the project.

Janine Clark describes a similar organisation of charitable work in Egypt, Jordan, and Yemen.[24] She suggests that the horizontal ties that make up middle-class networks create the conditions for the existence of many "Islamic Social Institutions" (ISI). These ISIs rely on personal relations for funding, to overcome bureaucratic obstacles, to recruit staff and volunteers, and for many other administrative issues. According to her, what holds the ISIs together is the strength and breadth of the middle-class networks that support them, though the benefits are not unidirectional. The members of these networks benefit from the support they provide to ISIs as much as the ISIs benefit from their contributions. These benefits are not necessarily material. A strong sense of solidarity, a feeling of inclusion and harmony, and the satisfaction of being part of a group working for a good cause are all significant outcomes of ISI involvement. However, there are undeniable yet indeterminable material benefits, as well. A businessman's donations to an ISI may initiate a commercial exchange between him and others in the network, a voluntary service may turn into paid employment, and a favour for one's charitable cause may be reciprocated with a favour of support to the charity of the other.

A similar observation is made by Osella and Osella in their study of the Muslim entrepreneurs of Kerala who made fortunes through their businesses in the Gulf states.[25] These wealthy men heavily invest in charitable projects, especially in the field of education, in their hometowns in Kerala. However, most of these projects also involve mobilisation of state resources, other businesspersons' donations, and local elites' participation. This is only possible because the Kerala rich are already implicated in a network that is formed by marriages between families, business partnerships, and gifts and favours of all sorts.

Clark's case studies in Egypt, Jordan, and Yemen,[26] and Osella and Osella's observations in Kerala support my research in Kayseri that networks are of prime importance to civic welfare provision, and that the reciprocal exchange of gifts and favours is what makes these networks function smoothly and keeps them geared towards further solicitation. Therefore, as argued above, the gift relations

---

24 Clark 2004.
25 Osella and Osella 2009.
26 Clark 2004.

that are the subject of this book do not exist between the donors and beneficiaries alone. Alongside the gift relations between intermediary *vakıfçı*s and beneficiaries, another gift circuit of vital importance in Kayseri is constituted by the gifts that flow between friends, colleagues, and relatives who donate, work for, or otherwise support the *vakıf*s.

This reliance on personal contacts encourages and justifies informality. Unless there is an absolute need to do the paperwork, formalising the flow of resources is not seen as necessary. Paperwork and formalisation are only mandatory for the immovables, like buildings or sites. On such occasions, protocols are drafted to legalise the conditions of the transfer previously agreed upon in private settings and terms. Certainly, all *vakıf*s are subject to annual government controls and they all keep ledgers. Yet, as what comes in also goes out quickly, there is little time to record every bit of money that goes into a *vakıfçı*'s bag or to keep logs of the mattresses waiting to be collected in a businessman's warehouse. The "iron cage of bureaucracy"[27] is antithetical to the ad hoc nature and fluidity of *hizmet*. Yet this lack of bureaucracy also opens room for a lack of accountability and transparency in the strict sense. Accountability is maintained at the personal and communal level, and transparency is not always sought after. There are thus widely-used shortcuts that go unquestioned, since the people know each other and have established long-term reciprocal relations. In Kayseri, doing *vakıf* work is all about establishing these relationships and increasing one's command over various forms of capital and their circulation within these networks. I will discuss this Bourdieuian point further with the help of an anecdote.

One day in October 2008, Beyaz was busy helping to settle a refugee family from the Caucasus in their new home in Kayseri. A Circassian himself, Beyaz had known the family since the early days of their arrival in Turkey. They were not registered beneficiaries of Kayseri Derneği, but he was willing to use his own resources to help them settle. The first task was to arrange accommodation. A friend of Beyaz took care of this, renting a flat for the family in one of the newly-built mass housing projects on the outskirts of the city, even paying the first month's rent. Beyaz was supposed to furnish the flat, as the family had nothing but their clothing. After telling me the story of their troubles, he made a list of basic household items and started his first round of phone calls. After a number of calls, he was promised a gas cooker, a sofa set, carpets of various sizes, a bunk bed and mattresses, a dinner table and chairs, a set of pots and pans, a small second-hand refrigerator, and a television set. Just half an hour after our initial conversation, the only items remaining on his list were a vacuum cleaner and

---

27 Weber 1985.

a washing machine. He told me that he actually had the washing machine. He had found one a while ago for somebody who had not shown up to collect it, so it could be of better use now. He checked his list of immediate necessities once more and told me to have a glass of tea and wait to see "how God would send the vacuum cleaner."

Beyaz's reach and ability to mobilise resources may be somewhat extraordinary, but the incident illustrates commonplace networking, resourcing, and outsourcing activities undertaken by all those involved with *vakıf*s in Kayseri. Being in this field, most importantly, entails capacities to orchestrate one's own as well as other people's material, social, and cultural resources. Beyaz's own network consists of fellow *vakıfçı*s, wealthy businessman, benevolent friends, public service employees, fellow members of a religious order, and people from his ethnic community. Within this broad and diverse network, he occupies an important node in the local charity field.

Beyaz is not a wealthy man himself; indeed, he actually lives on the verge of poverty. He looks after a family of five on his decent salary from Kayseri Derneği. Coming from an impoverished migrant family, he was a construction worker during his teens and twenties. Then, while he was working on a construction site in Medina, Saudi Arabia, he rediscovered Islam through some extraordinary dreams and coincidences. By the time he returned to Turkey, he was a devoted and practising Muslim who wished to be part of *hizmet*. Beyaz defines *hizmet* as being a servant of God by being a servant of "the universe". With this aim, he began working in *vakıf*s through the help of the religious group with which he was involved. He was soon established as a trustworthy actor in the field of beneficence in Kayseri. At the time of my research, lacking the financial resources to support his *hizmet*, Beyaz was working as a salaried employee of Kayseri Derneği. He held a decision-making position that allowed him a flexible work schedule, and so he spent a significant amount of time in the service of other *vakıf*s or coordinating gift-giving of all sorts, including the likes of the one described above.

Despite Beyaz having very limited economic and cultural capital in the Bourdieuian sense, his extensive social capital allows him to be a prominent actor in the field of beneficence in Kayseri. Bourdieu defines social capital as an aggregate of a person's at least partly institutionalised relationships of mutual acquaintance and recognition.[28] Within these relationships, one can pursue claims to the capital of others. Social capital gives a person command over other people's resources, reputations, and capabilities.[29] This allows even people who

---

28 Bourdieu 1986.
29 Coleman 1988.

lack the initial material or cultural capital to gain power and mastery in their fields.[30] When a person exercises command over other people's resources, a conversion of types of capital takes place. While Beyaz is relatively disadvantaged in terms of class and education, he has other resources that can be converted. He is in particularly good command of rhetoric that has a persuasive effect on his connections. His language is rich in religious references, but its efficacy is not solely dependent on this. It is powerful because it is shared. It speaks to the common sensibilities of the members of his circle, it is full of references to shared past experiences, it thrives on a mutual ethos, and employs signs referring to a particular imaginary – the imaginary of the *waqf*. If Beyaz's credibility is an accumulation of various mutual exchanges resulting in desired outcomes, his command of a shared language certainly has a multiplicative effect on this accumulation.

As much as a substantial amount of symbolic capital is required for one to be able to mobilise resources within networks, the networks themselves are also a powerful initiator of beneficence activities. They are created and maintained through relations of reciprocal exchange – gift-giving – among peers of different standings. What is exchanged are not simply words and prayers like "may God be pleased". The material basis of *hizmet* and all *vakıf* activities can also be found in gift exchange. Within the networks of beneficence, favours may be made with disinterested intentions, but they create an obligation to reciprocate anyway. Reciprocation often involves another act of *hizmet*. Thus, when the social ties between network members are strengthened, or at least maintained, resources for beneficence activities are guaranteed without any open agreement or contract. It is the mechanism of gift-giving that sustains both the social world of the *waqf* and its possibilities. How much this can go wrong will be illustrated in the Epilogue.

## The Gift of Giving

One silent afternoon in Kayseri Derneği, an elderly man in a smart suit appeared at the door. All the employees seemed to know him already; they all moved to greet him. He was Selim Korkmaz, one of the organisation's founders and an important donor; but he rarely visited. Behind him was a young woman in worn-out clothes holding a tiny baby in her arms. The baby was wrapped in a blanket. After greeting everybody, Korkmaz explained that earlier that day he had gone to the hospital for a routine health check. It was there that he crossed paths with the woman and the baby. She was at the hospital to get treatment for her child,

---

**30** Lewis 2010.

who appeared to have a serious debilitating condition in her feet. When Korkmaz inquired about her situation, she expressed her devastation, saying that the doctors had treated them badly and refused to care for the child. She felt sure it was because they were poor. Korkmaz decided to take them to Sinan Hospital for free treatment, but on the way, he stopped at Kayseri Derneği to offer the woman some in-kind help. While he was pushing the shopping cart in the market, filling it with one each of almost every item available, we were instructed to find new clothes for the woman and the baby. With the help of another employee, I collected several blouses, cardigans, and skirts from the shelves and gave them to the woman to see if she liked them. We then went to the racks together to find her a thick overcoat. I was holding and caressing the baby as she tried the coat on when Korkmaz appeared with a full cart and smiled at me. He said, "Do you know how lucky you are that you are now holding this baby? It is a blessing sent to you by God. That doctor asked for money. He has no idea what real luck is!"

This idea of being lucky or blessed for helping a fellow human being is widely shared among beneficence circles in Kayseri. To have the opportunity to do good is considered a Godly gift, an occasion created for you by God. It is also considered a gift in the sense of being gifted. It is inborn, therefore even the propensity to give is given by God. With both of these implications, it is a gift to be grateful for, and this is where human agency resides. One should recognise the gift, acknowledge it, accept it, and act accordingly. The doctor, with his market-orientedness, is considered pitiable because he did not recognise the gift, let alone take the initiative to accept it.

In the way people in the beneficence field in Kayseri see it, being able to participate in *hizmet* is a gift itself. Those who give feel they have already received something, that they have already been implicated in gift-giving. This goes against the assumption of premeditating subjects who think, decide, and donate, in that order. Instead, the understanding that gifting is itself a gift suggests that gift-giving precedes the subjects who enact it. By arguing that *hizmet* is a gift given to them, *vakıfçıs* imply that what they are actively doing is beyond their intentions, aims, and beliefs – they are merely implicated in it. Not ignoring the performative aspects of this claim, I see here the Derridean notion of the non-intentionality of the gift and the reason behind its effectiveness as the primary mechanism in the field of beneficence.[31]

---

31 Derrida 1997.

## Conclusion

In this chapter, I have delved into the theory of gift-giving in Kayseri, often expressed through the encompassing term *hizmet*. I have examined the diverse manifestations and facets of this concept, giving equal weight to its religious implications and its practical role within the gift-giving dynamics. Throughout this chapter, I have posited that labor, donations, favours, words, and prayers all take on the form of gifts in various ways. These acts of giving extend to the city, beneficiaries, customers, friends, and acquaintances who seek favours. Finally, they are also offerings to God, the ultimate recipient of these gifts. Thus, *hizmet* serves as fertile ground upon which to establish relationships, and it further enchants them with a religious discourse. The idioms and imagery reproduced within these relationships can also be seen as sources of obligation to participate in *hizmet* and, consequently, to give gifts. Furthermore, within the context of *hizmet*, the act of giving gifts is also perceived as a gift to the giver, implying an action that transcends the intentions and volition of the individual.

In this intricate web of relationships forged through gift-giving, even money takes on an unalienable and non-neutral character. It is designated by religious norms and the intentions of the donors. Moreover, *vakıfçıs* resist the detachment of their labor, its quantification, and its transformation into a mere element within a cost-benefit analysis. Despite the impersonal bureaucracy involved in the allocation of resources to beneficiaries or the market-like nature of charity fairs, donors and volunteers spare no effort in rekindling the enchantment and personalization of their gifts. They do so through prayers, religious discourse, and by operating within networks of personal acquaintances.

Nonetheless, *hizmet* is not solely a religious concept, and gifts are not exclusively given with religious references. In the upcoming chapter, I will discuss how the ultimate recipients of these gifts – namely, the beneficiaries of *vakıfs* – are determined and the various criteria that this process encompasses.

# 4 "Our Poor": Criteria, Entitlement, and Justice

In the previous chapter, we saw that while social networks can be sustained by gift circulations, they are also selective about access – a selectiveness performed through choice of lexicon, lifestyle, religious orientation, and ties to the city. Therefore, the gift cycles that make *hizmet* possible in any setting are not universally inclusive. Those who enter these gift cycles from the lowest end, often as receivers (at least in terms of material gifts), face even higher barriers. In order for their claims to be validated, they have to accept scrutiny, questioning, and investigation. Yet this questioning begins with a more universal understanding of entitlements as being born out of needs, not out of any other categorical belonging or identification. This is where I begin to investigate the workings of beneficiary selection in Kayseri *vakıf*s. Towards the end of the chapter, it will become clear that while this understanding of entitlements generally does not differ very much from any other means-test on paper, it informs the negotiations of justice in the embodied encounters between *vakıfçı*s and supplicants.

In Kayseri, workers and volunteers at *vakıf*s would call the beneficiaries of their organisations "our poor" (*fakirimiz* [s.] or *fakirlerimiz* [pl.]), with all the paternalist connotations involved. Our poor are those who are being cared for and assisted by the organisations. It is a designated term for those entitled to regular provisions or access to services. It distinguishes the poor provided for by *vakıf*s from those poor who are not, as well as from those provided for by different *vakıf*s. To become "our poor", one must go through processes of evaluation, investigation, and finally, selection. This chapter follows this complex and non-linear process and focuses on its elements: terms of investigation; bureaucratic paperwork; conceptions, articulations and relationality of justice; and daily encounters.

The underlying theme of the chapter comes from yet another name given to beneficiaries. In Kayseri, "our poor" are also commonly called *ihtiyaç sahipleri* (literally meaning "possessors of needs"), a phrase different than *muhtaç* (needy). In a paradoxical twist of language, people usually defined by what they lack come to be depicted by what they have. Poverty in that sense becomes something not determined by what is missing, but by what is out there, what is felt and lived. "Possessors of needs" have something recognisable, identifiable, and very legitimate, and by virtue of "possessing" needs, they also possess rights: rights to receive, to be assisted and cared for. Therefore, what "our poor" possess is the right to have their needs satisfied and their suffering alleviated.[1]

---

[1] For a discussion on where suffering and need fall in the humanitarian framework, see Bornstein and Redfield 2011.

Yet not every need qualifies someone as "our poor". Needs and situations are differentiated from one another through a number of norms and practices, and only some are deemed legitimate objects of intervention. Some needs are given priority over others, sometimes via a perceived hierarchy of needs (as in the case of prioritising the need for food over the need for clothing) but also depending on the capacities of organisations to meet them. Some organisations respond to immediate physical necessities, such as medical or sanitation needs, while others respond to needs for education or homemaking. Every *vakıf* defines and selects their poor according to their respective criteria while, at the same time, trying to match needs with the means they possess. Kayseri *vakıf*s face the challenges all humanitarian agents come across, and attempt to solve them by creating hierarchies and mechanisms of "triage".[2]

Even among needs that fall into the categories defined by individual *vakıf*s, not all are recognised or met. Distinguishing "valid" from "invalid" needs, as well as the urgent from the deferrable, even ignorable, requires more finely tuned screening techniques than simple determining whether a supplicant's needs fall within the recognised categories. "Who is the possessor of needs?" is the key question here, a question that immediately splits into a score of other questions: Is it a woman or a man? How old are they? Healthy or sick? Widowed? Married? With children? Without children? With school-aged children? Where are they living? Working? Retired? Able-bodied or disabled? Is there a family? Where are they from? What are they wearing? Golden bracelets? A worn-out summer jacket in January? Slippers? Heels? Do they have government support? Any support? Benefits? Aid? Are there any well-off family members? Such questions follow one another as the story of the supplicant becomes flesh and blood. The practice of digging for needs, truth, and urgency is also a practice of establishing categories for sorting aspects of a unique human story, making the person identifiable, recognisable, and ultimately legitimate.

This chapter is an attempt to outline those practices that create subjects who possess and utilise rights resulting from the recognition and legitimation of their needs. These can all be read as practices used to define a "just" basis for determining which needs should be tended to and what entitlements follow from them. Yet these practices, being attempts to locate a precept of justice (or justness) rather than being a product of it, are not iterations of predetermined procedures. Instead, they are singular, sometimes unpredictable, and often inde-

---

[2] Redfield 2011; Fassin 2007; Fassin 2010. Peter Redfield situates triage and sacrifice at the heart of humanitarian action and Didier Fassin gives a detailed account of the creation of hierarchies of humanity through humanitarian action.

terminate acts of judgement. They lean on some written and agreed upon norms about what need is, what right is, and what poverty is. Yet they equally circumvent, undermine, or challenge said norms. Hence, I will illustrate over the course of this chapter how these practices form and transform these norms within the fluidity and elusiveness of the quotidian, in the slowness and patience of the perfect continuous tense.

I argue that this fluid relationality is *the* location of justice (and, by implication, injustice). In the porous and fuzzy borders of norms, procedures, and categories, personal interactions can sustain their moral weight; stories and needs are forgiven their singularity and persons are recognised in their personhood. That is why the possessive pronoun in "our poor" speaks to something more than the story of registering, record-keeping, and administering. It tells of responsibility, responsiveness, and a performance of intimacy as much as it does a story of punishment, exclusion, and discipline. But this is getting too far ahead for the moment. Before moving towards the edges, let me first take you to the core, the core of representation and discourse, where categories, labels, check boxes, and computer software reign.

## Governing Through Categories

*Vakıf* workers in Kayseri are not alone using criteria to assess the validity of their supplicants' needs as well as their inability to meet those needs on their own. Indeed, a great bulk of scholarly work on poverty deals with the same problem. Seeking to create a reliable, effective, and realistic understanding of what poverty is, scholars, officials, and technicians of all sorts define and redefine what counts as basic human needs and by what means these criteria are satisfied. On the one hand, they try to set the minimums and maximums of each domain, classify needs and requirements, and establish norms that are expected to be applied universally. On the other hand, they seek ways to understand regional differences and translate those differences into international comparisons. Affiliated with a range of academic disciplines, particularly economics, these experts create indexes and charts that order countries according to their poverty levels, then subdivide these poverty figures by severity, region, gender, and age. They investigate how poverty is related to and/or correlated with other predefined social problems, like obesity,[3] malnutrition,[4] and life expectancy.[5] They also scrutinise how poverty is intertwined with race, gender, ethnicity, and age.[6] They develop schemes to help address problems accurately, given detailed explanations regarding the measurement of poverty through innumerable criteria. Institutions such as the World Bank, IMF, UN commissions, and international aid agencies pick up on and utilise this "data" to develop social and public policies on poverty relief.

In the social sciences, this literature of measuring, assessing, classifying, scaling, and ordering poverty and the poor has itself become a matter of analysis and criticism. Although this critical vein of literature became more widely respected after Foucault's ground-breaking intervention relating knowledge production with very specific modes of power, for more than a century, scholars had had the tendency to approach poverty not as an empirical truth but as a matter of social treatment. As early as 1908, Georg Simmel wrote:

> The poor, as a sociological category, are not those who suffer specific deficiencies and derivations, but those who receive assistance or should receive it according to social norms. Consequently in this sense, poverty cannot be defined in itself as a quantitative state, but only in terms of the social reaction resulting from a specific situation ... The individual state, in itself, no longer determines the concept, but social teleology does so; the individual is determined by the way in which the totality that surrounds him acts toward him.[7]

Simmel suggests that the answer to the question of what poverty is, could and should be derived from the *treatment it receives*, not from what it *is*. Therein, he underlines the contingent and historical nature of poverty. Taking a further step from that analysis has led social scientists to inquire as to what these definitions and treatments tell us, not only about poverty itself, but also about that particular society, its morals, regulations, social relations, divisions, and governmental mechanisms. How poverty is defined and treated at a certain moment and within a certain society tell us about the core conflicts, overarching ideas, and prevalent discourses of that time and place. Therefore, in a sense, the knowledge and discourse that envelop poverty convey less about the so-called poor than about those who speak of poverty.

The changes in the Western approaches to poverty in the past three centuries are illustrative on this account. With the pauperism debates of the late eigh-

---

[3] Pena and Bacallao 2000; Prentice 2006.
[4] Sen 1981; Tanumihardjo et al. 2007.
[5] Wilkinson 1992; Marmot 2005.
[6] Townsend 1993; Ravallion 1994.
[7] Simmel 1965, 138.

teenth and early nineteenth centuries there came a shift from "policing the poor" towards a "liberal mode of governance".[8] With this move, the previously local systems of relief were highly centralised. As the bureaucratic state assumed more responsibility for the well-being of its population, the private sphere of family became a wholly legitimate area of state intervention. The male breadwinner appeared as a category of social agency, held responsible for the material conditions of his family. Means tests and workhouse tests became the sole basis by which external relief was determined. This rupture paved the way to the modern bureaucratic welfare state as an effect of a larger transformation of power, or as Foucault would put it, a "governmentalisation of the state".[9] In par with what Foucault calls the rise of biopower this governmentalisation have targeted both the individual human body to optimise its capacities, and the population, to discipline its reproduction and health[10] always in an intricate and mutual relationship with modern capitalism.

Population became a matter of great concern only when the wealth of nations started to be evaluated not by territory but by the industriousness of their people. The productive capacities of every individual and the population as a whole then became the main object of intervention, resulting in the production of numerous techniques and great bodies of knowledge. Hence, addressing the well-being of a species-body means addressing the productive capacities of this species-body, which in turn certainly applies to poverty alleviation schemes and modern welfare technologies. Lydia Morris argues that, from Marx's lumpenproletariat/reserve army of labour to the underclass of today's social policy debates, in the modern era, the poor have always been conceptualised in relation to capitalism: as a matter of productivity, in terms of the healthy reproduction of the working class and/or as a potential source of insurgency against the structural inequalities created by capitalist relations of production.[11] Therefore, for more than the last two centuries of Western history, how to govern poverty has been a question of how to sustain capitalism.

Yet more recent debates on poverty alleviation and humanitarian aid point to a divergence from this phenomenon. Today's surplus labor is not the same as the reserve army of labor in the Marxian sense. As Tania Li convincingly argues, impoverishment is not a strategy of the global capital to lower the wages anymore.

---

8 Dean 1991.
9 Foucault 1976; Foucault 1991.
10 Foucault 1991.
11 Morris 2001.

Instead it is "a sign of their [the poor's] limited relevance to capital at any scale."[12] Although, for many, there is no hope to find secure employment, this transformation is accompanied by a neoliberal self-responsibilization. Self-improvement and self-help discourses place the blame for global redundance on the impoverished and dispossessed individual. Yet for the states, the situation creates a crisis of legitimate sovereignty when large segments of populations are disenfranchised through economic mechanisms. "Neoliberal welfare states" – states that rely on social assistance, not premium-based social protection – are the product of this crisis.[13]

In Kayseri, the issue of poverty is most often thought of together with the problematique of productive labour. Willingness to work is highly valued. Yet there are no systematic schemes to increase people's productivity with job trainings or to adorn them with entrepreneurial skills. The capacity to labor is assessed only to determine worthy recipients of aid. However, this chapter will show that even this idea is subject to debates when *vakıfçı*s encounter the conditions of the people with whom they work. Before coming to these controversies, however, I want to discuss the criteria and techniques employed by the city's *vakıf*s to differentiate between various needs and various supplicants.

## Who Will Be "Our Poor"?

An ordinary morning at Kayseri Derneği. Filiz is sitting behind the counter with her computer on; Beyaz is standing, checking some folders stacked on the counter, chatting with beneficiaries who are waiting for their turn to do shopping. The foyer is crowded with people. A young pregnant woman hesitantly opens the main door. She checks the crowd for a second, then approaches the counter. She does not look sure about what to do, and reluctantly says that she wants to register for provisions. Filiz points to Beyaz, telling her, "Our brother will take care of you." Beyaz asks, "How can I help you, sister?" The young woman repeats that she wants to register. Beyaz then says, "We have some criteria, we do not register just anybody. Are you married?" "Yes", the woman says, faintly pointing to her pregnant belly, "I am expecting in a month and we cannot even find a slice of bread to eat." Beyaz then asks about the husband, "What is he doing?" He appears to have been unemployed for the last four months. Beyaz then says, "I am sorry, but we cannot do anything about this. We do not help those who can work.

---

12 Li 2010, 67.
13 Ferguson 2015.

We help widows, or the husband should be disabled." The woman looks greatly disappointed at first, then with a glimpse of hope she says, "But my husband is disabled, he has a disability report from the public hospital." Looking confused, Beyaz asks about the rate of his disability. "70 percent," says the woman. "Do you receive aid from any other institution?" asks Beyaz. The woman shakes her head. "Ok then, sister, tell me your name and address; I will come to your house to see your situation. But you will need some documents; make sure to prepare them before I come," says Beyaz, and lists them: a certificate of poverty issued by the neighbourhood authority, the husband's disability report, and a detailed family registry document. While trying to register these in her mind the woman asks, "When are you going to come?" Beyaz says he could not say, but probably within a couple of weeks. The woman thanks him, reciprocates Filiz's smile, and leaves.

This encounter from October 2008 depicts an ordinary application for services with Kayseri Derneği. People come seeking assistance, Beyaz asks them certain questions to see if they fit the criteria. If they do not, he tells them about the rules and presents this as an excuse for rejecting their application from the start. If the case looks a bit more complicated or worth investigating, he then asks for further documents or schedules a home visit. The criteria look simple at first sight: The "head of the family" should either be absent (in jail, doing military service, or in the hospital), dead, or disabled. If the situation fits into any of these categories, the next requirement is that the supplicant woman should not be working with a salary or receiving any kind of pension. And the final criterion is that the supplicant, or anyone from the household, should not be receiving aid from any other *vakıf* in Kayseri. In short, and in the exact phrasing of a senior *vakıf* director, aid schemes in Kayseri (including municipal and public funds) "accept two types of families. Either they should be widowed and/or orphaned, or the head of the household should be unable to work." This categorisation points to the underlying prerequisites of the aid schemes: the male breadwinner and industriousness.

**The Male Breadwinner**

As well known and naturalised as it has become, the male breadwinner family structure is actually a very particular type of household and labour organisation, in which the husband plays the role of sole provider for his dependents, i.e., his wife and children, by working "outside". The wife makes her contribution to the household by working "inside", mostly in the form of unpaid domestic labour. Reproductive activities like cleaning, cooking, and child rearing then fall into the wife's area of responsibility. Yet there is a lot more to this system than simple explanations about the division of labour, and a huge feminist literature has grown out of these implications.

First, it is important to remember the historical specificity of this organisational structure. Although patriarchal relations have shaped how labour is organised in many different settings, feminist historians have shown in detail that it is the coming together of patriarchy and capitalism that has paved the way to the birth of the ideology of the male breadwinner.[14] In agriculture, family labour is a universal norm. Women and men may fulfil different roles, and their activities may be differently valorised, but there is no divide confining women to the domestic sphere and making her dependent on the husband's income-generating or subsistence activities. In fact, women's participation in such activities is essential.[15] In pre-capitalist Europe, female breadwinning activities were not the exception, and it was with the rise of individual wage labour and the separation of workplace and home that the male breadwinner became the norm.[16] But it was a norm that was only attainable among the upper and middle classes. Women and men in agriculture could never thrive with such tidy divisions, much less slaves or indigenous women in the colonies.

Still, as an ideal, the male breadwinner has proved potent, and has shaped the prevailing gendered establishment of Europe's citizenship regimes, and gradually, those elsewhere, as the capitalist mode of production spanned across the world. In a discussion of coverture in the U.S., Nancy Fraser and Linda Gordon describe how white men's civil citizenship was established through their status as household heads. Having dependents, just like property ownership, was established as a qualification for full citizenship.[17]

With the increasing dominance of the male breadwinner model in capitalist relations of production, and with established gendered civil citizenship categories at hand, a viable pattern for social citizenship was already in place. The ideal of the male-breadwinner family unit has cut across all varieties of social welfare regimes in Europe and North America and made its way to modern governmental establishments all around the globe. Although, in practice, the model did not hold except among middle class families for a few decades, it has survived counter practices, as well as geographical and country-by-country variations, as an ideal.

---

14 Janssens 1998.
15 Boserup 2007.
16 Oakley 1976.
17 Fraser and Gordon 1998.

In Turkey, the ideal found its bluntest expression in the civil code. Until radical changes were enacted in 2002, the Turkish Civil Code dictated in its infamous Article 152 that the head of the household was the husband. The husband was also held responsible for providing for his wife and children. Women could not work or establish businesses without the consent of their husbands until the Constitutional Court overturned the article in 1990. After a struggle spanning over two decades and taking the wind of EU accession talks at its back, Turkey's feminist movement succeeded in making the newly drafted civil code egalitarian in many respects. Now, at least according to law, the husband is no longer the head of the family. Spouses have equal responsibility and rights in running the matrimonial union. Women no longer need permission from their husbands for any kind of economic activity.

The new civil code stripped the male breadwinner model of its legal backing, yet the gendered nature of the labour market and the contribution-based social security system keeps women dependent on their husbands regardless of legal regulation. In other words, because of women's lower participation in formal, paid jobs and tragically lower property ownership rates, the de facto heads of families are still men. Moreover, a 2010 report showed that even among women with jobs outside the home, it is common practice for them to hand their earnings to their husbands.[18] Hence, it would be wrong to assume that even a structural change in labour markets or an egalitarian civil law is sufficient to shift this paradigm, because the resilience of the patriarchal family model cannot be explained by material conditions alone. As I have suggested above, the strength of the model does not necessarily stem from how accurately it holds with lived reality. Instead, it should be understood as a patriarchal model that serves to keep women subordinate even though it cannot keep its promise of providing for them. Thus, despite recent changes in the organisation of capitalism favouring women for low-paid, part-time, and informal jobs, and although women are increasingly taking part in income-generating activities in urban contexts, their status as housewives and dependents is not necessarily changing so quickly.

In Kayseri *vakıf*s the male breadwinner ideal is intact as an underlying assumption behind the criteria for acceptance to aid schemes. Not only is aid conditional upon the absence or disability of the male head of the household, but whether or not a woman is working is not an area of inquiry unless she holds formal and registered employment. Home-based income-generating activities are seen as natural extensions of housework and do not count as income. Yet for men, unregistered work (which is often the only option for male beneficiaries,

---

**18** Bingölçe 2010.

too) is an area of persistent inquiry. However, in poor households nationwide, women's home-based, informal jobs are both common and vital to the survival of the family, particularly when men's employment is intermittent and insecure.[19] Despite this well-reported fact, women's alleged dependency saves them from investigations of their informal work.

Although the norm looks solid and perfectly functioning at the level of the *vakıf* administrations, female volunteers and workers at these organisations continuously challenge the male-breadwinner archetype. Kayseri Derneği volunteers sporadically encourage beneficiary women to seek employment, often without the threat of cutting the benefits they receive from the organisation. In 2006, Kayseri Derneği women coordinated with a local geriatrics clinic to train their beneficiaries as professional carers. Some of these trainees were then employed by nursing homes. Even though there was no such training at the time of my research, I observed *vakıf* women mobilising their personal networks to find cleaning, babysitting, or patient care jobs for beneficiaries. The nature of these jobs takes us back to the question of women's place and the value of female labour, which is shared despite variation in attitudes regarding women's dependency.

**Productive Hands**

Eight days after the pregnant woman's application to Kayseri Derneği, I am travelling in Beyaz's van towards the outskirts of the city. It has been a tough day. We have already made seven visits. Two of the visited supplicants were not at home, so we left notes with neighbours. At another two, we found only teenaged girls at home. Beyaz asked some questions at the door, but we did not enter the flats. At another flat, there was an old woman looking after her three grandchildren. Her story was devastating; Beyaz approved her registration. After two more visits, we are finally making our way to a newly emerging neighbourhood called Esentepe. Yet finding the address proves to be almost impossible: the street we are looking for does not exist. In the end, we have to call the supplicant for clarification. The address seems to be correct. In fact, it had been correct a week ago, but the municipality changed the street names in the meantime.

Finally, we arrive at the newly built apartment block. The pregnant woman's husband meets us on the street. One of his legs is visibly shorter than the other one and seems dysfunctional – he limps heavily. He lets us in. We take off our

---

**19** Buğra and Keyder 2003; A. Bora 2002.

shoes and wait for him to guide us towards the living room. It is a new flat, barely furnished. In the living room, there is only a two-seater sofa and an armchair. There is not a single carpet in the whole house. A flower-patterned fabric has been laid on the floor of the living room as a weak substitute for a carpet. Although it is a three-bedroom flat, only one bedroom is furnished with a bed and a closet. In the kitchen, there is a small table and four chairs. The flat is otherwise completely empty. A two-year-old girl is sleeping on the armchair in the living room . Her visibly pregnant mother is sitting on the sofa. As we enter, she grabs a chair from the kitchen and leaves the sofa to us. Beyaz asks the man how long he has been unemployed. He says, "Four months." Beyaz asks whether he receives disability benefits. He says, "No, I cannot. My disability rate was 70 percent but then the public hospital took it down to 40 percent. Now I am not eligible." Beyaz looks thoughtful as this rate does not match the Kayseri Derneği criterion, which is 50 percent. He then asks, "Do you receive unemployment benefits?" "No," says the man again, "you have to accumulate 600 days of contributions in the system. It appeared that I only had 559." He continues, "I have been looking for a job since then, but with the financial crisis, nobody is hiring anymore." Beyaz then wonders what kind of a job he could do with his disability. "Anything that does not require standing all day long," he says. Beyaz nods appreciatively. He asks how long they have been married. The woman replies, "Three years," while she hands Beyaz the family registry and disability report. He briefly scans the documents, then tells them to come to Kayseri Derneği the next day to finalise their registration and to receive their first provisions. We leave. On the way back to Kayseri Derneği, Beyaz tells me that he barely held back his tears while we were there.

This is how a typical home investigation takes place. Not only at Kayseri Derneği, but among other *vakıf*s and public offices that offer aid schemes, as well, every application is finalised after a visit. These visits are designed to obtain first-hand evidence of poverty, but they also allow negotiation of the organisational criteria as supplicants have more chances to tell their stories in this setting. What is negotiated during the specific occasion I portrayed above is one of the core criteria shared by all aid institutions: the male head of the household's inability to work.

If a household with a male "head" (or with a son above school age) is to be registered to an aid scheme, there should be justifiable reasons for doing so. To be working is the norm for men and to not be working for any reason is seen as deficit. If this "abnormality" cannot be justified, it becomes treated as a moral deviance. Idleness and laziness are seen as social vices that should not be encouraged or supported. This discourse is so pervasive that the *vakıfçı*s of Kayseri often have to desperately defend themselves against accusations of "encouraging laziness" and "attracting the idle masses to town." Instead of discarding this discourse in its entirety, *vakıfçı*s negotiate its terms and participate in its constitution by establishing criteria and categories to distinguish "the lazy" from "the unable".

Being unable to find a job does not usually count as a legitimate reason for not working. Quite to the contrary, such an explanation is often seen as an excuse for "laziness". I have heard the argument "Nobody can claim he could not find a job in Kayseri. There are always some openings in the industrial zone" more than once. But in fact, there aren't always jobs awaiting applicants. During my period of fieldwork, the effects of the international financial crisis were almost palpable, with factories laying off workers one after another. During this period, DISK, one of the largest federations of labour unions, announced that the Kayseri Industrial Zone had reduced its capacity by 16,000 workers between 2007–2008.[20] Moreover, in 2008, the unemployment rate in Kayseri was 11.1 percent, slightly above the national rate of 11 percent for Turkey. Finding employment in Kayseri was no easier than anywhere else. When the effects of the crisis became undeniable, the image of Kayseri as an industrial haven where jobs were plentiful came under discussion by the *vakıfçı*s themselves. Many were in favour of including the unemployed in aid schemes, but their own resources had also been negatively affected by the crisis. Every time someone attempted to begin a conversation on the issue, it would come to an abrupt conclusion as soon as the issue of means – and thus the impossibility of further inclusion – was brought to the table.

Notwithstanding these limitations and mindsets, every application is still an occasion for the negotiation of norms and criteria. As in the story of the disabled man above, the findings of an investigation are weighed against each other to manoeuvre what could be deemed an unfit case towards entitlement. At this stage of human contact, the particularity of needs and the singularity of the story affect the outcome as much as established norms do. A wife due to give birth in the very near future, a visible disability (even though the degree of severity did not meet *vakıf* standards), the absence of many ordinary household items, and the man's expression of his willingness to work, while not objectively quantifiable, are certainly recognisable as evidence of "genuine" need, and thus an entitlement, by the family. In that particular moment, being "just" appears to manifest itself as a disregard for regulations (which are taken as the basis for justice), counterweighing them against the "realities" of the singular. The moral weight of these realities provides leverage against the claims of discursive truth in the norms and standards. The cultural significance of a pregnant woman is one source of leverage, and the missing furniture and appliances are another. But the most important is the supplicant man's willingness to work.

---

20 Radikal 2009.

## The Hardworking and the Beggar

A desire and determination to work are highly appreciated among the *vakıfçı*s of Kayseri. Women volunteers appreciate and support beneficiary women's attempts to invent income-generating activities like lacemaking or knitting. Directors express their desire to include the working poor in aid schemes but complain about the insufficiency of their resources. Even those in formal and regular jobs on minimum wage are considered worthy of support. Yet, they are left out of schemes, again, due to limited funds. Industriousness and productivity are thought of highly but are not accompanied by systematic attempts to make the beneficiaries more productive or to increase their worth in labour markets. Except for sporadic efforts by women (like the geriatrics training mentioned before), such enterprises fall outside of the area of activity of the *vakıf*s, and *vakıfçı*s settle for mobilising these nuances in drawing distinctions between supplicants. In that sense, attempts at governing the productive capacities of the poor are minimal.

Although having a job or even being able to work disqualifies one for aid schemes, there are many registered beneficiaries of Kayseri Derneği and Yardımlaşma Vakfı who are like the husband of the pregnant woman. This situation is often justified with a desire to reward the hardworking for their efforts. The hardworking, here, are positioned against the beggar and the indolent. In this comparison, the hardworking are mostly described in terms of being responsible and independent, and of accumulating just (*helal*) earnings. Beggars may be responsible but are perceived as lacking in just earnings and honour. And the indolent seem to lack all of the above; indeed, they generate a sense of outrage among the *vakıfçı*s. I recall, for example, an occasion when Beyaz returned from a home visit annoyed and furious. He had gone to investigate the home of a construction worker who had been unemployed for a fairly long time. Yet, when Beyaz arrived there at 11 a.m. on a weekday, he found the supplicant man just getting up. Beyaz lectured the man about the vices of laziness and questioned his sense of responsibility, as well as the genuineness of his need, asking, "How can an unemployed man sleep until noon instead of going out and looking for work? If you are not willing to take care of yourself, do not expect us to do so."

Idleness is a common theme in discussions of poverty and welfare provisions. From the workhouses of seventeenth-century Britain[21] to the unemployment benefit regulations of modern welfare states[22], examples of tests for idleness and precautions against it are plentiful in European history. Lydia Morris describes in

---

21 Polanyi 1957; M. Dean 1991.
22 Fox-Piven and Cloward 1972; Katz 1989.

detail how poverty has been moralised in England since the sixteenth century, when landless masses began flowing into cities.[23] The regulations that followed the famous Poor Law of 1601 sought ways of administering the mostly vagrant poor. Practices like assigning each to a parish and confining the able-bodied poor to workhouses were all aimed at fighting the "idleness and vagrancy" of the victims of the Great Enclosure and the effects of early capitalism. Coming to the nineteenth century's New Poor Law, pauperism was commonly seen "by implication as a wilful choice of the idle, who were to be denied community membership not just by physical removal to the workhouses, but also by moral condemnation."[24] As Morris illustrates, the equation of poverty with idleness and moral degradation has travelled through discourses of eugenics, the lumpenproletariat, and Social Darwinism, well into twentieth-century discussions on the culture of poverty and welfare dependency.

Within this framework, beggars have been doubly condemned and often criminalised as sources of social vice, manifesting idleness, intentionally declining work, and parasitically living off other people's earnings.[25] But, notwithstanding the observable similarities in today's Kayseri, it would be wrong to attribute universality to this discourse. Discussing how begging has been perceived in Muslim societies, Amy Singer notes that until the end of the nineteenth century, beggars were widely tolerated and sustained in the Islamic World.[26] Even when begging was criticised, it was not done so on the basis of social morality, but formulated within terms of faith in God. An outspoken critic of begging, Al-Ghazali argued in the twelfth century that, although it may be permissible in certain situations, begging was not laudable for two reasons:

> First, begging suggested that one's belief in God is flawed, either through lack of confidence that God would provide or by the intimation that a person might somehow share in God's attributes, either as a provider or as a source of shame for the one who begs. Second, begging risked testing another believer in an inappropriate manner by demanding charity and so perhaps compelling a person to give to or refuse someone for the wrong reasons...[27]

This attitude towards begging as a test of one's faith or as a risk to another's moral standing is paradigmatically different from an approach to begging as a social ill or moral vice. Here, problems associated with begging are those of the rela-

---

23 Morris 2001.
24 Ibid., 36.
25 Ibid.
26 Singer 2008.
27 Ibid., 169.

tionship between a person and God, and with the person from whom charity is demanded. There is not a society or a population involved whose well-being could be threatened by such an act, nor is there a concern about idleness. In this view, working to earn money may be encouraged, yet not working is not stigmatised.

Nadir Özbek reports that until 1750, there had not been a single attempt to eradicate begging or to make use of the productive capacities of the poor in the Ottoman Empire.[28] Later, sporadic and unsystematic attempts to regulate begging emerged in large urban areas. Yet, well into the twentieth century, beggars had their own guilds and their own legal status in the cities. Officially, begging was treated like any other vocation.[29] Around 1890, public discourse around beggars changed markedly. Beggars began to be characterised in newspapers as an urban disturbance. Singer approaches this change in discourse, which could only be attributed to the influence of the bureaucratic elite, as a manifestation of desires for modernisation.[30] Pamuk makes a similar observation and contends that the Ottoman elite adopted a Western gaze, looking at their urban spaces with contempt and curiosity, and attempted to erase whatever this gaze was attracted to.[31] Özbek notes the irony of the situation, observing that even the descriptions of beggars on the streets of Istanbul were direct translations from French newspapers.[32]

In the end, laws criminalising begging and vagrancy, the first of which was issued in 1909, were generally ineffective. There were a few deportations from Istanbul, and even fewer prosecutions, but no attempt to nudge beggars towards work, even though this was the manifest aim of the law. In the republican era, begging has been seen as a petty offence and punished arbitrarily with a minimal monetary fine.[33] Despite these laws, there have been only sporadic efforts to arrest and penalise beggars. In the public discourse, however, begging is increasingly perceived as a form of organised crime, with beggars being forced to work on the streets by gang leaders.[34] Hence, they have come to be seen either as victims or profiteers of a criminal organisation, which in turn has little to do with genuine need.

In the *vakıf*s of Kayseri, begging and its local variation, "gathering", are almost unanimously despised. Part of this ire is created by shared opinions about idleness and parasitism, yet there are other issues affecting attitudes towards beggars, as well. To provide a more complete picture, I should clarify the meaning

---

28 Özbek 2002.
29 Ibid., 74.
30 Singer 2008.
31 Pamuk 2006.
32 Özbek 2002, 82, note 37.
33 Article 33, Resmi Gazete 2005.
34 See, for example, ATO 2004.

of "gathering" (*toplayıcılık*). In the vernacular language of Kayseri *vakıfçı*s, a gatherer is a person who collects aid from various *vakıf*s and public institutions and then allegedly sells some of these aid items for cash. Among *vakıfçı*s, not only are gatherers' intentions and moral stances continuously questioned, the genuineness of their need is also under suspicion. They are seen as professionals wasting already limited resources. With their "fake" needs and cons, they are *vakıfçı*s' and social workers' anathema par excellence. Beggars are usually lumped together with gatherers as professional liars, storytellers, and performers of poverty and misery.

In addition to suspicions about the morality of supplicants, this manifest disdain towards beggars and gatherers points to two phenomena. The first is related to issues of funding, while the second presents concerns about justice. There is strong agreement between the directors, workers, and benefactors of *vakıf*s in Kayseri on the purported negative effects of gatherers on the field of beneficence. Benefactors want to be confident in the fate of their donations – that they are spent for the right reasons to meet the just and genuine needs of the poor in Kayseri. Personal networks of trust are the sole sources of this guarantee. All *vakıf*s rely on these networks of trust to collect regular donations, and thus to sustain their activities. Because trust is built around personal recognition, it is equally common for it to be lost with a counter-story. Stories of gatherers and beggars who abuse *vakıf*s are argued to have a geometrically increasing effect on the trustworthiness of these organisations and their workers. In order to fight this problem, eight of the most prominent *vakıf*s in Kayseri cooperated with the Kayseri Metropolitan Municipality to create a shared database. Known as Database of Households in Need of Help (*Yardıma Muhtaç Hane Bilgi Sistemi*, HBS), this database was built by the Social Services Directorate of the Metropolitan Municipality. The idea behind HBS was to scan for poverty in the city and to register everybody whose income fell under a certain level. According to the municipal officer who initiated the project, there were four motives behind this tremendous task. First, to create a social risk map by registering those who are disabled, widowed, etc. Second, to avoid wasting resources by preventing duplicate aid. Third, to maintain the trust of benefactors. And fourth, to guarantee that no one who needed help was missed by the aid schemes.

The municipality initiated the HBS project in 2005. In 2006, 15,000 households, totalling approximately 60,000 citizens, were surveyed. The objective was to have surveyed the whole population of 911,984 people by the end of 2009.[35] Despite these ambitious goals, as of 2011, not a single survey has been added

---

35 TÜİK 2009.

to the original 15,000. Therefore, at the time of this research, the declared aims of creating a social risk map and all-inclusive database of *ihtiyaç sahipleri* were postponed, if not quietly abandoned. We were then left with the other two aims: preventing duplicate aid and creating trust.

In order to achieve the first goal, the municipality donated computers to participating *vakıf*s and organised training sessions to teach *vakıf* employees how to use the database. During my fieldwork, six of the participating eight *vakıf*s were regularly entering data into the system. They also entered their registered beneficiaries, further developing the database. With these entries, duplicate aid could be detected immediately after the introduction of the system, and these beneficiaries were given the chance to choose one *vakıf* and give up the rest. Now, a crucial part of the assessment and registration processes became cross-checking supplicants' declarations that they were not receiving any aid with the information in the system. As previous entries were also accessible, it was possible for *vakıf* workers to question the supplicants regarding the reasons why their entitlements had been withdrawn by another *vakıf*.

Left in the hands of the *vakıfçı*s, this highly developed and centralised surveillance tool served some practical needs of the organisations. Disregarding the municipality's requests that all fields of the questionnaire be completed, *vakıf*s entered only the names and addresses of supplicants, and the type of aid scheme to which they were registered. They did not collect any data regarding family members, their ages, education levels, income-generating activities, health conditions, household needs, hometowns, or migration histories, as requested by the municipality. Nor did they create records for rejected applications. In the end, the initial design of the project, which had aimed to document and govern the welfare of poor citizens, gave way to a more pragmatic use with one aim: detecting scams and fraud. With this tool, *vakıf* directors' hands were strengthened in their attempts to persuade potential benefactors.

The second facet of the disdain expressed towards beggars and gatherers is related to ideas and concerns about justice. Some *vakıfçı*s occupy positions that involve assessing needs, outlining the rights that might derive from these needs, and helping beneficiaries turn entitlements into means to meet their needs. How to prioritise between various needs and who to aid are decisions that must be made, and *vakıfçı*s unavoidably make judgements in the course of these decisions. In coming to decisions, they make claims to justice and justness. This particular sense of justice is essentially relational. This relationality exists first with reference to the dialogical character of the decision-making process, which involves at least two parties: the supplicant and the *vakıfçı*. Here, beggars are despised for the reasons articulated by al-Ghazali, especially for the notion of compelling a person to give charity for the wrong reasons. They are blamed for inappropriately and unnecessarily testing a fellow believer's faith and obedience to God's orders, i.e., being generous in giving.

Justice is also relational in that it always refers to third parties not directly involved in the process of judgement. These third parties are other beneficiaries, other supplicants, and even unknown others who have needs but have not made demands based on those needs. They are the "others" alluded to in excuses like, "If we register you, it would be an injustice to others we have rejected on the same grounds." They are the consolidated "people" referred to in such phrases as, "Still be grateful, there are people who are worse off than you," and named when it is argued that, "We accepted so-and-so, now we have to be just!" Hence, all judgements and decisions refer to this sometimes intimately known, sometimes anonymous mass of others who possess needs. Need is recognised and treated with distributive and comparative aspects of justice in mind. Within this context, helping professional beggars and gatherers whose needs are not justifiable is a breach of justice, a violation of somebody else's rights.

There is one more aspect to this overly present relationality. Kayseri *vakıfçı*s can be seen as often doing care work with resources that are not their own. They see themselves as intermediaries between benefactors and beneficiaries – between the owners of means and the possessors of needs, respectively. As Sena, a *vakıfçı* and a municipal worker, once commented, they "hunt someone else's bird with someone else's stones". Occupying this intermediary position, *vakıfçı*s find themselves in situations in which they are charged with deciding where and on whom to spend donations. Yet, administering someone else's money has implications beyond having to maintain trust to keep receiving funds. As I discussed in detail in the previous chapter, donations carry a history of their own, traces of previous owners. The intentions of benefactors and whether the money is *zakat* or *sadaqah* restrict the areas in which the money could be spent.

As I described earlier, *zakat* in particular can only be given to certain groups of people to meet certain needs. *Vakıfçı*s carry this burden of managing the beneficence of others while remaining loyal and just to their cause and their intentions. Judgement, an attempt to be just, therefore involves relationality in one more sense, that of having an indissoluble connection to benefactors via the medium of their donations. Spending these (almost) borrowed resources on beggars and gatherers, whose needs and conditions are questionable, is considered an injustice to the benefactors, as well.

However, in accordance with the principle of relationality in its first sense – as an interaction between *vakıfçı*s and supplicants – there are always variations in the ways *vakıfçı*s deal with beggars. For example, the director of Sinan Vakfı follows a principle of never turning anyone away empty-handed. So, even if she knows perfectly well that the person in front of her is a professional beggar and that their story is not true, she does not risk refusing any genuine need. She describes her solution to the problems of justice and righteousness as one of practicality: she does not spend *vakıf* resources or any *zakat* or *sadaqah* portion of what was given to her for distribution; she uses only her own resources on supplicants she cannot trust. In this way, she re-calibrates the relationship as one between herself and the supplicant only.

Another variation of this is performed by the Kayseri Derneği employees working in the *vakıf*'s Turkish bath. These two female employees told me that they actively hid information about a beneficiary they knew to be a beggar. The employees knew this woman personally, and because the beneficiary woman begged only when she ran out of basic necessities, they did not perceive her behaviour as indolence or parasitism. In their eyes, this was a subsistence activity. In the last instance, not all begging was the same, nor were everyone's stories.

**Possessions**

Recall the home visit I mentioned earlier, and recall what the supplicants' home looked like. After we came back to Kayseri Derneği that afternoon, Beyaz continued to dwell on the emptiness of the house. His impression had heavily influenced his decision, and what he was most touched by was that emptiness, those missing items we were so used to seeing in every other flat: carpets, sofa sets, dining tables, cupboards, dressers, chests, televisions, radios, computers, kitchen appliances, etc. Otherwise, the flat looked new, clean, and in good condition.

During these investigations, poverty must be materialised in front of the *vakıfçı*s to convince them of the genuineness and urgency of need. This expectation signals an underlying assumption about poverty, that it is an observable material condition, in such a way that one can recognise penury almost at first sight. Most important is this visual recognition: what the investigator sees, and then codes as signs of wealth or poverty, is taken as proof. Yet, there are also moments when poverty manifests itself through other senses; the smell of damp, a shiver from the coldness of a room, or the coughing of a sick child are all jotted down in a mental note.

Partly due to decision-makers in Kayseri *vakıf*s often being those who make the home visits, no written or recorded material is produced in these investigations. Typically, no photographs are taken, nor forms completed, though this is not a uniform practice and is a matter of an ethics debate among *vakıf* workers. For example, within the municipal bureaucracy, investigators are often low-level employees, while only their directors have the authority to make decisions regarding the distribution of provisions like daily bread or hot dishes from municipal soup kitchens. In this case, investigators are asked to provide visual evidence when a case becomes controversial. In one such situation, Sena, the secretary to the Director of Social Services, went to visit a persistently demanding supplicant's home with a camcorder. After a very tense visit, she returned with footage, which then travelled around the municipality. I watched it on Sena's computer. The whole of the footage was of the household items in the supplicant's home. The voices of both Sena and the supplicant woman were heard in discussion off-screen, but even without seeing their faces it was apparent that the woman's strenuous efforts to tell her story did not catch Sena's attention. Rather, her gaze was directed towards the woman's possessions: extra carpets stacked behind the door and rooms crammed with furniture.

There were many other reasons (like her grown-up children and their earnings) for the rejection of this woman's demands, but this intrusive footage and in particular the abundance of carpets provided the municipality the most solid grounds for their negative decision. What the supplicant possessed was taken as proof of wealth, and wealth is always taken as a disqualifier. Indeed, detecting signs of wealth is the main component of investigations. In Kayseri *vakıf*s this is done in a very informal and personal way. Larger international aid organisations use official investigation forms on which all possible household items are listed, from washing machines to mobile phones, and these forms are then presented to decision-making bodies to paint a picture of the family's degree of poverty. These investigative processes are very much quantified and objectified, and in that sense different from those at Kayseri *vakıf*s; nonetheless, all share the assumption that poverty is detectable through what a household possesses or lacks.

Home investigation, or a home visit as some *vakıfçı*s say to sugar-coat it, is structurally an intrusive surveillance technique. It exposes the inside of a person's home, their belongings, living arrangements, possessions or lack thereof, and even the contents of their refrigerator to a stranger's eyes. Some *vakıfçı*s are sensitive to the violation this investigative strategy involves and develop techniques to turn the occasion into a possibility to create an intimate connection, as will be seen in the next chapter. This awareness has motivated some *vakıf*s to develop policies that avoid documenting poverty, especially with photographs and video recordings, because the insult of such a practice adds to the injury of the poor. Yet there are cases like Sena's in which no one seems to care. Although how the situation is handled makes a big difference, home investigations in general emphasise the imbalance of power and create shame in the beneficiaries that is manifested alongside an anxiety over what their possessions might tell the investigator.

With this anxiety, supplicants sometimes feel the need to warn against the impression investigators may take from the appearance of their homes. Some tell how wealthy they once were, others disclose which items were the gifts of benevolent neighbours and relatives. Supplicants try to shift the focus of investigation from possessions to income; as one woman said, "We have all the fancy furniture, but at the end of the day you cannot eat your sofa." These arguments are often found to be plausible, but how to get to the truth under the glossy layer of commodities is a matter of discussion, and a uniform resolution is impossible to achieve. Possessions, then, become another item of negotiation during home visits. In attempts to be just in decision-making, even car ownership might at times be ignored, while at other times a new mobile phone may create suspicion.[36]

## Responsibilisation and Moralisation

The disabled supplicant with the almost empty house comes to Kayseri Derneği the next morning, as he was instructed. He is driven to the market by his brother and mother. They enter the building together and look around for Beyaz. After welcoming them, I go to find him. Beyaz is in the kitchen fetching his tea, but comes back hastily, greets them, and takes the man's documents to finalise the registration. The man and his family are now entitled to 80TL (€40) worth of goods every month from the market. Because the earliest scheduled shopping day for his neighbourhood is quite a while later, Beyaz tells him to take his first shopping trip then and there, as an extra. When the man enters the market to fill his shopping cart, Beyaz calls on Emre to fetch four carpets from the depot and instructs me to find clothes for the expected baby. Emre brings the carpets, I leave the baby overalls and vests, along with some other items for the mother, next to the cashier. When I go out to the foyer, I hear Beyaz and the man's brother talking. It appears that the brother is a municipal constable, in a moderately paying, stable position. Beyaz reproaches him saying, "What kind of a brother are you? If you had bought one carpet each year with your constable's salary, that little kid would not have had to grow up on bare floors."

As we have seen with the idea of the male breadwinner and through discussions around idleness, the issue of responsibility always accompanies poverty

---

[36] See Prochaska 2008 for a comparison with the practice of "district visiting" in Victorian England.

discourses. It is not necessarily one of individualised liberal responsibility.[37] Nor does it always take the shape Morris describes – blaming the poor for their poverty, although this is occasionally the case.[38] But certainly the *vakıfçı*s of Kayseri do try to assign responsibility to others, not necessarily in the sense of holding these others responsible for their current situation, but in the sense of requesting that one take responsibility for alleviating the effects of poverty. As seen in this anecdote, it is almost always family members who are invited to take on this responsibility. Siblings, fathers, children, and even more distant relatives are expected to take care of their fallen kinsmen (especially kinswomen). It is seen as a natural responsibility, causing great dishonour if not taken. So, the application and assessment process includes inquiries about family members, both to learn whether or not they are dependent on the supplicant, and because they are viewed as possible assets, just like a house or a pension.

A detailed family registry (one of the documents required from every prospective beneficiary) is often used as a reference point for this inquiry. The document lists marital status and kin from both older and younger generations, i.e., spouse, father, mother, and children, as well as siblings if the supplicant is not married. In addition to names, the registry details the ages and civil statuses of all listed, along with information regarding death, adoption, marriage, and divorce. With the help of the registry, *vakıfçı*s ask about the vocations and whereabouts of those who might be held responsible for the well-being of the supplicant. In the case of older beneficiaries these are often the children, for young widows they are the parents and brothers.

If these family members are poor themselves, their morals are not questioned. But if they are well off, *vakıfçı*s question why they did not help. This line of questioning works in two interrelated ways and directions. It makes the familial tie an issue of both responsibility and morality; because familial care responsibilities are taken as natural, their absence is seen as a moral deviance – either on the part of the "irresponsible" relative or the non-receiving supplicant. By extension, if the wrongdoing may seem to reside with the supplicant, this causes suspicion that leads to further scrutiny. For women supplicants such suspicion has additional implications. For example, in one case, the morals of a young, divorced woman were called into question because she was not receiving any support from her father or brothers, who had objected to her divorce.

---

**37** See Dean 1991.
**38** Morris 2001.

If responsibility is mostly sought from men, morality is often treated as a female issue.[39] Similarly, and with close relation to family honour, morality is assumed to reside in women and hence comes under greater attack when women fall destitute. The most imminent and immediate risk purportedly faced by women upon losing the support of their male relatives is losing their sexual honour. Thus, choosing women as the prime target of beneficence not only stems from the idea of female dependency but also from ideas about the fragility and weakness of female morality. One of the primary tasks of aid organisations is to help women "protect" themselves by providing them a certain level of material assurance (to keep them away from male abuse and prostitution).

## Justice as Relationality

So far, I have illustrated the prevailing norms at Kayseri *vakıf*s that define certain people as eligible to receive provisions. At the same time, I have given examples of how these norms are sidestepped, challenged, and discussed; that is, how they are tactically used by *vakıfçı*s to reach judgements about people's needs and means. I have also briefly argued that non-uniformity in the decision-making process is related to *vakıfçı*s' concerns about justice and being just. These concerns are an intrinsically relational phenomenon. So far, I have delineated three levels of this relationality: the dialogical relationship between *vakıfçı*s and supplicants, the *vakıfçı*s' distributive responsibility to "possessors of needs", which also refers to unrelated third parties, and the ties between the *vakıfçı*, the beneficiary, and the benefactor established through inalienable donations.

Yet, there is one more dimension of this relationality that has been left undiscussed: relations with God, as an omnipresent transcendental judge. For the *vakıfçı*s of Kayseri, the reason they do what they do is often very simple: they claim to do it for the sake of God. Religious texts and teachings invariably value charitable work, caring about and for others in society. For beneficence workers, being a *vakıfçı* is itself an act of piety directed towards gaining God's mercy. At the same time, it is also a burden, a risky business compared to other forms of piety, like daily prayers or fasts. What makes this kind of work risky and troublesome (*veballi*) is the possibility of committing an injustice, since there is an ultimate judge who will evaluate all judgements. If charity is done to please God, and if it is certain that God is particularly displeased by injustice, the risk of making unjust decisions becomes overwhelming. This fear is what Neriman describes as "what

---

39 For a similar observation from Lebanon, see Jawad 2009b.

keeps me awake at night," and what makes Beyaz consider giving his efforts up in favour of a safer life track. This is also why, on the first morning of clothing distribution, the Kayseri Derneği volunteer women were worriedly talking among themselves:

> Hatice: I considered not participating in this. I am so afraid of doing injustice. God save us, it is such a responsibility!
>
> Sabahat: And what is worse is we are giving away other people's donations... I am losing my mind when I think about it; what if I give one person more and the other less?
>
> Ferda: You should not think this much. It is also a matter of *kısmet* [God given luck, chance, also sometimes fate] you know. For one person you cannot find anything to fit despite all your efforts. Then comes another person and beautiful items almost present themselves. It is her *kısmet*... But, of course, we should not overlook any obvious injustice.

What is striking here is that these *vakıfçı*s usually stand behind their acts and argue their justness. However, they are still afraid. They may judge their own actions and decisions as just, but theirs is not the final evaluation. Despite all norms, religious precepts, texts, teachings, guidance, and bureaucratic mechanisms, God's judgement is not accessible to human beings. It is a deeply affective unknown. Without having access to this unknown and ultimately righteous judgement, the capacities of human beings for justice are limited from the start. This incapacity indefinitely postpones a final and ascertainable judgement. This dimension of relationality, i.e., a continuous reference to an omnipresent, ultimate, but not-immediate judge is, aside from other dimensions, what gives the assessment and decision-making processes their plasticity and fluidity. Within all these relational considerations, no one criterion has any more meaning than as a tactically and selectively used rhetorical tool for arguing about what is just and what is unjust.[40]

Bourdieu suggests that "[h]abitus is in cahoots with the fuzzy and the vague. As a generative spontaneity which asserts itself in the improvised confrontation with endlessly renewed situations, it follows a *practical logic*, that of the fuzzy, of the more-or-less, which defines the ordinary relation to the world".[41] The practices of *vakıfçı*s and the judgements they have to make in the course of becoming *just vakıfçı*s, exhibit this fuzzy logic. Every encounter is an opening to reconsider

---

**40** See Schielke 2019 for a discussion of the open potentials of the believers' relationships with God.
**41** Bourdieu 1987; quoted in Wacquant 1992, 22; Wacquant's translation.

the criteria of acceptance, past decisions, and acts, as well as the people who are not immediately affected by these decisions but whose presence haunts the encounter right from the start. Even if the official criteria of their respective organisations, shared assumptions, stereotyping and prepossessions delimit *vakıfçıs'* field of action, with every life story heard or witnessed, they reposition themselves and manoeuvre not only *within* but also *with* these limits – challenging, bending, reinterpreting or silently ignoring.

## Conclusion

In this chapter, I explored how *vakıfs* choose their beneficiaries and the grounds on which this selection is based. I also sought to illustrate the principles and assumptions underlying the most naturalised criteria, like the male breadwinner, industriousness, family responsibility, or what a poor household should rightfully possess. However, as I have contended, neither these criteria nor the assumptions on which they are based are absolute in their applicability. *Vakıfçıs* in decision-making positions within *vakıfs* strive for a justice that cannot be guaranteed through the strict application of these rules. Every encounter demands individualised treatment, however slight the differences between scenarios might be, and this treatment depends greatly on the interaction between *vakıfçı* and supplicant. It is thus during this interaction that the relational aspects of justice unfold.

I also argue that God is incorporated into gift-giving through this relationality, not by an absolute dictum to give. Therefore, the ethnographic material and analysis presented in this chapter challenge the notion of a "nonhumanitarian Islamic ethics of giving" proposed by Amira Mittermaier.[42] Mittermaier argues that by moving charity out of the relational realm between human beings and placing it in the relation between the individual giver and God, Islamic giving becomes oblivious to emotions evoked by human misery, as well as the criteria that make this misery recognisable.[43] As I have illustrated throughout this chapter, justice in the charitable contexts of Kayseri concerns itself with relations at many levels, none of which negates other human beings as significant parties

---

[42] Mittermaier 2019

[43] Here Mittermaier's reading is informed by the critical scholars of humanitarianism, who problematise the reliance of humanitarian impulse on the emotions of pity and compassion, which are selective, derogatory and contingent. See Ticktin 2011; Bornstein 2012; Fassin 2012. As illustrated in this chapter but will be discussed more in detail in the next one, such compassion plays a significant role in Kayseri beneficence field, yet not as the only determinant.

to the question of justice. Moreover, these relations and concerns are very much informed by certain criteria, which are more profane than sacred.

According to Mittermaier, by positing that giving is simply a presentist duty, Islamic ethics of giving resists the developmentalist as well as neoliberal agendas of aid. However, as presented in the previous pages, giving in Kayseri refers to multiple registers and is shaped by a multitude of dictums, alongside the ones coming directly from religious beliefs. My interlocutors would feel comfortable saying that they give to earn God's blessings. Yet both their discussions with each other and the criteria they set to make sources meet the ends, as well as their embodied practices, point to an array of discourses and social repertoires they tap into. When these discourses conflict with each other – such as the precept of the male breadwinner conflicting with the dictum to feed the hungry – God is brought back to the scene as the ultimate procurer of justice. However, this incorporation is different from giving solely to please God. In the context I studied in Kayseri, people are pulled into and implicated in giving for a variety of reasons. Moreover, this giving is highly selective through criteria that are not very different from their Western counterparts, but are made negotiable with reference to other norms.

In *Seeing Like a State*, James Scott discusses how "the poor" are made "legible" by fitting terms, categories, and characteristics that are observable, assessable, and amenable to the management and information regimes of modern bureaucracy.[44] He calls this phenomenon a "tunnel view" of reality. "Tunnel view" is an appropriate metaphor with which to end this chapter. Seen through categories, schemas, and check boxes, is always a fragment of reality, a fragment that is understandable and governable. Yet a larger chunk of reality lurks outside the tunnel, complex and unbounded. Attempts by Kayseri *vakıfçıs* to create more accurate, sharpened, and finer criteria by which to judge their claimants never ends. Yet, outside these criteria, outside the tunnel in the multi-relational and multi-referential practice of justice, they are in the realm of care and of ethical complexities. These two realms will be the subject of the next chapter.

---

44 Scott 1998.

# 5 Embodied Ethics of Being a *Vakıfçı*

Among those who work in the field of beneficence in Kayseri, a significant distinction is made between *vakıfçı* – the men and women of a *vakıf* – and *hayırsever* – benefactors or philanthropists. Although these two categories are often used descriptively, they are also notably value laden. *Vakıfçı* refers to those who put their labour, time, and energy into charitable work, whether in private or institutional settings. They are the volunteers, employees, managers, and active board members of charitable organisations. They may also be men and women without any institutional engagement but who are still known for "devoting their lives" to beneficence. *Vakıfçı*s have close contact with the people they aid. *Hayırsever*, on the other hand, literally means "those who love doing good deeds," connoting less hands-on involvement, but moral and financial support from outside as benefactors. *Hayırsever*s are usually not involved in the daily operations of institutions but rather support them through donations, particularly preferring large-scale projects like the construction of schools or mosques. Of course, most *vakıfçı*s financially support their institutions and engage in private benefaction via donations, too, so it is not possible to establish this distinction by focusing on the kind and quality of what is given.[1]

Proximity to beneficiaries is what distinguishes *vakıfçı* from *hayırsever*. The philanthropists rarely meet the people their contributions affect unless invited by organisations to observe how they are being put to use. But these occasions are less about engagement than they are about overseeing the use of money. In contrast, being a *vakıfçı* involves extensive encounters with the persons in need, as well as occasionally establishing long-term, sustained relations.

This distinction between *vakıfçı* and *hayırsever* has important gender and class dimensions. In corollary with the uneven distribution of property ownership among men and women in Turkey, the *hayırsever*s of Kayseri are almost exclusively men. Although schools or soup kitchens named after women are quite common, this is the result of an established tradition in which husbands or sons sponsor civic gifts in commemoration or in the name of women from their families. Yet, among *vakıfçı*s, men and women are equally active, either as volunteers or as paid employees. Again, as a direct derivative of ownership of wealth, *hayırsever*s exclusively belong to the upper classes, while among *vakıfçı*s some

---

[1] An earlier and shorter version of this chapter was published as Alkan Zeybek, Hilal. 2012. "Ethics of Care, Politics of Solidarity: Islamic Charitable Organisations in Turkey." In *Ethnographies of Islam: Ritual Performances and Everyday Practices*, eds. Thomas Pierret, Baudouin Dupret, Paulo G. Pinto, and Kathryn Spellman-Poots, 144–52. Edinburgh: Edinburgh University Press.

Open Access. © 2023 the author(s), published by De Gruyter. This work is licensed under the Creative Commons Attribution-NonCommercial-NoDerivatives 4.0 International License.
https://doi.org/10.1515/9783111156552-006

industrialists actively work within the organisations they founded, as do workers, who try to survive with their part-time salaries.

In this chapter, I focus on the formation of *vakıfçı* subjectivities by exploring their processes of ethical self-formation. Ethics here refers to an intersubjective and relational phenomenon that finds both its content and its expression in practices of care (both for the self and others) rather than in defined norms and values. Thus, my discussion in this chapter of the formation of ethical beings particularly refers to the development of capacities to care and give.

## Ethical Bodies, Embodied Affects

In *Politics of Piety*, Saba Mahmood discusses the premises of positive ethics in understanding ethical and pious agency. According to Mahmood, in post-Enlightenment thinking, ethics is often conceived of as an abstract system of principles, values, and regulations.[2] In this Kantian tradition, ethical reasoning is more heavily emphasised than ethical practices, which are either seen as habits that do not qualify as virtues or as actualisations of some abstract values and principles. By this understanding, ethics always begins within the person (with critical reasoning) and usually, but not always, creates a change in their behaviour. Therefore, the direction of ethical transformation is from inside to outside. Yet in positive ethics – Aristotelian ethics – moral actions are seen not as contingent but constitutive elements of the content of the ethical norm.[3] Therefore, the variety of relationships that can be established between the constitutive elements of the self (including the body, affects, volition, and reason) and the accepted norm become a matter of analysis.[4] This variety allows transformation to travel in the opposite direction – values and attitudes changing with the alteration of actions and behaviours. Rituals, prayers, fasts, and meditation may all be counted as classic examples of technologies of transformation that start from the outside. In this vein, I approach the formation of an ethical being through the ongoing processes of becoming a *vakıfçı* as a matter of adopting actions, donning new stances, and meticulously working on behaviour.

In the Kayseri beneficence field there are, of course, religiously informed norms that are clear and hardly surprising: a *vakıfçı* should be indiscriminately compassionate to all creatures of God, be patient, gentle, and humble. These

---

2 Mahmood 2005, 119.
3 Ibid., 120.
4 Ibid.

norms are repeated piously as they represent the will of God in the name of being good Muslims. While such ethical arguments, and actors' identification with and employment of these arguments, are important, inquiry should extend beyond them to explore multiplicity and ambivalence in the bodily cultivation of religious ethics. Doing so would allow us to understand how norms are inhabited, challenged, or desired.

As I have mentioned, *vakıfçı*s have first hand, face-to-face encounters with the beneficiaries and supplicants, and they are responsible for the immediate caregiving and caretaking activities that their organisations offer. Their daily contact with beneficiaries and supplicants lead *vakıfçı*s to revise their attitudes (not always intentionally) and force them into situations they would have otherwise avoided. They are impelled by the singularity of the encounter and the intimate content of the care relationship. Their position forces them to alter their embodied dispositions against the poor and poverty. Let me illustrate this with an example.

When I asked the female volunteers of Kayseri Derneği how volunteering affected their lives, Aliye explained, "I have gone beyond myself. I used to refrain from eating strangers' food, but I've started eating it. I used to refrain from sitting down in a poor house, but I started to do that. I've witnessed great changes in myself, and I am very happy about it."

Aliye is a wealthy woman aged over sixty. She covers her hair with chic silk scarves and always wears elegant clothes. Her golden-rimmed eyeglasses and rings of precious stones give away her upper-middle-class position at first sight. She is now responsible for running the public bath of a charitable organisation in Kayseri, where she interacts with the poorest women and children of the inner city. Catering to those who do not have access to running water, she is at ease with women roaming around the bath naked, making casual and friendly conversation or smoking in the foyer without the slightest embarrassment about their nakedness. And there, Aliye sits, chats with them, checks their papers, and fortnightly shares the Turkish bath experience, including being washed by one of the bath employees. Users of the bathhouse usually bring some food with them and offer to share their food with employees, including Aliye. She accepts and reciprocates with her own food offerings. She and two employees, who had once been beneficiaries before being offered employment a couple of years prior, eat lunch with a score of naked and half-naked women and children hanging around. Having once been uncomfortable entering homes in slums, Aliye now has the most intimate contact with their inhabitants, albeit not completely free of conflict and restlessness.

Aliye's experience is not unique. Other *vakıfçı*s, too, narrate similar stories and are routinely affected by similar daily encounters. These narratives, first, indicate the dispositions these women have had all their lives: that poverty is dirty, even disgusting, which therefore leads to a very visceral and bodily repulsion. Notwithstanding the stories of the poor-but-tidy as a possible exception, there is always a reluctance to establish physical ties with the poor: eating their food, cuddling their kids, and visiting their homes creates discomfort. Second, uprooting these dispositions is possible but only through a tedious, tense, and multidirectional process. Let me now briefly dwell on the first point to explore the question of what this feeling of disgust does to those who exhibit "class racism"[5] and have the means to distance themselves from poverty.

### Affects of Poverty (for the Well-Off)

According to Sara Ahmed, emotions reside neither in the subject who feels them, nor in the object that gives rise to those feelings.[6] Instead, emotions are a matter of how objects and subjects come into contact. Therefore, the encounter is always read via a lived history that creates the emotions. Certain bodies become objects of disgust as they evoke histories of accumulated and associated signals through skin colour, nakedness, odour, and sight, within frameworks of racism, misogyny, or class relations. However, that these signs are contingent does not in any way diminish the material reality and effects of the emotion evoked. Disgust affects the bodies that are pushed into shame in more profound, degrading, and harmful ways,[7] but here my focus is solely on the effects on those who feel disgust.

Disgust in particular entails proximity between the subject and the object, and it immediately urges bodies to withdraw for fear of contamination. Disgust attests to the fragility and permeability of the skin and the body's openness to such threats from the outside, no matter if these threats have any objective basis. And with this immediate bodily reaction, disgust functions as the mechanism for abjection.[8] Bodies that cannot be contacted, bodies that have contagious qualities, are created in the moment of disgust. Yet, neither the emotion itself, nor the effects and "borders" it produces, can simply be reversed through reflexive processes. "Emotions shape the very surfaces of bodies, which take shape through the repetition of actions over time, as well as through the orientations towards

---

5 Balibar 2010.
6 Ahmed 2004.
7 See, for example, Sennet and Cobb 1972; Tomkins 1995; Erdoğan 2007; Lorde 2007; Jo 2013.
8 Kristeva 1982; Lorde 2007.

and away from others."⁹ Therefore, emotions bear a weight more onerous than those of psychic states, and they are difficult to erase. Reinforced by a lifetime of material and discursive iterations, the contingent associations that entangle certain cues with certain emotions can only be undone via diligent bodily work. In our case, this bodily work is significant in its possibility for subverting abjection by not invoking or reinforcing shame in the beneficiaries of these organisations.

Accounts of poverty alleviation and containment describe in detail how the emotions of disgust and fear of contamination have shaped policies addressing the poor and are affected by the discourses that inform those policies.¹⁰ Images of beggars with missing limbs and open wounds, pauperised women threatening the psychological and physiological well-being of society through sexually transmitted diseases, and street children sneaking into clean family homes may all be recalled from a vivid reservoir of social imagery.¹¹ Even if these seem too marginal to invoke a common feeling of disgust, milder images of shanty towns with open gutters, leaky ceilings, and that very particular smell of dampness feel all too familiar, evidence that poverty itself is often perceived as dirty. In Kayseri, these images are intensified with reference to local Roma and Kurds, who are doubly stigmatised when poor. With or without an element of racialisation, these images and recollections of poverty work through sensations and bodily responses.

The narratives of *vakıfçı* women in Kayseri are no different in making use of such sensationalist images. A very palpable sense of lacking, not only of certain comforts or basic survival requirements but also of assumed hygiene and cleanliness standards, accompanies their vivid descriptions of poverty. Yet, in a twist, disgust is replaced with compassionate contact in a particular strain of these stories. The common antagonist in this type of narrative is Nevin Akyurt. Nevin Akyurt came from a prominent Kayseri family but did not have much wealth of her own. Instead, she had a vast network both thanks to her family connections and her work in local media. She was also known to have an extraordinarily warm and outgoing personality. Until her death in 2004, after a decade-long fight against cancer, Akyurt had been the local heroine of the *vakıf* field in Kayseri. She mobilised the wealthy to attend to the needs of the city's poor by establishing several *vakıf*s and encouraged women to take an active part in their operations. Yet, as these women's stories attest, the most impressive aspect of her dedication were her private acts of benevolence, which often involved intimate care.

---

**9** Ahmed 2004, 4.
**10** M. Dean 1991; Morris 2001.
**11** Morris 2001.

Consider what two of her disciples told me during our informal conversations at different times:

> Neriman: One day, she took me along to [visit] Zehra. She was taking continuous care of that lady, who had serious mental health problems. We went to her place, which was simply a dump. She was living there with several wild dogs she used to sleep with, cuddling. I guess this was the way she protected herself and also stayed warm. She was a wild lady, never letting anybody close. She used to scream and attack strangers who approached her. But she trusted Nevin Abla deeply. So when we went there I was really frightened by the scene and by her looks. I hesitated to get out of the car. Nevin Abla told me to follow her. We approached Zehra. She had that bewildered and dangerous spark in her eyes. Then she recognised Nevin Abla and visibly relaxed. Nevin Abla went to her side, patted her hair, and talked with her. She asked Zehra to get into the car. Then, we took Zehra to Nevin Abla's house, where she personally washed her. Then she made Zehra sit on the carpet and started to pick lice from her hair. She cut her hair, washed her clothes, and later we took her back to her place. I could not possibly have touched that woman, but Nevin Abla was like this. There was a lot we should have learnt from her.

> İpek: There was a very old couple, living on their own in a rotting apartment. She found them somehow. The old lady was paralysed, so she was in diapers. Her husband was doing his best, but his condition was also miserable. Nevin Abla used to visit them regularly, change the diapers, clean the lady up, wash her, and take their clothes to her house to wash. She would even comb the lady's hair and embrace her like a child.

We learn more: Nevin Akyurt would never hesitate to enter anyone's home, sit and eat what was offered. She would play with their children. She would dress the most terrible of wounds. In any case, she would establish physical contact with the people she was trying to help, as a natural requirement of care. There is certainly a disciplinary aspect to this extension of care, which will be discussed later in the chapter. For now, I will stick to how Akyurt's example is interpreted among Kayseri *vakıfçı*s. The legend of Nevin Akyurt first and foremost relies on transgression of the usual physical boundaries between strangers – boundaries enacted especially through the emotion of disgust. These boundaries, certainly, have very strong class and ethnic dimensions. The most significant quality of Akyurt, in the eyes of the *vakıfçı*s, is this extension of intimate care across difference and social distance.

Yet all these stories carry a sense of exceptionality; they are almost always followed with the addendum that it was not possible for Akyurt's disciples to match her example, that she was extraordinary. By being exceptional, anecdotes about Akyurt often function as reminders and invocations of the normality of recoiling in disgust, while at the same time alluding to the possibility that this norm may not be set in stone. In that sense, the legend of Akyurt provides a regulative ideal, one which is unreachable but, in striving to mimic her, opens a path towards ethical transformation.

This ethical transformation, as exemplified by Akyurt and expressed in the self-narratives of Aliye and the other *vakıfçı*s, does not necessarily imply a radical change in the conception of the poor as dirty. While it has led to a habitual presumption that they are not, behavioural change on their part neither begins nor ends with such a change in assumptions. It is rather a piecemeal transformation that resides in action more than in a reflexive questioning of beliefs and conceptions. The crux of the ethical transformation is to act it out even before internalising it.

At the risk of losing sight of nuances and personal differences, I can sketch an overview of the process as such: a person decides to do some "good" for the needy of her town for any number of reasons. She certainly has the aforementioned negative predispositions and embodied feelings, but figures being there will push her into situations she has never experienced before. As she acts out her decision, sometimes even in spite of herself, these actions settle in her body and conscience, slowly evolving into an ethical habitus.

**Positive Ethics**

In order to explore "the work that bodily practices perform in creating" this ethical subject,[12] I return to the work of Saba Mahmood and the source of her inspiration, Michel Foucault. In his later work, Foucault approached ethics as "care for oneself", by which he meant the operations of a person on his or her own soul, thoughts, body, and feelings.[13] This is different from the established conception of ethics as a product of mental capacities and contemplation. Foucault's notion of ethics is primarily embodied and acted out. This approach is built on the notion of ethics in Greek antiquity, especially Aristotle. Given the influence of Aristotle on paradigmatic Islamic scholars like Al-Ghazali and Ibn Khaldun, Mahmood observes a very similar understanding and practice of ethical formations in Islam.[14]

According to Aristotle, "states of character arise out of like activities", and virtue inhabits one's body only through effort. Virtue is not something we have as part of our nature, but it is natural to strive for it and to be able to build towards

---

12 Mahmood 2005, 160.
13 Foucault 1997a; Foucault 1997b.
14 Mahmood 2005.

it.¹⁵ Yet, virtue is learned only through acting virtuously. Continuing with Aristotle, "for the things we have to learn before we can do them, we learn by doing them, e.g. men become builders by building and lyre players by playing the lyre; so too we become just by doing just acts, temperate by doing temperate acts, brave by doing brave acts."¹⁶

Doing in order to become requires a significant level of discipline and repetition because it is only in this way that a virtue becomes ingrained in character and habitus, which drive an unconscious, unpremeditated repertoire of actions like those of Nevin Akyurt. The idea of acquiring virtue by relentlessly acting it out has significant ontological implications. First, it implies an understanding of the human body not as the vessel for inner qualities but as an agent for sowing and fostering these qualities. It is a body that is formed by the ethical transformation it is performing. Therefore, it is malleable and affective, as well as effective and active. In order to explain this paradoxical notion, I will borrow from Mahmood's reading of the Foucauldian concept of docility. She argues that:

> The capacity for action is enabled and created by specific relations of subordination. To clarify this paradox, we might consider the example of a virtuoso pianist who submits herself to the often painful regime of disciplinary practice, as well as to the hierarchical structures of apprenticeship, in order to acquire the ability – the requisite agency – to play the instrument with mastery. Importantly, her agency is predicated upon her ability to be taught, a condition classically referred to as 'docility'. Although we have come to associate docility with the abandonment of agency, the term literally implies the malleability required of someone in order for her to be instructed in a particular skill or knowledge.¹⁷

This brings us to docility, which means not only being submissive and controlled, but also plastic enough to be formed, taught, and shaped; hence, docility has the capacity to subject one to discipline and also to situations that may create pain, discomfort, or anxiety. As a condition of ethical formation, docility involves both being open to the interventions and interlocutions of trusted masters-of-the-trade and subjecting oneself to tedious control and repetition.¹⁸ It involves acting upon the self as much as it involves allowing others to act upon that self. While discussing my methodology, I suggested, upon reflection on my experiences in Kayseri, that rendering oneself docile is a precondition for embodied and internalised learning. Now, I expect, the methodological and substantive significance of these

---

**15** See Laidlaw 2013, for a wider discussion on the ever-presence of striving for ethics and virtue in everyday life.
**16** Aristotle 2002, bk. 2:1.
**17** Mahmood 2005, 29.
**18** Cf. Allahyari 2000.

are better linked. If docility means allowing one's dispositions to change through repetition of bodily performances and being receptive to pedagogical formation by a mentor, in Kayseri Nevin Akyurt served as a mentor of this kind to whom most of today's *vakıfçı*s have submitted themselves.

## Discipline

Just as care for the self involves discipline of the self, care for the other contains an aspect of discipline as well. Remember the statements from Nevin Akyurt's friends and disciples that I used to illustrate the significance of the transgression of bodily boundaries among Kayseri *vakıfçı*s. One more strikingly consistent theme in these stories was that Akyurt cleaned the people she cared for. She took Zehra into her home, washed her, and picked lice from her hair. She washed the old lady and changed her diaper. Akyurt was certainly caring for these people in a very corporal sense, but at the same time, hers was an effort to make their bodies meet her standards. What she recognised as a need – cleanliness – was at the same time a terrain of discipline and control. This mutuality of care and discipline crystallised before my eyes when I witnessed Neriman and Beyaz's failed attempts to "help" a family.

One day, Neriman received a call from a woman about a neighbouring flat that was full of garbage. This neighbour called Neriman for help after the stench had become unbearable and their efforts to convince the mother of the household to clean had ended in a violent argument. Neriman called Beyaz, and they went to see the condition of the flat. It was so full of all sorts of junk that it was no longer possible to enter some of the rooms. The household consisted of two teenage girls, their hoarding mother, and bedridden father. The conditions of the two young girls, the terminally ill father, and the mentally ill mother moved Neriman and Beyaz deeply and they decided to do something for the family. Registration with the Kayseri Derneği aid scheme was the first and easiest step to take. They then convinced the girls to empty the flat, made arrangements to keep the family away during that process, and finally called the municipality to ask for trucks. Then, everything in the flat except a few items of personal use was loaded onto the trucks and taken to the city dumping grounds. Neriman had the flat cleaned and whitewashed. Both she and Beyaz used their contacts to find new furniture and finally took the family to their renewed and refurbished home, expecting them to be happy and grateful. But the mother was inconsolably upset with the situation. Neriman tried to arrange psychiatric care for her, but she refused and finally chased us out of the flat. Neriman did not give up. She was determined to "save the girls, even if it was impossible to help the mother." However, his proved equally difficult.

I met the girls in Neriman's office a few weeks after the big cleaning operation. Neriman invited them to share the latest developments on the issue of after-school tuition they had said they needed. Then, we all got into Beyaz's van and went to see the flat. The girls were not happy with this idea, but they obeyed Neriman's wish. The interior of the flat was covered with traces of muddy cat paws. All sorts of rubbish lay on the floor and furniture. The flat was filled with a smell that made breathing almost impossible. Without a word, Beyaz went outside to wait for us. I sincerely wished I could have joined him, as I nearly fainted from the smell. Neriman was totally disheartened. In a sweet voice (actually, in an almost weeping tone) she begged the girls to keep the flat clean. They stared blankly back at her. She shifted to an angrier tone and told them of the amount of work she had undertaken to make the flat "a habitable place". Both girls appeared indifferent to the lecture. Neriman was helpless, so we left. On the way back, she was truly upset and shed a few tears. She told me how many times she had told the girls to keep the flat clean, even promising to bring them gifts on the condition of cleanliness. Apparently, nothing had worked. Gradually, Neriman gave up the effort and left the family to themselves.

From our conversations throughout this process and from the way she approached the girls, I knew Neriman really cared about the family and their well-being. She did what she thought was best to care for them, yet she neither managed to establish the relationship she wanted with the girls, nor could she accomplish her task of cleaning the flat. However, on the way to failure, she showed me how care was intricately related to discipline (or in this case, even to coercion). This problématique of discipline requires further attention.

In a Foucauldian sense, discipline is a modality of power that aims to affect the conduct of individuals in prescribed ways. Foucault's intellectual interest had been in the technologies of discipline that people were subjected to via total institutions like prisons or asylums, and on the disciplines (as professions) that institutionalised these technologies through the production of knowledge.[19] A significant number of these disciplinary professions are related to care work, like medicine and psychiatry. There is also an expanding literature that employs Foucauldian thinking to approach others like poverty alleviation,[20] social work,[21] and nursing.[22]

---

19 Foucault 1975; Foucault 1976.
20 M. Dean 1991.
21 Gilliom 2001.
22 Hugman 1991.

According to the British sociologist Nick Fox, the social sciences have approached the issue of care mostly with a focus on this dimension of discipline.[23] Fox calls this dimension "the vigil of care", with reference to Florence Nightingale, who christened vigilance as one of the pillars of the nursing profession. Care, practised as vigil, is an activity of surveillance and an exertion of disciplinary power over those being cared for. While Fox limits his analysis to the discourse of care, this vigil becomes even more prominent in the daily experience of care relationships, just as it became evident in Neriman's campaign against the "junk-house" and its inhabitants.

Discipline is also evident in the creation and application of selection criteria for beneficiaries, as this process has the potential to push beneficiaries into a rigid table of categories. As discussed in the previous chapter, house inspections performed to cross-check applicants' stories and to witness first-hand the level of poverty can well be seen as prime disciplinary techniques. These techniques turn applicants and their lives into an object of a *vakıfçıs'* gaze, which sweeps rooms, furniture, and household members to ensure the applicants' conditions qualify them for registration. As in the case of municipal worker Sena and her camcorder, technological devices can be used to extend the gaze to those unable to be present for the first-hand evaluation.

However, as I suggested earlier, these inspections also often serve as an opportunity for the applicants to detail their story, establish a personal connection with *vakıfçıs*, and negotiate the terms and conditions of care, as much as they form a backdrop for disciplinary interventions. They offer the applicants a feeling of recognition, and the *vakıfçıs* satisfaction from their work. According to Fox, what takes place on such occasions of mutual understanding is "care-as-gift"; a possibility, he argues, that is severely overlooked in the social sciences.[24] He identifies care-as-gift with feelings and virtues he derives from Hélène Cixous' work:[25] generosity, trust, love, affection, benevolence, patience, and curiosity. In Cixous' formulation, these "feminine' qualities of the Gift" are contrasted with the elements of "the masculine realm of the Proper": property, propriety, possession, identity, and dominance.

Fox's understanding of gift is strictly unidirectional (as in "pure" altruism).[26] Therefore, it does not recognise the fact that even gift relations can be disciplinary, although they are enacted with such genuine feelings as compassion or altruism.

---

23  Fox 1995.
24  Ibid.
25  Cixous, 1996.
26  Fox 1995.

As I elaborated earlier, a gift is primarily a relationship, not a thing that is given. Within this relationship, power and status can be played out, as can equality and mutual respect. I therefore suggest focusing on the encounter itself and locating discipline and gift where they belong – in the realm of intersubjectivity, rather than categorically naming some practices "discipline" and others "gift".[27]

Such a view would also critique one aspect of Foucault's understanding of ethics as care for the self. Foucault's genealogy may appear to be strictly about the self: an inward looking, non-porous, and unified self that diligently performs mental, spiritual, and corporeal work on itself. Although he mentions in passing that care for oneself is a precondition of care for others and vice-versa,[28] the problem of others on this ethical quest remains under-theorised. All in all, however important it is to recognise embodiment and the element of discipline, Foucault's view needs development from the standpoint of recognising ethics as one's relationship to the other.[29] Thus, it should be clear that the core of the ethical transformation I have been describing in relation to Kayseri *vakıfçıs* is necessarily located in encounter with others; it is self-formation that is not contained within the self, but which comes into being in the realm of the social, in personal relations and connections. It can therefore only be understood using an intersubjective approach. Intersubjective theory is vast and a conclusive discussion is beyond the scope of this book. But, there is one strand of scholarly work that owes a lot to intersubjective theory and must be considered here: the ethics of care. I contend that this is a particularly relevant way of shifting the locus of ethics from the individual to the relationship. If ethics is an activity, as Aristotle claims, then, within the realm of *vakıf* work, it is the activity of extending care to others.

## An Ethics of Care

In contemporary social science literature, questions concerning the issue of care have often been dealt with by feminist scholars, who work relentlessly to move this subject from its "peripheral" location – where it is conceived as a "natural" maternal attitude – towards political, ethical, and psychological debates surrounding the issues of human societies. Care is an act of concern for the other, as well as an active undertaking emerging from this concern. It is a fundamental

---

27 For a critique of the lopsided views on care as gift (with an understanding of gift as wholly positive) and a discussion of how the debates evolved in the 2010s, see Thelen 2021.
28 Foucault 1997b.
29 Gilligan 1982.

part of human lives, in good times and in bad, in sickness and in health. It is a daily necessity for human life, and not merely in times of crises, as in the case of hospital care. Therefore, it is worth every effort to revalue care in all its societal dimensions.[30] However, in this section I will offer only a very selective reading of this literature, delving into the intersubjective and relational aspects of care.

Joan Tronto defines care via certain "core values" and phases: (1) attentiveness and caring about, (2) responsibility and taking care of, (3) competence in meeting needs and care giving, and (4) responsiveness and care receiving.[31] These values have since informed many theorisations of the ethics of care.[32] Thus, a brief exploration can help clarify the concept of care as it is used in this chapter.

According to Tronto, attentiveness is the starting point of any caring relationship.[33] Care begins with caring about, and hence a recognition of a need, which captures the attention. Without attentiveness it is not possible to meet needs, as they would not even be acknowledged as such. Attentiveness is especially related to understanding the other's needs, their particularity as a separate human being, and the requirements of this particularity. Yet, Tronto's conceptualisation of attentiveness is too dependent on voluntaristic and rationalist assumptions.[34] As Wendy Hollway argues, on the contrary, attentiveness stems from processes that are less volitional than it first seems, usually functioning at an unconscious and embodied level.

The second value, responsibility, assumes the duty of meeting recognised needs. It is therefore similar to answering a call and taking action. Through responsibility, the abstract notion of "caring about" turns into a solid and practical "caring for". Yet, simply assuming responsibility does not make one capable of providing "good-enough" care. The performance of care requires skills, habits, and bodily orientations that cannot be obtained in a moment; rather, they can only be aggregated over a lifetime of care experiences. This brings us to the third requirement of care: competence. Competence in the provision of care only comes with practice, as care can only be learned by doing. Finally, responsiveness as a skill is about the interaction between the giver and receiver of care, about the openness of each to the other's situation and reactions. This value, along with attentiveness, emphasises the intersubjective nature of care relations.

---

30 In the past decade care has become a pivotal topic and received interest from a wider range of disciplines. See, for example, de la Bellacasa 2017; Chatzidakis et al. 2020; Thelen 2021; Gabauer et al. 2022.
31 Tronto 1993, 106–7.
32 Sevenhuijsen 1998; Sevenhuijsen 2003a; Sevenhuijsen 2003b; Komter 2005; Hollway 2006.
33 Tronto 1993.
34 Hollway 2006.

Wendy Hollway, a critical psychologist informed by psychoanalysis and object relations theory, identifies two developmental processes that are key to acquiring these values: identification and differentiation. Hollway notes that although these processes are chronological in that they appear at infancy, they are also simultaneous over a lifetime.[35] All our lives, identification is vital for recognising and responding to others' needs, while differentiation is critical in order not to dominate and oppress the other with the act of care. Hollway bases her theorisation of the capacity to care on the "tension between experiencing the other's needs and one's own difference".[36]

Similarly, Richard Sennett suggests that, in order to care, one should initially and *falsely* assume somebody else's pain as one's own. So, an act of care "begins as a mistake", but at that moment of identification, one should recognise that the carer and the cared for are actually separate beings with different needs.[37] This simultaneous occurrence of the "mistake" of identification with the other and the correction of this "mistake" is the precondition for mutual respect.

When differentiation and identification are seen not as rivalling processes but as orthogonal axes of the process of subjectivity formation in relational terms, attentiveness and responsiveness find their true basis.[38] But, it is important to acknowledge the inherent ambivalence and fluidity of these qualities and the phases of care that accompany them. The axes of identification and differentiation both have extreme ends towards which one can slide. The swing between assumptions of omniscient knowledge about the other's needs and effective differentiation, as well as the swing between over-identification (hence, unbearable pain) and dis-identification (abjection/othering), is possible in every care scenario. Sometimes, the pain of identification is so high that the other's needs may be completely ignored. Sometimes, the caregiver exercises domination over the one in need, operating under the assumption that all the needs and desires of the other are transparent to the caregiver. Other times, the individual feels their autonomy is under threat because of the neediness of the other. Yet there are also times in which care may become a pleasure in itself because of the pleasure/ relief it provides to the cared for. Capacities to care can best be conceptualised as capacities to manage the swing of these pendulums in such a way that the particular needs of the other are both recognised and met within the intersubjective

---

[35] Hollway 2006.
[36] Ibid., 125.
[37] Sennett 2003.
[38] Hollway 2006, 109.

space of conscious, unconscious, bodily, verbal, and affective communication, as acknowledged by mutually interrelated individual subjects.

Kayseri *vakıfçı*s cannot always manage the swings of the pendulum between identification and differentiation. All the scenarios listed above are observable in their interactions with beneficiaries. There are times when the needs of a beneficiary are completely overlooked, usually with excuses made about the unavailability of resources. Other times, identification is so strong that an encounter leads to sleepless nights and feelings of pain and incapacity. There are even cases, as with what happened between Neriman and the two girls, when a *vakıfçı*'s disciplinary care, coupled with little differentiation of herself from those whom she cares for, end in emotional outburst. But there are also times in which, for some, the act of care leads to satisfaction and a feeling of mutual recognition and understanding. How this is to be achieved and how the balance is to be maintained is a matter of constant discussion among the *vakıfçı*s themselves. Warning each other, reflecting on past conduct, and critiquing the actions of third parties all help to shape and maintain a norm as a way of coming to terms with this highly affective swing. Yet, as they commonly acknowledge, this tension is only lived through and managed by an accumulation of embodied and unconscious knowledge stemming from experience.

In order to explicate the dimension of embodiment further, I will cite Hollway, wherein she defines identification:

> The psychoanalytic concept of identification embraces processes that are conscious and unconscious, embodied, affective and cognitive, both primary (unthought) and secondary (thought) processes. Without the psychological capacity to identify with others across the boundary that comes to define one individual from another, compassion and concern would be impossible. We can only know what another person is experiencing through empathy or 'fellow feeling'; that is, *through using ourselves as an instrument of understanding.*[39] (Italics mine)

Hollway's idea of using ourselves as instruments to understand the other's experience illustrates the level of significance the role that bodies (not only as flesh and blood, but also as the locus of senses, sentiments, and reactions) play in the process of identification. Maurice Hamington develops this aspect of care further with the concept of "caring knowledge".[40] For him, caring knowledge is most importantly knowledge of the body; bodies communicate and understand more than what is available to the consciousness. Consider the body that recoils with a sense of disgust even when the subject's intentions had been to remain

---

39 Hollway 2006, 14.
40 Hamington 2004.

respectful. Or consider the involuntary cry of the witness to an accident, as if she herself has been hit. Identification, in that sense, is most importantly the embodied knowledge of having a body that is fragile and a psyche that hurts, bleeds, enjoys, and longs just like others. Of course, identification does not imply the subject understands the other to be exactly like the self. Healthy development goes hand in hand with the process of differentiation and the recognition of the other as a unique self.[41] It also means approaching the body as the site of otherness, of divergent needs and sensitivities.

In an attempt to think about the ethics of care through the phenomenological lens of Merleau-Ponty, Hamington approaches care as a phenomenon that is ultimately embodied, and argues that bodies are not only objects or instruments of care, but that they are also the very possibility of care.[42] This possibility is related to the unarticulated and often unconscious (and also involuntary) nature and primacy of the body's knowledge and its communication of this knowledge through behaviours. Following from this, as Hamington argues, "as a corporeal potential, care can be cultivated or diminished through practices and habits."[43] Similarly, Selma Sevenhuijsen argues that "the core idea of the ethic of care in my view is that care is a practice, and that it is crucial for developing a moral attitude – and thus also a moral vocabulary – of care by engaging in the practice of care. By doing so, care can in fact grow into a disposition, a part of our everyday thinking and doing."[44]

The *vakıfçı*s of Kayseri practice care to fulfil their duties through their everyday work. They learn by doing, by bodily involvement; and, as I have suggested before, they experience an ethical transformation as part and parcel of this bodily involvement. This transformation shifts their boundaries and potentially their notions of dirtiness and cleanliness, which are often indexes of racial and class discrimination.[45] What requires emphasis here is that care as a practice of ethics is not a process that begins and ends with an individual self. It is a relational and intersubjective phenomenon, an interaction, an exchange. As such, care has an ontological proximity to gift, and certain aspects of gift relations could well be extrapolated to offer a deeper comprehension of care relations.

---

41 Hollway 2006.
42 Hamington 2004.
43 Ibid., 5.
44 Sevenhuijsen 2003b, 18; quoted in Hollway 2006, 9–10.
45 For a wider discussion of how cleanliness functions as a tool of distinction see Douglas 1966.

## An Ethics of Giving

In June 2009, I spent a day with Nihal and Fatma, travelling all around Kayseri in Nihal's car. These two women had participated in the founding of a small *vakıf* and had remained involved with it as volunteers. The organisation helped poor couples who wanted to marry but did not have the means to do so, and that day we were on a mission to do applicant home visits. With the help of sponsors, the organisation provided basic household items, furniture, a wedding gown for the bride, and a suit for the groom. They would also cover associated legal fees. Its employees used a checklist for preliminary applicant assessments with the aim of verifying their poverty and/or orphanage. This was followed by the home visits to cross-check the stories.

On that day, our trip began with getting lost on the outskirts of the city so badly that we spent more than an hour finding the first address, which had been inadequately reported. The applicant's house was situated in a garden, typical of the summer homes of Kayseri's wealthy, but it was visibly old and run down. It was a lovely day, so although the lady of the house invited us in, Fatma and Nihal preferred to sit on the benches in the garden. When we were settled, the lady rushed back inside to make us tea, despite Fatma and Nihal's objections. When she came back, she told us that she was trying to arrange her son's wedding. Although her family were once known as wealthy natives of Kayseri, she was facing difficulties because all the family's wealth had been lost as a result of her ex-husband's lifestyle. She was concerned that her application remain hidden because she did not want her in-laws to learn about their financial problems. Fatma was particularly taken by the story and openly empathised with the woman's wish. After checking with Nihal (without saying a word, but by exchanging a knowing glance and a nod) Fatma then approved the application and explained the necessary next steps. We sat there for almost an hour, sipped two glasses of tea, and as we were leaving Fatma and Nihal hugged the woman and kissed her youngest child, a ten-year-old boy, affectionately.

At our second stop on the other end of the city, we were welcomed into a shanty house, bereft of even the most basic household items. There, the mother of the house offered us peanuts and tea. Again, we spent nearly an hour chatting about the story of the bride-to-be. Fatma and Nihal offered them advice on how to get more than the routine package, consisting of a bedroom set, an oven, and a sofa set. We left the house hugging and kissing everyone – including the neighbours, who happened to drop by while we were there. When we got to the car, Fatma told Nihal to put a note on the family's file indicating that they should be given extra food boxes.

There were ten addresses on our list that day and it was already past noon, so Nihal and Fatma discussed refusing any food or drinks and cutting the visits as short as possible. They wished to stick to their primary aim, which was investigation. But we ended up eating a plateful of cherries at our next stop. Fatma and Nihal had to spare the next day (which was a Sunday) finishing the visits, since we managed to make it to fewer than half of the addresses on our list.

On that day, Fatma and Nihal exemplified many of the elements of care that define *vakıfçı* ethics in Kayseri. They were attentive to the applicants' stories and responsive to their particular needs. They were also congenial in their attitudes and established physical contact freely and frequently. They were well equipped to ease the anxiety the applicants likely felt in relation to being inspected. Moreover, they looked quite comfortable receiving offerings from beneficiaries. I suggest that all of these elements of conduct has strong ethical and political implications.

I discussed the meaning and significance of touch earlier in this chapter and suggested that crossing the physical boundaries created by established emotional histories is an important aspect of extending care to the beneficiaries of Kayseri *vakıf*s. But, unlike the examples from Nevin Akyurt's life, those instances of contact are not often directed towards any concrete physical need, like dressing wounds or washing the elderly or the disabled. Physical contact, in the form of a hug, a firm handshake, or a helping hand for changing socks and shoes, usually performs a different function: recognition of the other as a fellow human being, and therefore, in a very subtle way, subverting the abjection that often taints similar encounters. Hence, what Fatma and Nihal actually gave through their tight embraces was the gift of recognition.

The second element that requires attention is Fatma and Nihal's ease at accepting offerings from beneficiaries. While they declared to the host each time that it was exceptional for them to accept anything from applicants, the proceedings of the day attested otherwise. They never refused anything or established boundaries that would have hinted at a refusal from the start. If their discourse of not accepting gifts was a declaration of a certain understanding of professionalism, their practices referred to a more powerful calling, or better entrenched ethical values about personal relations: a gift obliges acceptance.

This obligation is worth dwelling on. Moments of contact between *vakıfçı*s and beneficiaries involve an obvious inequality of power, despite the *vakıfçı*s' best intentions. While one of the parties has an immediate need asking to be met, the other party has the power to decide whether or not to attend to that need. For *vakıfçı*s, it is easy to cause injury. For beneficiaries, shame and humiliation are never far off. How this inequality is to be managed is often posed as an ethical question. Resorting openly to the paradigm of the gift is an often-used strategy in the face of this question. In order to understand how gift helps resolve some of these tensions, we need to remember the features of it discussed in detail in the introduction. I elaborated there, contrary to common understandings of voluntariness, how gift is defined by obligation: obligation to give, obligation to accept, and obligation to reciprocate. Only when this cycle is smoothly completed, or when completion is left open over time, does the given thing acquire the status of gift. If the cycle is broken because of an interruption to the cycle of obligatory acts, this causes a crisis in the relationship that the gift upholds.

Keeping this in mind, it should be clear why refusing certain offerings might insult the beneficiaries with whom Fatma and Nihal were interacting. In the context of *vakıfçı*-applicant interactions, a glass of tea or a plateful of cherries constitutes a gift. When they are rejected without acceptable cause (like health problems), it becomes a problem of recognition of personal value, for a gift is inalienable from its giver. These small offerings are at the same time counter-gifts given in return for the *vakıfçıs*' interest in the supplicant's case, as well as for the anticipated support from the institutions. This brings us to another effect of gift: that it is utilised as an ethical means to handle inequality.

By obligating a return, the gift, essentially, has a levelling effect. Its reciprocal nature does not erase inequalities. But, because it recognises every actor involved in the gift relationship first and foremost as a giver, it is ontologically a relation between equals, i.e., persons who are equal in their capacity to give, even though what can be given may not be matching in value. In that sense everyone is rich enough to be able to give and everyone poor enough to receive something from the other. The positions of giver and receiver are interchangeable. Indeed, they have to be interchanged if the gift is to be completed. Thus, accepting beneficiaries' offerings (which include peanuts as well as prayers) is recognising them as givers. What they give does not have to match what they are given, for gift resists calculation and symmetry anyway. It does, however, allow for a restatement of dignity because, as Kayseri *vakıfçıs* often quote from the Prophet Mohammad, "the giving hand is superior to the receiving hand." Accepting a receiving hand's offerings is momentarily changing that equilibrium and turning the dictum on its head, opening room for a respectful relationship with interlocutors who are seen in their "full social existence".[46]

---

46 Rozakou 2012.

## A Tentative Conclusion: Respect

The distinction between *hayırsevers* and *vakıfçıs*, which rests on negotiations of proximity and distance with the beneficiaries, can be mapped onto the model developed by Turkish social scientist Tanıl Bora[47]. Reflecting on ways of fighting poverty, Bora suggests the analytical use of four typologies: social rights, charity, solidarity, and self-organisation. Social rights refer to the content of social citizenship as understood within the framework of welfare states, whereas self-organisation refers to community and grassroots organisations that either aim to provide relief through their own resources or which fight for the social rights. These two forms of welfare provision to needy members of society either address the state or turn to the community as a source of self-sufficiency. Charity and solidarity, on the other hand, share the characteristic of being dependent on other peoples' willingness to share their wealth with those in need, though the similarity between the two stops there. They are different in their implications and potentialities. While, according to Bora, charity is giving without establishing any personal relationships, with the recognition that a hint of intimacy may turn the encounter into one of obligation, solidarity aims for exactly that which charity seeks to avoid: establishing personal contact. Welfare provision through beneficence swings between charity and solidarity because of these characteristics, which reflect the rupture between *vakıf* workers and benefactors. Solidarity is the potential outcome of contact, not necessarily of the political convictions of the actors.[48]

At a time when the social sciences seem occupied with understanding the consequences of spatial segregation in urban centres, of gated communities and slums, of the spatial and hierarchical imprint of increasingly uneven income distribution, of network societies and redundant populations that are not even a node in these networks; in short, with social distances stretching to an unbearable extent, talking about potentialities for cross-class, cross-status solidarities established on such minor occasions and under conditions of gross inequality may seem utopian. Certainly, the encounters themselves do not guarantee any action towards creating social equality. On the contrary, they may turn into stages for the performance of class divisions, social stigma, and power inequality. Occa-

---

[47] T. Bora 2009.
[48] I do not exactly agree with Bora's classification, because what he sees as the core value in solidarity is well enacted in the charitable settings of Kayseri. What I find especially important, however, is his emphasis on contact as the distinguishing feature between conservative and potentially transformative acts of giving, whatever name we give to them.

sionally, however, when the parties involved are attuned to each other's stories and needs, something else may be born: mutual respect.

Richard Sennett's *Respect in a World of Inequality* diagnoses contemporary societies as suffering from a scarcity of respect, despite this precious substance being completely free of charge.[49] He then contemplates the structural sources of inequality and how disrespect is implicated in these inequalities in modern societies. Sennett argues that the modern code of respect includes three dicta that make it possible to be respected and to feel self-respect: "make something of yourself, take care of yourself and help others."[50] All three have the effect of emphasising and creating inequalities for a number of reasons. First, not everybody has the same capacity to make something out of themselves – people differ in their talents, mental capacities, and physical conditions. Moreover, during life courses, financial or physical independence can be lost, both due to aging or ill health and events like war, displacement, disaster, or job loss.[51] Second, not everybody is able take care of themselves. Dependency is an inescapable aspect of life, whether it comes in the form of disability, age-related health conditions, or poverty. And, finally, not everybody is given the same chances to help others and participate in community building. Welfare provision is a territory in which all three, especially the last two, of these bases for disrespect are structurally rife.

Sennett puts forth a couple of modest proposals to build respect within relations and encounters that are marked by inequality. As an antidote to the dictum of independence, he suggests admitting just claims of adult dependency. Clearly, *vakıfçılık*, in general, is based on a recognition of dependency. However, the question of what constitutes a just claim of dependency does not have an easy answer and, as I have shown, is open to contestation and negotiation. *Vakıf*s develop criteria to determine just bases for acceptance and rejection. In that sense, "seeing like a *waqf*" is not much different than "seeing like a state".[52] Official categories and acceptance criteria aim to make supplicants legible and manageable in a fashion similar to modern technologies of governmentality. However, as impossible as it is to argue that state policies are uniformly applied by "street-level bureaucrats",[53] it is equally unrealistic to assume that *vakıfçı*s uniformly follow the procedures of their respective organisations. Just like state employees who

---

[49] Sennett 2003
[50] Ibid., 260.
[51] See also Kittay 1999 for a detailed discussion on dependency from the perspective of feminist political philosophy.
[52] Scott 1998.
[53] Lipsky 2010.

interact with citizens on a daily basis, *vakıfçıs* have discretion over the extent to which they follow the procedures. In the context of *vakıf*s, deciding on who "our poor" will be, and thus who has needs that create rightful entitlements, requires a relational and fluid notion of justice, as illustrated in the previous chapter. Understanding the needs of the other, as I have also shown, is not a straightforward process. It is, in the intensity of encounter, about finding a momentary balance in the pendulum's swing between identification and differentiation, between using your own experience as a human being to understand the other and recognising the uniqueness of the other's condition and needs. But, first and foremost, it is a process of acknowledging others' vulnerability, incapacity, and dependency as merely human conditions.

The fluidity and flexibility of the notion of *just dependency* create tension between different actors in the field of beneficence in Kayseri. Both in the media and in private conversations, a local version of the proverb "give a man a *fish* and you feed him for a day; teach a man to *fish* and you feed him for a lifetime"[54] is enthusiastically recited by businessmen, high ranking local bureaucrats, and even by *hayırsevers* who find *vakıf* work useless, if not harmful. I once witnessed an outburst from Neriman when she was confronted with the same argument in a meeting of prominent townswomen. She first laughed angrily and then said, "Are you kidding? Who is going to learn fishing? The 80-year-old man or the widow with four small children? I would rather feed them all their lives than tell them this proverb once!"

Sennett's proposed precaution for hindering the potential of inequality hidden in the final code of respect, "help others", is to permit people to participate more actively in the conditions of their own care. What he means by this is not only encouraging independence when possible, but more importantly by allowing recipients to reciprocate.[55] With this assertion, Sennett invokes gift relations. The counter-gift that is offered by beneficiaries and accepted by *vakıfçıs* has a levelling effect. Certainly, it does not erase inequalities, nor does it finalise transactions, as it would in a commodity exchange, but it creates a subject who *gives* out of a subject who *receives*.

Mary Douglas candidly and famously asserts that "there should not be any free gifts. What is wrong with the so-called free gift is the donor's intention to be exempt from return gifts coming from the recipient."[56] It is this exemption

---

54 See James Ferguson's insightful book *Give a Man a Fish* for a wider discussion around this most widely used cliché. Ferguson 2015.
55 Sennett 2003.
56 Douglas 1990, 1.

(when invoked) that gives the benefactor an upper hand, strips the other party of its capacity to be a giver, and hurts him or her for always being on the same side of an asymmetrical relationship. On the other hand, asymmetry is unavoidable and even desirable in gift relations. Unlike market transactions, gift loathes symmetry, for it connotes calculation and contract.[57] What makes gift relations potentially equitable is the interchangeability of positions in this asymmetrical reciprocity. This is why Sennett firmly asserts that "reciprocity is the foundation of mutual respect."[58]

To conclude, with this discussion on respect, I do not intend to argue that *vakıfçıs* uniformly act according to these principles, reinforce the self-respect of the people they work with, and make them feel respected. *Vakıfçı* practices are heterogeneous; they vary from person to person, between organisations and on different occasions. Ultimately, all encounters are unique, and respect, being an intersubjective phenomenon, is contingent over space and time. Moreover, *vakıfçıs* do not enter the field of beneficence stripped of their long-existing dispositions and moral registers. While they try to construct *vakıfçı* subjectivities as just and pious persons, they also juggle these existing references, habits and values, and self-expectations regarding professional behaviour. Critique of others, and to a lesser degree self-critique, is a favourite pastime among *vakıfçıs* and a significant way of negotiating the contradictions and juxtapositions of varying registers. Reflecting on similar contradictions he observed among youth in Egypt, Schielke argues that pious commitment is "a fragile form of continuous self-suggestion rather than a cumulative self-perfection."[59] I can conclude this chapter with the proposition that a commitment to *vakıfçılık* is a similar form of self-suggestion, with its slippages, transgressions, and detours.

---

57 Young 1997.
58 Sennett 2003, 219.
59 Schielke 2009, 304.

# Epilogue

I am given a tour of the premises of a *vakıf* in Kayseri. There is a small storage room at the back, with its door open. Standing outside, I can see that it is full of boxes to be delivered to the beneficiaries. But there are also some odd items: several hand-woven, dark red, beautiful carpets, a couple of richly decorated daggers, and a number of embroidered, foreign pieces of headwear made of silk and wool. They look nothing like the donations waiting to be given to the registered poor. They are too flamboyant, too exotic, and obviously too precious. I ask what they are. The employee who is giving me the tour proudly says that they are the donations of a very high-level statesman, who is a native of Kayseri and a friend of the founders of the *vakıf*. He gave the items as gifts to be sold at a charity fair and turned into cash for the *vakıf*. I go in to have a closer look and comment that some of the items look like they are from Central Asia. The employee smiles and explains that they are gifts the statesman received from foreign envoys. Noticing my astonished look, he quickly adds, "you know, he receives hundreds of them, and they accumulate in Ankara." I nod. He takes it as agreement, and we continue with the tour.

I have revisited this disconcerting incident many times during and after my fieldwork. From one perspective, the statesman was misusing state property. Those gifts were given to him not because of who he was as a person, but because he was the representative of the state. Thus, the gifts belonged to his office and by extension to the state. They should have been registered as inventory and kept safe as state property. Yet there was truth in the statement that there were hundreds of such objects lying in storage in Ankara without any public benefit. Wouldn't it be more fitting to the notion of public property that they be put to public use? Selling them at a charity fair would certainly benefit the public, because the money would be used for welfare provision for the poor. I could see the point, yet couldn't help being perturbed.

Even if one followed the employee's logic, there was much to be concerned about. There was certainly no formal procedure to decide where these gifts would be donated; the decision was made on the basis of friendships. And, there was obviously no differentiation made between public and private property; the items were considered gifts from the statesman, not as public resources redirected to the *vakıf*. Yet, in this international circulation of gifts from a Central Asian state to the storage room of a *vakıf* in Kayseri, later to be transformed into food boxes for the needy, the intentions were all "good". Neither the donors nor the intermediaries would financially benefit from the exchange. And yet, while the beneficiaries of the *vakıf* would reap the monetary benefits, it was the relationship between the founders of the *vakıf* and the statesman that would thrive.

I now see that this ambiguity, this grey zone in which different ethical precepts collide, is the locus of welfare as gift. In this grey zone, where and how the resources were created is not judged by the canon of modern bureaucratic accountability. However, this does not mean that anything goes. There are other considerations at play. Throughout this book, I have laid out the practices that facilitate the realisation of welfare as gift and the precepts that define the boundaries of its legitimacy, such as the social markings of the money, the obligations that arise from social and kinship relations, and the religious canon. As a testament to Marcel Mauss' statement that "gift is a total social phenomenon" I considered how gifts related to other economic activities, the creation of social networks, the making of religious sentiments, and the formation of ethical subjectivities.

Gifts embody, crystallise, and sometimes bridge several contradictions: public–private, autonomy–dependency, and interestedness–disinterestedness. These contradictions and how they are experienced and overcome in the daily worlds of beneficence, is one of the major topics I explored in depth. I also argued that these contradictions (or, rather, false dichotomies in understanding the gift) create a fertile ground for of the transformation of Turkey's welfare regime from an employment-based social security system with narrow coverage to a means-tested social assistance system with a wide reach and broad base.

In this new regime, non-state actors play a significant role. In Turkey, giving is mostly personal and donations to institutions are low in comparison, for example, to Indonesia or the USA. Yet, the World Giving Index documents a significant increase in Turkey in giving to complete strangers as well as donations to organisations. Between 2011 and 2022 both numbers almost doubled: from 40 percent to 75 percent for giving to strangers, and from 14 percent to 33 percent for donations.[1] The low scores in 2011 do not necessarily mean less giving, but may point to a preference for giving to people who were not complete strangers, as suggested by a 2016 national study that found that 88 percent of people in Turkey preferred person-to-person giving.[2] The overall change in the composition of giving can be related to several factors, such as urbanisation and spatial segregation, as well as to the growing significance of non-state welfare organisations. Between 2010–2020, the number of registered associations increased by almost 50 percent,

---

[1] CAF 2022, 22 and CAF 2011, 24.
[2] Çarkoğlu and Aytaç 2016. The CAF data was generated via the question Did you donate to an organisation last month?", while Çarkoğlu and Aytaç asked their respondents what they would prefer, not what they did. This may explain the difference in numbers.

up to 122,000.³ The number of *vakıf*s also increased from 5002 in 2010⁴ to 6302 in 2022, 1003 of which are state-founded Social Solidarity *Vakıf*s (SYDVs).

While there is a general increase in numbers, there is no transparency about the volume of the financial operations of the civic sector. However, the extraordinary growth of a few *vakıf*s with organic ties to the government and president is plain to see. They are often the protagonists of corruption scandals making the headlines in the opposition news outlets, although no investigations or indictments follow.⁵ They have been given fundraising advantages, tax exemptions, and most importantly they have been on the receiving end of massive estate allocations through cooperation agreements with ministries and municipalities⁶ These arrangements have not only strengthened these foundations financially but have also turned them into major providers of some welfare and education services. They mostly target school children, youth, and women with the provision of accommodation, scholarships, and trainings.

The transfer of public resources to such organisations does not always follow direct routes. In one famous case, a large corporation made a huge donation to the Turkish Red Crescent to be transferred to one such *vakıf*, later to be wired to the *vakıf*'s sister organisation in the US to finance their construction project in the heart of New York City.⁷ By making the donation to the Red Crescent, the corporation allegedly gained tax advantages. Thus, at least part of the final donation came out of the state treasury. Moreover, the corporation had previously won several public bids with extraordinarily low sums and acquired land in controversial ways. Therefore, the donation can also be read as the reciprocation of those favours.⁸ The main shareholder of the company is a personal acquaintance of President Erdoğan, and the president's son and daughter are involved with the *vakıf*s mentioned. The gifts that allegedly circulate in this close-knit network are tremendous and do not necessarily come from individuals' or companies' holdings; rather, they often come from public property. Moving up from the storage room of a local *vakıf* to the national scale, the same mechanism seems to be at work, with consequences that can hardly be imagined by my modest interlocutors in Kayseri.

As I have detailed throughout the book, but especially in the last three chapters, giving is framed as a matter of ethics in the context of welfare provision. It

---

3 İlke 2021.
4 VGM 2011, 32.
5 See, for example, Cumhuriyet 2019; Özmen 2021.
6 Ünker 2022.
7 Independent Türkçe 2020.
8 Özgür 2020.

means that the gift act falls within the realm of ethical assessments and justice. Hence, it involves great risks, especially concerning one's standing before God. How, what, and to whom to give are burning questions that require re-evaluation on each occasion to ensure – as much as mortal human beings can do – righteousness. These re-evaluations are also necessary because giving is an enforcer of personal relationships and is implicated in them. On this slippery ground, the street-level actors of welfare as gift struggle to maintain their relations with each other, the beneficiaries, the donors, and with God. They strategically make use of the hierarchy inducing features of gift giving, as well as its levelling mechanisms, as a manifestation of respect for the beneficiaries, to navigate the ethically dangerous waters of poverty alleviation.

Gifts can be heartfelt, but they are hardly ever given out of the blue. They are often responses – to previous gifts, requests, unnamed feelings of being obliged, religious dictum, expectations based on social standing, familial positions, and so on. Every middle-class parent in modern Western(ised) cultures knows that there is no voluntariness in buying children birthday presents. Every guest at a wedding in Turkey knows better than not to bring an appropriate gift of money or gold. Some gifts must be given if the relationships created via them are to survive. Welfare as gift is no different. As social assistance – provided by state or non-state agents – becomes more common and regular, it is not only the obligation to reciprocate that becomes stronger, but also to keep giving. There are only so many times a gift can go ungiven. Eventually, the relationship breaks or transforms. When state officials present public services and provisions as their personal gifts, or the gifts of a political party, what is expected in return is loyalty. Analyses of voting patterns in Turkey illustrate that this strategy has, so far, functioned well.[9] However, according to a 2019 national survey, social assistance is increasingly considered a right that can be demanded when not delivered.[10] Thus, while the gift spiral is being extended, entitlements are being created. "Shadow gifts"[11] haunt the real gifts when materialised gifts fall short of expectations. What will come after welfare as gift is yet an open question. The emergence of a new regime of social citizenship is one possible scenario if the provisions are sustained. The collapse of the personalised relationship between the givers and receivers is another if the gifts stop being delivered. In the meantime, gifts continue to have ever wider consequences: ethical transformations at the individual level, and transformations of ethics at the societal level, each at the opposite end of the spectrum.

---

**9** Yörük 2022.
**10** Konda 2019, cited in Yörük 2022.
**11** Copeman and Banerjee 2021.

# Bibliography

Abu-Lughod, Lila. 1988. "The Dutiful Daughter." In *Arab Women in the Field: Studying Your Own Society*, eds. Soraya Altorki and Camilla Fawzi El-Solh, 139–62. Syracuse, New York: Syracuse University Press.

Abu-Lughod, Lila. 1999. *Veiled Sentiments: Honor and Poetry in a Bedouin Society*. Berkeley and London: University of California Press.

Aburaiya, Issam. 2009. "Islamism, Nationalism, and Western Modernity: The Case of Iran and Palestine." In "The Culture of Conflict in Israel and Palestine," eds. Rachel Werczberger and Boaz Huss. Special issue, *International Journal of Politics, Culture, and Society* 22, no. 1 (March): 57–68.

Açar, Onur. 2009. "A Critique of Liberal-Conservative Approach to Poverty in Turkey: The Case of Deniz Feneri Association and Social Assistance and Solidarity General Directorate." PhD thesis, Middle East Technical University, Ankara.

Adaş, Emin Baki. 2006. "The Making of Entrepreneurial Islam and the Islamic Spirit of Capitalism." *Journal for Cultural Research* 10, no. 2 (August 18): 113–37.

Ahmed, Sara. 2004. *The Cultural Politics of Emotion*. Edinburgh: Edinburgh University Press.

Alkan Zeybek, Hilal. 2012. "Ethics of Care, Politics of Solidarity: Islamic Charitable Organisations in Turkey." In *Ethnographies of Islam: Ritual Performances and Everyday Practices*, eds. Thomas Pierret, Baudouin Dupret, Paulo G. Pinto, and Kathryn Spellman-Poots, 144–52. Edinburgh: Edinburgh University Press.

Alkan, Hilal. 2021. "The Gift of Hospitality and the (Un) Welcoming of Syrian Migrants in Turkey." *American Ethnologist* 48, no. 2 (May 16): 180–91.

Allahyari, Rebecca Anne. 2000. *Visions of Charity: Volunteer Workers and Moral Community*. Berkeley and Los Angeles: University of California Press.

Altorki, Soraya. 1988. "At Home in the Field." In *Arab Women in the Field: Studying Your Own Society*, eds. Soraya Altorki and Camilla Fawzi El-Solh, 49–68. Syracuse, New York: Syracuse University Press.

Altorki, Soraya, and Camillia Fawzi El-Solh, eds. 1988. *Arab Women in the Field: Studying Your Own Society*. Syracuse, New York: Syracuse University Press.

Aristotle. 2002. *Nicomachean Ethics*. Translated by Joe Sachs. Newburyport: Focus Publishing.

Arjomand, Said-Amir. 1998. "Philanthropy, the Law, and Public Policy in the Islamic World Before the Modern Era." In *Philanthropy in the World's Traditions*, eds. Warren Frederick Ilchman, Edward L. Queen, and Stanley Nider Katz, 109–32. Bloomington: Indiana University Press.

Aybars, Ayse Idil, and Dimitris Tsarouhas. 2010. "Straddling Two Continents: Social Policy and Welfare Politics in Turkey." *Social Policy & Administration* 44, no. 6 (December): 746–63.

Baer, Gabriel. 1997. "The Waqf as a Prop for the Social System (Sixteenth–Twentieth Centuries)." *Islamic Law and Society* 4, no. 3 (January 1): 264–97.

Balibar, Etienne. 2010. "Class Racism." In *The Ethnicity Reader: Nationalism, Multiculturalism & Migration*, eds. Maria Montserrat Guiberno and John Rex, 369–80. London: Polity Press.

Barrientos, Armando. 2013. *Social Assistance in Developing Countries*. Cambridge: Cambridge University Press.

Betz, Hans-Georg, and Carol Johnson. 2004. "Against the Current–Stemming the Tide: The Nostalgic Ideology of the Contemporary Radical Populist Right." *Journal of Political Ideologies* 9, no. 3 (August 6): 311–27.

Bhattacharya, Tithi, ed. 2017. *Social Reproduction Theory: Remapping Class, Recentering Oppression.* London: Pluto Press.

Bilefski, Dan. "Turks Knock on Europe's Door with Evidence That Islam and Capitalism Can Coexist." *New York Times*, August 27, 2006.

Bingölçe, Filiz. 2010. *Süper Kadın Süper Zor: Türkiye'de Kadına Yönelik Ekonomik Şiddet.* Istanbul: Ekonomi Muhabirleri Derneği.

Bode, Ingo. 2006. "Disorganized Welfare Mixes: Voluntary Agencies and New Governance Regimes in Western Europe." *Journal of European Social Policy* 16, no. 4 (November 1): 346–59.

Bonner, Michael, Mine Ener, and Amy Singer, eds. 2003. *Poverty and Charity in the Middle Eastern Contexts.* Albany, New York: State University of New York Press.

Bora, Aksu. 2007. "'Olmayanın Nesini İdare Edeceksin?': Yoksulluk, Kadınlar Ve Hane." In *Yoksulluk Halleri: Türkiye'de Kent Yoksulluğunun Toplumsal Görünümleri*, ed. Necmi Erdoğan, 97–132. Istanbul: İletişim Yayınları.

Bora, Tanıl. 2009. "Sadaka, Sosyal Yardım, Dayanışma, Örgütlenme." *Birikim* 241 (May): 19–23.

Bornstein, Erica. 2009. "The Impulse of Philanthropy." *Cultural Anthropology* 24, no. 4 (October 9): 622–51.

Bornstein, Erica. 2012. *Disquieting Gifts: Humanitarianism in New Delhi.* Stanford, California: Stanford University Press.

Bornstein, Erica, and Peter Redfield. 2011. "An Introduction to the Anthropology of Humanitarianism." In *Forces of Compassion: Humanitarianism Between Ethics and Politics*, eds. Erica Bornstein and Peter Redfield, 3–30. Santa Fe: SAR Press.

Boserup, Ester. 2007. *Woman's Role in Economic Development.* London: Earthscan.

Bourdieu, Pierre. 1986. "The Forms of Capital." In *Handbook of Theory of Research for the Sociology of Education*, ed. John G. Richardson, 241–58. New York: Greenwood Press.

Bourdieu, Pierre. 1987. *Choses Dites.* Paris: Editions de Minuit.

Bourdieu, Pierre. 1997a. "Marginalia-Some Additional Notes on the Gift," 231–41. In Schrift 1997.

Bourdieu, Pierre. 1997b. "Selections from The Logic of Practice," 190–230. In Schrift 1997.

Brooke, Steven. 2019. *Winning Hearts and Votes: Social Services and the Islamist Political Advantage.* Ithaca, New York: Cornell University Press.

Brubaker, Rogers. 2017. "Why populism?" *Theory and Society* 46, no. 5 (October 26): 357–85.

Buğra, Ayşe. 1999. *Islam in Economic Organizations.* Istanbul: TESEV Yayınları.

Buğra, Ayşe. 2007. "Poverty and Citizenship: An Overview of the Social-Policy Environment in Republican Turkey." *International Journal of Middle East Studies* 39, no. 1 (February): 33–52.

Buğra, Ayşe. 2015. "Philanthropy and the Politics of Social Policy." In *New Philanthropy and Social Justice*, ed. Behrooz Morvaridi, 117–36. Bristol: Policy Press.

Buğra, Ayşe. 2020. "Politics of Social Policy in a Late Industrializing Country: The Case of Turkey." *Development and Change* 51, no. 2 (January 11): 442–62.

Buğra, Ayşe, and Aysen Candaş. 2011. "Change and Continuity Under an Eclectic Social Security Regime: The Case of Turkey." *Middle Eastern Studies* 47, no. 3 (May 19): 515–28.

Buğra, Ayşe, and Çağlar Keyder. 2003. *New Poverty and the Changing Welfare Regime of Turkey.* Ankara: United Nations Development Programme.

Buğra, Ayşe, and Çağlar Keyder. 2006. "The Turkish Welfare Regime in Transformation." *Journal of European Social Policy* 16, no. 3 (August 1): 211–28.

Buğra, Ayşe, and Sinem Adar. 2008. "Social Policy Change in Countries Without Mature Welfare States: The Case of Turkey." In "Poverty and Social Exclusion," eds. Biray Kolluoğlu and Deniz Yükseker. Special issue *New Perspectives on Turkey* 38 (Spring): 83–106.
Cammett, Melani, and Lauren M. MacLean, eds. 2014. *The Politics of Non-State Social Welfare*. Ithaca: Cornell University Press.
Çarkoğlu, Ali. 2006. "Türkiye'de Bireysel Bağışlar Ve Vakıf Uygulamalarında Eğilimler." TÜSEV Yayınları, no. 40. Istanbul: TÜSEV.
Carlson-Thies, Stanley. 2001. "Charitable Choice: Bringing Religion Back into American Welfare." In "Religion, Politics, Policy." Special issue *Journal of Policy History* 13, no. 1 (January): 109–32.
Çelik, Aziz, and Meryem Koray. 2015. *Himmet, Fıtrat, Piyasa-AKP Döneminde Sosyal Politika*. Istanbul: İletişim Yayınları.
Cheal, David J. 1988. *The Gift Economy*. New York: Routledge.
Choudhury, Masudul Alam. 1983. "Principles of Islamic Economics." *Middle Eastern Studies* 19, no. 1 (January): 93–103.
Cixous, Helen. 1996. "Sorties: Out and Out: Attacks/ Ways Out/ Forays." In *The Newly Born Woman*, eds. Helen Cixous and Cathrine Clement, 63–132. London: I.B. Tauris.
Çizakça, Murat. 2000. *A History of Philanthropic Foundations: The Islamic World from the Seventh Century to the Present*. Istanbul: Boğaziçi University Press.
Çizakça, Murat. 2011. *Islamic Capitalism and Finance: Origins, Evolution and the Future*. Cheltenham: Edward Elgar Publishing.
Çınar, Menderes. 1997. "Yükselen Değerlerin İşadamı Cephesi: MÜSİAD." *Birikim* 95 (May): 52–56.
Clark, Janine A. 2004. *Islam, Charity, and Activism: Middle-Class Networks and Social Welfare in Egypt, Jordan, and Yemen*. Bloomington: Indiana University Press.
Clifford, James. 1986. "Introduction: Partial Truths." In *Writing Culture: The Poetics and Politics of Ethnography*, eds. James Clifford and George E. Marcus, 1–26. Berkeley: University of California Press.
Cnaan, Ram A., and Stephanie C. Boddie. 2002. "Charitable Choice and Faith-Based Welfare: A Call for Social Work." *Social Work* 47, no. 3 (July): 224–35.
CNN Türk. 2007. "Erdoğan'dan valilere kömür dağıtın çağrısı." *CNN Türk*, 24 December 2007. https://www.cnnturk.com/turkiye/erdogandan-valilere-komur-dagitin-cagrisi
Coleman, James S. 1988. "Social Capital in the Creation of Human Capital." In "Organizations and Institutions: Sociological and Economic Approaches to the Analysis of Social Structure," Supplement *American Journal of Sociology* 94: 95–120.
Copeman, Jacob, and Dwaipayan Banerjee. 2021. "Actual and Potential Gifts: Critique, Shadow Gift Relations and the Virtual Domain of the Ungiven." *Anthropological Theory* 21, no. 1 (March): 28–49.
Dallal, Ahmad. 2004. "The Islamic Institution of Waqf: A Historical Overview." In *Islam and Social Policy*, ed. Stephen P. Heyneman, 13–43. Nashville: Vanderbilt University Press.
Dalton, George. 1965. "Primitive Money." *American Anthropologist* 67, no. 1 (February): 44–65.
De Landa, Manuel. 1997. *A Thousand Years of Nonlinear History*. Brooklyn: Zone Books.
Dean, Hartley, and Zafar Khan. 1997. "Muslim Perspectives on Welfare." Journal of Social Policy 26, no. 2 (April 1): 193–209.
Dean, Mitchell. 1991. *The Constitution of Poverty: Towards a Genealogy of Liberal Governance*. London: Routledge.

Deeb, Lara. 2008. *An Enchanted Modern: Gender and Public Piety in Shi'i Lebanon*. Princeton: Princeton University Press.
Demirel, Ömer. 2000. *Osmanlı Vakıf-Şehir İlişkisine Bir Örnek: Sivas Şehir Hayatında Vakıfların Rolü*. Ankara: Türk Tarih Kurumu Basımevi.
Derrida, Jacques. 1997. "Time of the King," 121–47. In Schrift 1979.
Doğan, Ali Ekber. 2007. *Eğreti Kamusallık: Kayseri Örneğinde İslamcı Belediyecilik*. Istanbul: İletişim Yayınları.
Douglas, Mary. 1990. "Foreword." In Marcell Mauss: *The Gift: The Form and Reason for Exchange in Archaic Societies*. London: Routledge Classics.
Douglas, Mary. 1966. *Purity and Danger: An Analysis of Concepts of Pollution and Taboo*. London: Routledge and Kegan Paul.
Eisenstein, Charles. 2011. *Sacred Economics: Money, Gift, & Society in the Age of Transition*. Berkeley: North Atlantic Books.
Elveren, Adem Y. 2008. "Social Security Reform in Turkey: A Critical Perspective." *Review of Radical Political Economics* 40, no. 2 (Spring): 212–32.
Elyachar, Julia. 2010. "Phatic Labor, Infrastructure, and the Question of Empowerment in Cairo." *American Ethnologist* 37, no. 3 (August): 452–64.
Erdoğan, Necmi. 2007. "Yok-sanma: Yoksulluk-Mâduniyet Ve 'Fark Yaraları'." In *Yoksulluk Halleri*, ed. Necmi Erdoğan, 47–96. Istanbul: İletişim Yayınları.
Ergin, Osman. 1953. "İstanbul'un Fethinden Sonra Şehir Nasıl İmar Ve İskan Edildi?" *R.T.M.* 41: 2352–64.
European Stability Initiative. 2005. "Islamic Calvinists: Change and Conservatism in Central Anatolia." Istanbul: European Stability Initiative.
Esping-Andersen, Gøsta. 1990. *The Three Worlds of Welfare Capitalism*. Cambridge: Polity.
Faroqhi, Suraiya. 2000. *Subjects of the Sultan: Culture and Daily Life in the Ottoman Empire*. London: I.B. Tauris.
Fassin, Didier. 2007. "Humanitarianism as a Politics of Life." *Public Culture* 19, no. 3 (September 1): 499–520.
Fassin, Didier. 2010. "Inequality of Lives, Hierarchies of Humanity. Moral Commitments and Ethical Dilemmas of Humanitarianism." In *In the Name of Humanity*, eds. Ilana Feldman and Miriam Ticktin, 238–55. Durham: Duke University Press.
Fassin, Didier. 2012. Humanitarian Reason: *A Moral History of the Present*. Berkeley and Los Angeles: University of California Press.
Fennell, Lee Anne. 2002. "Unpacking the Gift: Illiquid Goods and Emphatetic Dialogue." In *The Question of the Gift: Essays Across Disciplines*, ed. Mark Osteen, 85–102. London: Routldege.
Ferguson, James. 2007. "Formalities of Poverty: Thinking About Social Assistance in Neoliberal South Africa." *African Studies Review* 50, no. 2 (September): 71–86.
Ferguson, James. 2010. "The Uses of Neoliberalism." *Antipode* 41, no. 1 (March 25): 166–84.
Ferguson, James. 2015. *Give a Man a Fish: Reflections on the New Politics of Distribution*. Durham: Duke University Press.
Ferguson, James, and Akhil Gupta. 2002. "Spatializing States: Toward an Ethnography of Neoliberal Governmentality." *American Ethnologist* 29, no. 4 (November): 981–1002.
Flanigan, Shawn Teresa. 2010. *For the Love of God: NGOs and Religious Identity in a Violent World*. Sterling: Kumarian Press.
Foucault, Michel. 1975. *Discipline and Punish: The Birth of the Prison*. New York: Random House.

Foucault, Michel. 1976. *The History of Sexuality: An Introduction*. New York: Vintage.
Foucault, Michel. 1991. "Governmentality." In *The Foucault Effect: Studies in Governmentality*, eds. Graham Burchell, Colin Gordon, and Peter Miller, 87–104. Chicago: University of Chicago Press.
Foucault, Michel. 1997a. "On the Geneaology of Ethics: An Overview of Work in Progress." In *Ethics, Subjectivity and Truth: Essential Works of Foucault, 1954–1984*, vol. 1, ed. Paul Rabinow, 253–80. New York: New Press.
Foucault, Michel. 1997b. "The Ethics of the Concern of the Self as a Practice of Freedom." In *Ethics, Subjectivity and Truth: The Essential Works of Foucault 1954–1984*, vol. 1, ed. Paul Rabinow, 281–301. New York: New Press.
Fox, Nick. 1995. "Postmodern Perspectives on Care: The Vigil and the Gift." *Critical Social Policy* 15, no. 44–45 (October): 107–25.
Fox-Piven, Frances, and Richard Andrew Cloward. 1972. *Regulating the Poor: The Functions of Public Welfare*. London: Tavistock Publications.
Fraser, Nancy, and Linda Gordon. 1998. "Contract Versus Charity: Why Is There No Social Citizenship in the United States?" In *The Citizenship Debates: A Reader*, ed. Gershon Schafir, 113–30. Minneapolis: University of Minnesota Press.
Charities Aid Foundation. 2011. "World Giving Index 2011: A Global View on Giving Trends." CAF Publications. London: Charities Aid Foundation. https://www.cafonline.org/docs/default-source/about-us-publications/world_giving_index_2011_191211.pdf.
Charities Aid Foundation. 2022. "World Giving Index 2022: A Global View on Giving Trends." CAF Publications. London: Charities Aid Foundation. https://www.cafonline.org/docs/default-source/about-us-research/caf_world_giving_index_2022_210922-final.pdf.
Gabauer, Angelika, Sabine Knierbein, Nir Cohen, Henrik Lebuhn, Kim Trogal, Tihomir Viderman, and Tigran Haas, eds. 2022. *Care and the City: Encounters with Urban Studies*. New York and Abingdon: Routledge.
Gavison, Ruth. 1992. "Feminism and the Public/Private Distinction." *Stanford Law Review* 45, no. 1 (November): 1–45.
Geertz, Clifford. 1972. "Deep Play: Notes on the Balinese Cockfight." *Daedalus* 101, no. 1 (Winter): 1–37.
Gerber, Haim. 1980. "Social and Economic Position of Women in an Ottoman City, Bursa, 1600–1700." *International Journal of Middle East* 12, no. 3 (November): 231–44.
Gerber, Haim. 2002. "The Public Sphere and Civil Society in the Ottoman Empire." In *The Public Sphere in Muslim Societies*, eds. Miriam Hoexter, Shmuel Noah Eisenstadt, and Nehemia Levtzion, 65–82. Albany: SUNY Press.
Gibson-Graham, J. K. 1996. *The End Of Capitalism (As We Knew It): A Feminist Critique of Political Economy*. Minneapolis: University of Minnesota Press.
Gilligan, Carol. 1982. *In a Different Voice: Psychological Theory and Women's Development*. Cambridge, Massachusetts: Harvard University Press.
Gilliom, John. 2001. *Overseers of the Poor: Surveillance, Resistance and the Limits of Privacy*. Chicago: The University of Chicago Press.
Godbout, Jacques T., and Alain Caille. 1998. *The World of the Gift*. Montreal: McGill-Queen's University Press.
Goldberg, Gertrude S., and Marguerite G. Rosenthal, eds. 2002. *Diminishing Welfare: A Cross-National Study of Social Provision*. Westport: Greenwood Publishing Group.
Gouldner, Alvin W. 1960. "The Norm of Reciprocity." *American Sociological Review* 25, no. 2 (April): 161–78.

Graeber, David. 2004. *Fragments of an Anarchist Anthropology*. Chicago: Prickly Paradigm Press.
Gregory, Chris A. 1982. *Gifts and Commodities*. London: Academic Press.
Cumhuriyet. "TÜGVA, Ensar, makam araçları... Bütün yolsuzlukları tek tek açıkladı." https://www.cumhuriyet.com.tr/haber/tugva-ensar-makam-araclari-butun-yolsuzluklari-tek-tek-acikladi-1450320, posted June 21, 2019.
Gümüşcü, Şebnem, and Deniz Sert. 2009. "The Power of the Devout Bourgeoisie: The Case of the Justice and Development Party in Turkey." *Middle Eastern Studies* 45, no. 6 (November 17): 953–68.
Hamington, Maurice. 2004. *Embodied Care: Jane Addams, Maurice Merleau-Ponty, and Feminist Ethics*. Chicago: University of Illinois Press.
Haneda, Masashi, and Toru Miura. 1994. *Islamic Urban Studies: Historical Review and Perspective*. London: Kegan Paul.
Harmsen, Egbert. 2008. *Islam, Civil Society and Social Work: Muslim Voluntary Welfare Associations in Jordan Between Patronage and Empowerment*. Amsterdam: Amsterdam University Press.
Hecker, Pierre, Ivo Furman, and Kaya Akyıldız, eds. 2022. *The Politics of Culture in Contemporary Turkey*. Edinburgh: Edinburgh University Press.
Hoexter, Miriam. 2002. "The Waqf and the Public Sphere." In *The Public Sphere in Muslim Societies*, eds. Miriam Hoexter, Shmuel Noah Eisenstadt, and Nehemia Levtzion, 119–38. Albany: SUNY Press.
Hollway, Wendy. 2006. *The Capacity to Care: Gender and Ethical Subjectivity*. London: Routledge.
Hoşgör, Evren. 2011. "Islamic Capital/Anatolian Tigers: Past and Present." *Middle Eastern Studies* 47, no. 2 (March 3): 343–60.
Hugman, Richard. 1991. *Power in Caring Professions*. London: Macmillan.
İLKE. 2021. "Sivil Toplumun On Yili: 2010–2020." Alan İzleme Raporları, no. 4. Istanbul: İLKE İlim Kültür Eğitim Vakfı. https://ilke.org.tr/sivil-toplumun-on-yili-alan-izleme-raporu-2010-2020.
Independent Türkçe staff and agencies. "Ensar Vakfı: Kızılay üzerinden yapılan bağışlar ABD'ye gitti." *Independent Türkçe*, October 31, 2020. https://www.indyturk.com/node/125581/haber/ensarvakf%C4%B1k%C4%B1z%C4%B1lay-%C3%BCzerinden-yap%C4%B1lan-ba%C4%9F%C4%B1%C5%9Flar-abdye-gitti.
Isik, Damla. 2014. "Vakıf as Intent and Practice: Charity and Poor Relief in Turkey." *International Journal of Middle East Studies* 46, no. 2 (May): 307–27.
Isin, Engin F. 2005. "Citizenship After Orientalism: Ottoman Citizenship." In *Citizenship in a Globalizing World: European Questions and Turkish Experiences*, eds. Fuat Keyman and Ahmet İçduygu, 31–51. London: Routledge.
Isin, Engin F. 2007. "Ottoman Awqaf, Turkish Modernization, and Citizenship." In *Remaking Turkey: Globalisation, Alternative Modernities, and Democracy*, ed. Emin Fuat Keyman, 3–15. Plymouth: Lexington Books.
Isin, Engin F., and Alexander LeFebvre. 2005. "The Gift of Law: Greek Euergetism and Ottoman Waqf." *European Journal of Social Theory* 8, no. 1 (February 1): 5–23.
Isin, Engin, and Ebru Üstündağ. 2008. "Wills, Deeds, Acts: Women's Civic Gift-Giving in Ottoman Istanbul." *Gender, Place and Culture* 15, no. 5 (September 18): 519–32.
Janssens, Angélique. 1997. "The Rise and Decline of the Male Breadwinner Family? An Overview of the Debate." In "The Rise and Decline of the Male Breadwinner Family?." Supplement 5 *International Review of Social History* 42 (September): 1–23.

Jawad, Rana. 2007. "Human Ethics and Welfare Particularism: An Exploration of the Social Welfare Regime in Lebanon." *Ethics and Social Welfare* 1, no. 2 (Juli 9): 123–46.
Jawad, Rana. 2009a. "Religion and Social Welfare in the Lebanon: Treating the Causes or Symptoms of Poverty?" *Journal of Social Policy* 38, no. 1 (January 1): 141–56.
Jawad, Rana. 2009b. *Social Welfare and Religion in the Middle East: A Lebanese Perspective*. Bristol: Policy Press.
Jawad, Rana, and Burcu Yakut-Cakar. 2010. "Religion and Social Policy in the Middle East: The (Re)Constitution of an Old-New Partnership." *Social Policy & Administration* 44, no. 6 (October 12): 658–72.
Jenkins, Tim. 1998. "Derrida's Reading of Mauss." In *Marcel Mauss: A Centenary Tribute*, ed. Wendy James and N. J. Allen. New York/Oxford: Berghahn Books.
Jessop, Bob. 1999. "The Changing Governance of Welfare: Recent Trends in Its Primary Functions, Scale, and Modes of Coordination." *Social Policy & Administration* 33, no. 4 (December): 348–59.
Jo, Yongmie Nicola. 2013. "Psycho-Social Dimensions of Poverty: When Poverty Becomes Shameful." *Critical Social Policy* 33, no. 3 (May 9): 514–31.
Karatani, Kojin. 2008. "Beyond Capital-Nation-State." *Rethinking Marxism* 20, no. 4 (September 3): 569–95.
Katz, Cindi. 2002. "Vagabond Capitalism and the Necessity of Social Reproduction." *Antipode* 33, no. 4 (December 16): 709–28.
Katz, Michael B. 1989. *The Undeserving Poor: From the War on Poverty to the War on Welfare*. New York: Pantheon Books.
Kayaalp-Aktan, Pınar. 2007. "The Endowment Deed of the Atik Valide Mosque Complex: A Textual Analysis." In F*eeding People, Feeding Power: Imarets in the Ottoman Empire*, eds. Nina Ergin, Christopher Neumann, and Amy Singer, 261–73. Istanbul: Eren Yayınları.
Keyder, Çağlar, Nazan Üstündağ, Tuba Ağartan, and Çağrı Yoltar, eds. 2007. *Avrupa'da Ve Türkiye'de Sağlık Politikaları: Reformlar, Sorunlar, Tartışmalar*. Istanbul: İletişim Yayınları.
Keyman, Fuat, and Berrin Koyuncu Lorasdağı. 2010. Kentler. Istanbul: Doğan Kitap.
Khadduri, Madjid. 2012. "Maṣlaḥa." In *Encyclopaedia of Islam*, Second Edition, eds. P. Bearman, Th. Bianquis, C.E. Bosworth, E. van Donzel, W.P. Heinrichs. http://dx.doi.org/10.1163/1573-3912_islam_SIM_5019.
Khan, M. Fahim. 1995. *Essays in Islamic Economics*. Leicester: The Islamic Foundation.
Kittay, Eva Feder. 1999. *Love's Labor: Essays on Women, Equality, and Dependency*. Hove: Psychology Press.
Kochuyt, Thierry. 2009. "God, Gifts and the Poor People: On Charity in Islam." *Social Compass* 56, no. 1 (March 1): 98–116.
Komter, Aafke E. 2005. *Social Solidarity and the Gift*. New York: Cambridge University Press.
Kristeva, Julia. 1982. *Powers of Horror: An Essay on Abjection*. New York: Columbia University Press.
Kuran, Timur. 2001. "The Provision of Public Goods under Islamic Law: Origins, Impact, and Limitations of the Waqf System." *Law and Society Review* 35, no. 4: 841–98.
Kuran, Timur. 2016. "Legal Roots of Authoritarian Rule in the Middle East: Civic Legacies of the Islamic Waqf." *The American Journal of Comparative Law* 64, no. 2 (July 1): 419–54.
Kutchins, Herb. 2001. "Neither Alms Nor a Friend: The Tragedy of Compassionate Conservatism." *Social Justice* 28, no. 1 (Spring): 14–34.
Laidlaw, James. 2000. "A Free Gift Makes No Friends." *Journal of Royal Anthropological Institute* 6, no. 4 (December): 617–34.

Laidlaw, James. 2013. *The Subject of Virtue: An Anthropology of Ethics and Freedom*. New York: Cambridge University Press.

Leisering, Lutz, and Armando Barrientos. 2013. "Social Citizenship for the Global Poor? The Worldwide Spread of Social Assistance." In "Exploring Global Social Citizenship: Human Rights Perspectives," eds. Benjamin Davy, Ulrike Davy, and Lutz Leisering. Special issue *International Journal of Social Welfare* 22, no. 1 (May 29): 50–67.

Levi-Strauss, Claude. 1987. *Introduction to the Work of Marcel Mauss*. London: Routledge and Kegan Paul.

Lewis, Jenny M. 2010. *Connecting and Cooperating: Social Capital and Public Policy*. Sydney: University of New South Wales Publishing.

Lipsky, Michael. 2010. *Street-Level Bureaucracy: Dilemmas of the Individual in Public Services*. New York: Russell Sage Foundation.

Lomnitz, Larissa Adler. 1988. "Informal Exchange Networks in Formal Systems: A Theoretical Model." *American Anthropologist* 90, no. 1 (March): 42–55.

Lorde, Audre, and Cheryl Clarke. 2007. *Sister Outsider: Essays and Speeches*. Berkeley: Crossing Press.

Mahmood, Saba. 2005. *Politics of Piety: The Islamic Revival and the Feminist Subject*. Princeton: Princeton University Press.

Makdisi, George. 1981. *The Rise of Colleges: Institutions of Learning in Islam and the West*. Edinburgh: Edinburgh University Press

Malkki, Liisa H. 2015. *The Need to Help: The Domestic Arts of International Humanitarianism*. Durham: Duke University Press.

Mardin, Şerif. 1991. "The Just and the Unjust." *Daedalus* 120, no. 3 (Summer): 113–29.

Marmot, Michael. 2005. "Social Determinants of Health Inequalities." *The Lancet* 365, no. 9464 (March 19): 1099–104.

Marshall, Thomas H. 1992. [1950]. *Citizenship and Social Class*. London: Pluto Press.

Maududi, Abul A'la. 1984. *Economic System of Islam*. Lahore: Islamic Publications Limited.

Mauss, Marcel. 1990 [1925]. *The Gift: The Form and Reason for Exchange in Archaic Societies with a Foreword by Mary Douglas*. London: Routledge Classics.

Meriwether, Margaret Lee. 1997. "Women and Waqf Revisited: The Case of Aleppo. 1770–1840." In *Women in the Ottoman Empire: Middle Eastern Women in Early Modern Era*, ed. Madelene Zilfi, 128–152. London: Brill.

Mittermaier, Amira. 2019. *Giving to God: Islamic Charity in Revolutionary Times*. Oakland, California: University of California Press.

Morgan, Kimberly J., and Andrea Louise Campbell. 2011. *The Delegated Welfare State: Medicare, Markets, and the Governance of Social Policy*. New York: Oxford University Press.

Morris, Lydia. 2001. *Dangerous Classes: The Underclass and Social Citizenship*. London and New York: Routledge.

Muehlebach, Andrea. 2019. *The Moral Neoliberal: Welfare and Citizenship in Italy*. Chicago: University of Chicago Press.

Narayan, Kirin. 1993. "How Native is a 'Native' Anthropologist?" *American Anthropologist* 95, no. 3 (September): 671–86.

Nasr, Vali. 2005. "The Rise of 'Muslim Democracy'." *Journal of Democracy* 16, no. 1 (January): 13–27.

Navaro-Yashin, Yael. 2002. *Faces of the State. Secularism and Public Life in Turkey*. Princeton: Princeton University Press.

O'Neill, John. 2005. "What Gives (with Derrida)?" *European Journal of Social Theory* 2, no. 2: 131–45.
Oakley, Ann. 1976. *Housewife*. Harmondsworth: Penguin.
Osella, Filippo, and Caroline Osella. 2009. "Muslim Entrepreneurs in Public Life Between India and the Gulf: Making Good and Doing Good." *Journal of the Royal Anthropological Institute* 15: 202–21.
Owens, Geoffrey Ross. 2003. "What! Me a Spy? Intrigue and Reflexivity in Zanzibar." *Ethnography* 4, no. 1 (March): 122–44.
Özbek, Nadir. 2002. *Osmanlı İmparatorluğu'nda Sosyal Devlet: Siyaset, İktidar Ve Meşrutiyet 1876–1908*. Istanbul: İletişim Yayınları.
Özbek, Nadir. 2003. "Imperial Gifts and Sultanic Legitimation During the Late Ottoman Empire, 1876–1909," 203–20. In Bonner et al. 2003.
Özdemir, Ali Murat, and Gamze Yücesan-Özdemir. 2008. "Opening Pandora's Box: Social Security Reform in Turkey in the Time of AKP." *South-East Europe Review* 4: 469–83.
Özgür, Bahadır. 2002. "Torunlar-Kızılay-Ensar: Bir Hokus Pokus Hikâyesi." *Gazete Duvar*, October 30, 2020. https://www.gazeteduvar.com.tr/yazarlar/2020/01/30/torunlar-kizilay-ensar-bir-hokus-pokus-hikayesi.
Özhaseki, Mehmet. "Hakkında." https://www.mehmetozhaseki.com.tr/hakkinda/, accessed June 15, 2023.
Özmen, Ünal. "TÜGVA TÜRGEV'dir, peki TÜRGEV nedir?." *Bir Gün*, October 15, 2021. https://www.birgun.net/makale/tugva-turgev-dir-peki-turgev-nedir-362167.
Pamuk, Orhan. 2006. *Istanbul: Memories and the City*. London: Faber and Faber.
Pamuk, Şevket. 1987. *The Ottoman Empire and European Capitalism, 1820–1913: Trade, Investment, and Production*. New York: Cambridge University Press.
Parry, Jonathan. 1986. "The Gift, the Indian Gift and the 'Indian Gift'." *Man* 21, no. 3 (September): 453–73.
Pena, Manuel, and Jorge Bacallao. 2000. *Obesity and Poverty: A New Public Health Challenge*. Washington, DC.: Pan American Health Organization.
Pinon, Pierre. 1987. "Sinan's Kulliye's: Inscriptions into the Urban Fabric." *Environmental Design* 1–2: 106–11.
Pioppi, Daniela. 2004. "From Religious Charity to the Welfare State and Back: The Case of Islamic Endowments (waqfs) Revival in Egypt." EUI Working Papers RSCAS, no. 2004/34. Florence: European University Institute.
Polanyi, Karl. 1957. *The Great Transformation: The Political and Economic Origins of Our Time*. Boston: Beacon Press.
Prentice, Andrew M. 2006. "The Emerging Epidemic of Obesity in Developing Countries." *International Journal of Epidemiology* 35, no. 1 (February): 93–99.
Prochaska, Frank. 2008. *Christianity and Social Service in Modern Britain: The Disinherited Spirit*. New York: Oxford University Press.
Puig de la Bellacasa, Maria, ed. 2017. *Matters of Care: Speculative Ethics in More Than Human Worlds*. Minneapolis: University of Minnesota Press.
Radikal. 2009. "İki Yılda Yüz Binlerce Kişi İşsiz Kaldı." *Radikal* (December 11).
Ravallion, Martin. 1994. *Poverty Comparisons. Fundamentals of Pure & Applied Economics*. Income Distribution. London: Routledge.
Read, Rosie, and Tatjana Thelen. 2007. "Introduction: Social Security and Care after Socialism: Reconfigurations of Public and Private." *Focaal* 50: 3–18.

Redfield, Peter. 2008. "Sacrifice, Triage, and Global Humanitarianism." In *Humanitarianism in Question*, eds. Michael Barnett and Thomas G. Weiss, 196–214. Ithaca: Cornell University Press.

Resmi Gazete. 2005. *5326 Sayılı Kabahatler Kanunu*. https://www.resmigazete.gov.tr/eskiler/2005/03/20050331M1-2.htm

Roumpakis, Antonios. 2020. "Revisiting Global Welfare Regimes: Gender, (In) Formal Employment and Care." *Social Policy and Society* 19, no. 4 (November 1): 677–89.

Rozakou, Katerina. 2012. "The Biopolitics of Hospitality in Greece: Humanitarianism and the Management of Refugees." *American Ethnologist* 39, no. 3 (August): 562–77.

Rozakou, Katerina. 2016. "Socialities of Solidarity: Revisiting the Gift Taboo in Times of Crises." *Social Anthropology/Anthropologie Sociale* 24, no. 2 (May): 185–99.

Rudner, David West. 1987. "Religious Gifting and Inland Commerce in Seventeenth-Century South India." *The Journal of Asian Studies* 46, no. 2 (May): 361–79.

Sadeq, Abul Hasan M. 2002. "Waqf, Perpetual Charity and Poverty Alleviation." *International Journal of Social Economics* 29, no. 1–2: 135–51.

Sahlins, Marshal. 1972. *Stone Age Economics*. New York: Aldine de Gruyter.

Saraceno, Chiara. 2002. *Social Assistance Dynamics in Europe: National and Local Poverty Regimes*. Bristol: Policy Press.

Schielke, Samuli. 2009. "Being Good in Ramadan: Ambivalence, Fragmentation, and the Moral Self in the Lives of Young Egyptians." *Journal of Royal Anthropological Institute* 15, no. 1 (March): 24–40.

Schielke, Samuli. 2019. "The Power of God: Four Proposals for an Anthropological Engagement." *ZMO Working Papers*, no. 13. Berlin: Leibniz-Zentrum Moderner Orient.

Schrift, Alan D. 1997. *The Logic of the Gift. Toward an Ethic of Generosity*. New York: Routledge.

Scott, James. 1998. *Seeing Like a State: How Certain Schemes to Improve the Human Condition Have Failed*. New Haven: Yale University Press.

Şeker, İskender. 2008. *Bir Farklılığın Hikayesi: Hayırseverlerimiz*. Kayseri: Kayseri Ticaret Odası.

Selçuk, Orçun. 2016. "Strong Presidents and Weak Institutions: Populism in Turkey, Venezuela and Ecuador." *Southeast European and Black Sea Studies* 16, no. 4 (October 10): 571–89.

Sen, Amartya Kumar. 1981. *Poverty and Famines: An Essay on Entitlement and Deprivation*. Oxford: Clarendon Press.

Şen, Mustafa. 2010. "Transformation of Turkish Islamism and the Rise of the Justice and Development Party." *Turkish Studies* 11, no. 1 (May 10): 59–84.

Sennett, Richard. 2003. *Respect in a World of Inequality*. New York: W. W. Norton & Company.

Sennett, Richard, and Jonathan Cobb. 1972. *The Hidden Injuries of Class*. Cambridge: Cambridge University Press.

Şentürk, Ömer Faruk. 2007. *Charity in Islam: A Comprehensive Guide to Zakat*. New Jersey: The Light.

Servet, Jean-Michel. 2007. "The Principle of Reciprocity by Karl Polanyi: Contributions to a Definition of Solidarity-Based Economy." *Revue Tiers Monde* 190, no. 2 (September 12): 255–73.

Sevenhuijsen, Selma. 1998. *Citizenship and the Ethics of Care: Feminist Considerations on Justice, Morality, and Politics*. London: Routledge.

Sevenhuijsen, Selma. 2003a. "The Place of Care: The Relevance of the Ethics of Care for Social Policy." In *Labyrinths of Care: The Relevance of the Ethics of Care Perspective for Social Policy*, eds. Selma Sevenhuijsen and Alenka Švab, 13–41. Ljubljana: Mirovni Institute.

Sevenhuijsen, Selma. 2003b. "Trace: A Method for Normative Policy Analysis from the Ethic of Care." In *The Heart of the Matter: The Contribution of the Ethic of Care to Social Policy in Some New EU Member States*, eds. Selma Sevenhuijsen and Alenka Švab, 13–46. Ljubljana: Peace Institute.
SGK. 2011. "SGK İstatistik Yıllıkları 2010." Ankara: Sosyal Güvenlik Kurumu. https://www.sgk.gov.tr/Istatistik/Yillik/fcd5e59b-6af9-4d90-a451-ee7500eb1cb4/.
Shami, Seteney. 1988. "Studying Your Own: The Complexities of a Shared Culture." In *Arab Women in the Field: Studying Your Own Society*, eds. Soraya Altorki and Camilla Fawzi El-Solh, 115–38. Syracuse: Syracuse University Press.
Silber, Ilana F. 1998. "Modern Philanthropy: Reassessing the Viability of a Maussian Perspective." In *Marcel Mauss: A Centenary Tribute*, eds. Wendy James and N. J. Allen, 134–50. New York/Oxford: Berghahn Books.
Silber, Ilana F. 1995. "Gift-Giving in the Great Traditions: The Case of Donations to Monasteries in the Medieval West." *European Journal of Sociology/Archives Européennes De Sociologie* 36, no. 2: 209–43.
Simmel, Georg. 1964. "The Metropolis and Mental Life." In *The Sociology of Georg Simmel*, ed. Kurt Heinrich Wolff, 11–19. Glencoe: Free Press of Glencoe.
Simmel, Georg. 1965 [1908]. "The Poor." *Social Problems* 13, no. 2 (Autumn): 118–40.
Singer, Amy. 2008. *Charity in Islamic Societies*. New York: Cambridge University Press.
Singer, Peter. 2009. *The Life You Can Save: How to Do Your Part to End World Poverty*. New York City: Random House.
Strathern, Marilyn. 1990. *The Gender of the Gift: Problems with Women and Problems with Society in Melanesia*. Berkeley: University of California Press.
Tanumihardjo, Sherry A., Cheryl Anderson, Martha Kaufer-Horwitz, Lars Bode, Nancy J. Emenaker, Andrea M. Haqq, Jessie A. Satia, Heidi J. Silver, and Diane D. Stadler. 2007. "Poverty, Obesity, and Malnutrition: An International Perspective Recognizing the Paradox." *Journal of the American Dietetic Association* 107, no. 11 (November): 1966–72.
The Care Collective, Andreas Chatzidakis, Jamie Hakim, Jo Litter, and Catherine Rottenberg. 2020. *The Care Manifesto: The Politics of Interdependence*. London and New York: Verso Books.
Thelen, Tatjana. "Care As Belonging, Difference, and Inequality." *Oxford Research Encyclopedia of Anthropology*, May 26, 2021. https://doi.org/10.1093/acrefore/9780190854584.013.353.
Thelen, Tatjana. 2023. "Die Gabe als Kritik – Eine sozialanthropologische Perspektive." In *Geben, Nehmen, Teilen: Gabenwirtschaft im Horizont der Digitalisierung*, eds. Michael Hunter and Birger P. Priddat, 65–80. Frankfurt/New York: Campus Verlag.
Thomas, Nicholas. 1991. *Entangled Objects: Exchange, Material Culture, and Colonialism in the Pacific*. Cambridge, Massachusetts: Harvard University Press.
Ticktin, Miriam I. 2011. *Casualties of Care: Immigration and the Politics of Humanitarianism in France*. Berkeley and Los Angeles: University of California Press.
Titmuss, Richard Morris. 1997. *The Gift Relationship: From Human Blood to Social Policy*. London: LSE Books.
Tomkins, Silvan. 1995. *Exploring Affect: The Selected Writings of Silvan S. Tomkins*, ed. E. Virginia Demos. New York: Cambridge University Press.
Topbaş, Osman Nuri. 2006. *Vakıf İnfak Hizmet*. Istanbul: Ekram Yayınları.
Townsend, Peter. 1993. *The International Analysis of Poverty*. New York/London: Harvester Wheatsheaf.

Transparency International. 2023. "Corruption Perceptions Index 2022." Berlin: Transparency International. https://images.transparencycdn.org/images/Report_CPI2022_English.pdf.
Tripp, Charles. 2006. *Islam and the Moral Economy: The Challenge of Capitalism*. Cambridge: Cambridge University Press.
Tronto, Joan C. 1993. *Moral Boundaries: A Political Argument for an Ethic of Care*. New York: Routledge.
Tuğal, Cihan. 2009. *Passive Revolution: Absorbing the Islamic Challenge to Capitalism*. Stanford: Stanford University Press.
Turam, Berna. 2007. *Between Islam And the State: The Politics of Engagement*. Stanford: Stanford University Press.
Turkey. Ankara Ticaret Odası. 2004. "Dilenen Türkiye." Ankara: Ankara Ticaret Odası.
Turkey. Sosyal Yardımlaşma ve Dayanışma Genel Müdürlüğü. 2010. "2009 Yılı Faaliyet Raporu." Ankara: T.C. Başbakanlık Sosyal Yardımlaşma ve Dayanışma Fonu Genel Müdürlüğü. http://www.sp.gov.tr/upload/xSPRapor/files/MkpW4+SYDGM_09_FR.pdf
Turkey. Vakıflar Genel Müdürlüğü. 2011. "2010 Yılı Faaliyet Raporu." Ankara: T.C. Başbakanlık Vakıflar Genel Müdürlüğü. https://cdn.vgm.gov.tr/genelicerik/genelicerik_216_260519/2010_yili_faaliyet_raporu.pdf
Turkey. Türkiye İstatistik Kurumu. 2009. "İl Düzeyinde Temel İşgücü Göstergeleri 2008." Ankara: Türkiye İstatistik Kurumu.
Turner, Victor. 1980. "Social Dramas and Stories about Them." *Critical Inquiry* 7, no. 1 (Autumn): 141–68.
Ünker, Pelin. "Türgev ve Ensar Vakfı Nasıl Denetleniyor?" *Deutsche Welle*. Retrieved from https://t24.com.tr/haber/turgev-ve-ensar-vakfi-nasil-denetleniyor,1036780. https://www.dw.com/tr/t%C3%BCrgev-ve-ensar-vakf%C4%B1-nas%C4%B1l-denetleniyor/a-61942846, accessed August 17, 2023.
Van Kersbergen, Kees, and Philip Manow, eds. 2009. *Religion, Class Coalitions, and Welfare States*. Cambridge: Cambridge University Press.
Vaughan, Genevieve. 2007. *Women and the Gift Economy: A Radically Different Worldview Is Possible*. Toronto: Inanna Publications and Education.
Verbit, Gilbert P. 2002. *The Origins of the Trust*. Bloomington: Xlibris.
Wacquant, Loïc J. D. 1992. "Toward a Social Praxeology: The Structure and Logic of Bourdieu's Sociology." In *An Invitation to Reflexive Sociology*, eds. Loïc J. D. Wacquant and Pierre Bourdieu, 1–60. Chicago/London: University of Chicago Press.
Weber, Max. 1985. *The Protestant Ethic and the Spirit of Capitalism*. London: Unwin Paperbacks.
Weiner, Annette B. 1992. *Inalienable Possessions: The Paradox of Keeping-While Giving*. Berkeley: University of California Press.
Weintraub, Jeff. 1997. "The Theory and Politics of the Public/Private Distinction." In *Public and Private in Thought and Practice: Perspectives on a Grand Dichotomy*, eds. Jeff Weintraub and Krishan Kumar, 1–42. Chicago: University of Chicago Press.
Werbner, Pnina. 1990. "Economic Rationality and Hierarchical Gift Economies: Value and Ranking Among British Pakistanis." *Man* 25, no. 2 (June): 266–85.
Wilkinson, Richard G. 1992. "Income Distribution and Life Expectancy." *BMJ* 304, no. 6820 (January 18): 165–68.
Yavuz, M. Hakan. 2020. *Nostalgia for the Empire: The Politics of Neo-Ottomanism*. New York: Oxford University Press.
Yoltar, Çağrı. 2020. "Making the Indebted Citizen: An Inquiry into State Benevolence in Turkey." *PoLAR: Political and Legal Anthropology Review* 43, no. 1 (June 13): 153–71.

Yörük, Erdem. 2012a. "Welfare Provision as Political Containment: The Politics of Social Assistance and the Kurdish Conflict in Turkey." *Politics & Society* 40, no. 4 (November 13): 517–47.

Yörük, Erdem. 2012b. "The Politics of the Turkish Welfare System Transformation in the Neoliberal Era: Welfare as Mobilization and Containment." PhD diss., Johns Hopkins University, Baltimore.

Yörük, Erdem. 2022. *The Politics of the Welfare State in Turkey: How Social Movements and Elite Competition Created a Welfare State*. Ann Arbor: University of Michigan Press.

Yörük, Erdem, Ibrahim Öker, and Gabriela Ramalho Tafoya. 2022. "The Four Global Worlds of Welfare Capitalism: Institutional, Neoliberal, Populist and Residual Welfare State Regimes." *Journal of European Social Policy* 32, no. 2 (May): 119–34.

Young, Iris Marion. 1997. "Asymmetrical Reciprocity: On Moral Respect, Wonder, and Enlarged Thought." In *Intersecting Voices: Dilemmas of Gender, Political Philosophy, and Policy*, ed. Iris Marion Young, 38–59.

Zelizer, Viviana A. Rotman. 1994. *The Social Meaning of Money: Pin Money, Paychecks, Poor Relief and Other Currencies*. New York: BasicBooks.

Zencirci, Gizem. 2015. "From Property to Civil Society: The Historical Transformation of Vakifs in Modern Turkey (1923–2013)." *International Journal of Middle East Studies* 47, no. 3 (August): 533–54.

Zubaida, Sami. 2001. "Civil Society, Community and Democracy in the Middle East." In *Civil Society: History and Possibilities*, eds. Sudipta Kaviraj and Sunil Khilnani, 232–49. Cambridge: Cambridge University Press.

# Index

Abdulhamid II 62
Abu-Lughod, Lila 37, 38, 40
AKP (Justice and Development Party) 2, 4, 5, 6, 11, 13, 25, 31
Akyurt, Nevin 2, 35, 123, 124, 126, 127, 136
Al-Ghazali 53, 106, 109, 125
Aristotle 125, 126, 130
authoritarian 8, 12, 13, 57, 63
beggar 105, 106–110, 111
benefaction 6, 78, 119
beneficence 3, 9, 10, 13, 17, 18, 19, 24, 27, 41, 42, 65, 66, 73, 75, 78, 79, 80, 90, 91, 110, 115, 117, 119, 120, 138, 140, 141, 144
body as a research tool 36–38
Bora, Tanıl 137
Bourdieu, Pierre 17, 18, 67, 88, 89, 116
Buğra, Ayşe 5, 6, 9, 10, 29, 57, 58, 59, 102
bureaucracy 6, 9, 10, 54, 61, 62, 86, 87, 88, 92-93, 97, 107, 111, 116, 118, 144
charity 1, 9, 21, 30, 52, 57, 66, 70, 78, 82, 83, 87, 89, 106, 107, 109, 115, 117, 137, 138
~ fair 33, 37, 69–77, 82, 92
charitable giving 9, 10, 20, 21, 44, 63, 78, 83, 85
charitable organization XI, 11, 12, 13, 22, 24, 36, 45, 77, 87, 119, 121
charitable sector 8
citizenship XI, 7, 19, 45, 48, 49, 55, 56, 63, 100
social citizenship 6, 9, 19, 57, 60, 61, 64, 100, 137, 146
Cixous, Hélène 129
commodity exchange 3, 6, 140
dependency 100, 101, 102, 106, 114, 115, 138, 139, 140, 144
Derrida, Jacques 15, 49, 75, 91
discipline 23, 36, 95, 97, 126–130
double movement 5
Douglas, Mary 21, 84, 134, 140
Durkheim, Emile 16
Erdoğan, Recep Tayyip 13, 61, 62, 63, 145
ethics of care 24, 130, 131, 134
family 8, 19, 29, 46, 48, 51, 52, 58, 94, 97, 99, 100, 101, 109, 114, 115, 117

kinship 5, 8, 16, 18, 81, 114, 144
Foucault, Michel 96, 97, 125, 128, 130
gender 23, 24, 38–41, 42, 43, 68, 69, 95, 96, 100, 101, 119
gift 10, 13, 14, 15–23, 24, 26, 31, 41, 42, 45, 49, 52, 54, 56, 61–68, 76, 77, 79, 80, 86, 87, 88, 90–93, 117, 140, 144, 146
~ circuit / ~ cycle 22, 31, 42, 65, 88, 93
~ ethics 134–137
~ as critique XIII
~ as a total social phenomenon 3, 144
civic ~ 27, 49, 60, 61, 63, 86, 119
religious ~ 9
labour as ~ 72–73
money as ~ 81–85
prayer as ~ 74–75
welfare as ~ XII, 3, 14, 19, 23, 49, 54, 63, 144
God 12, 20, 21, 22, 23, 49, 52, 54, 56, 65, 66, 68, 73, 74, 76, 80, 81, 82, 86, 89, 91, 92, 106, 107, 110, 115, 116, 117, 118, 120, 146
governmentality 24, 49, 96, 97, 139
Green Card 58, 59
habitus 16, 18, 125, 126
Hamington, Maurice 15, 133, 134
*hizmet* 65–92
Hollway, Wendy 131–134
honour 15, 16, 18, 19, 105, 115
humanitarianism 21, 24, 52, 78, 79, 93, 94, 97, 117
humanitarian reason 21
imaginary 9, 11, 14, 23, 45, 48, 56, 60, 61, 63, 65, 86, 90
Isin, Engin 47, 49, 50, 55, 56, 63, 78
Islamic Calvinism 28
Islam and capitalism 23, 25, 29, 30
Islamic Social Institutions 87 22
justice 20, 21, 24, 31, 93, 94, 95, 104, 108–111, 115, 116, 117, 118, 139, 146
Kuran, Timur 12, 50, 83
Mahmood, Saba 37, 120, 125, 126
Mardin, Şerif 54, 62
*maslaha* 53

Mauss, Marcel 3, 7, 13, 15, 16, 17, 65, 73, 75, 80, 144
Mehmed II 12
Mittermaier, Amira 21, 76, 117, 118
moral selving 24
Morris, Lydia 97, 105, 106, 114, 123
native anthropologist 35
nonhumanitarian ethics 21, 117
Özbek, Nadir 62, 107
*oturma* 39, 40
Polanyi, Karl 5, 6, 7, 15, 17, 105
poverty XI–XII, 2, 21, 24, 57, 61, 80, 93, 95, 96, 98, 103, 105, 106, 108, 111, 112, 113, 114, 121, 122, 123, 129, 135, 137, 139
~ alleviation 3, 4, 6, 8, 10, 24, 30, 48, 58, 59, 97, 123, 128, 146
the poor XII, 3, 4, 13, 14, 19, 20, 21, 22, 46, 47, 48, 51, 59, 60, 62, 80, 81, 93, 95–98, 105, 107, 108, 112, 114, 118, 121, 122, 123, 125, 139, 143
deserving / undeserving poor 24
Protestant Ethic 28
Rashid el-Din 47
reciprocity 3, 6, 7, 8, 9, 10, 17, 18, 21, 22, 55, 73, 76, 141
redistribution 3, 6, 7, 9, 16, 17, 20, 60
respect 8, 22, 24, 129, 132, 133, 137–141, 146
root paradigms 62
*sadaka / sadaqah* 20, 22, 81, 82, 83, 85, 110, 111
Scott, James 118, 139
Sennett, Richard 132, 138, 139, 140, 141
Silber, Ilana 20, 21, 22, 65
Simmel, Georg 84, 96
Singer, Amy 10, 13, 20, 47, 48, 50, 51, 53, 79, 106, 107
social assistance 4, 5, 8, 9, 10, 11, 14, 26, 58, 59, 60, 98, 144, 146
social capital 70, 89
social networks 19, 22, 93, 144
Social Security Institution (SGK) 58, 59
solidarity 15, 17, 22, 23, 60, 87, 137, 138
spy 23, 36
symbolic capital 18, 90
Titmuss, Richard 15, 17, 80
triage 94
Tronto, Joan 131

Turkish-Islamic Synthesis 11
underclass 97
*vakıf* 12, 14, 26, 27, 31, 45, 46, 56, 57, 59, 60, 66, 67, 69, 70, 71, 77, 78, 81, 82, 88, 90, 93, 94, 102, 107, 108, 109, 111, 112, 117, 123, 130, 139, 140, 145
Social Solidarity *Vakıf*s (SYDV) 59–60, 61, 145
*vakıfçı* 12, 19, 45, 57, 70, 82, 85, 88, 109, 110, 115, 117, 119, 120, 123, 133, 136, 137, 141
*vakıfçılık* 45, 139, 141
*waqf* 10, 11, 12, 20, 23, 45–57, 60, 61, 62, 63, 64, 86, 90, 139
charitable ~ / ~*khayri* 51–52
and civil society 11, 12, 43, 45, 48, 49, 63
family ~ / ~ *ahli* 51
and public sphere 43, 45, 48
Weiner, Annette 18
welfare provision 3, 6, 11, 12, 30, 45, 48, 49, 51, 57, 58, 60, 61, 63, 64, 71, 87, 138, 139
non-state ~ 2, 3, 6, 22, 31, 144
state-provided welfare 13
welfare expenditure 5
welfare state 7, 8, 54, 60, 100, 105, 138
neoliberal ~ 98
populist ~ 5
Southern European ~ 8, 58
corporatist welfare regime 5, 9, 57, 58
Turkish welfare regime 57–59
social assistance state 5, 6, 14
World Bank 8, 60, 96
*zekat / zakat* 20, 78, 81, 82, 85, 110, 111,
Zelizer, Viviana 84